CREATING AN INFORMED CITIZENRY

FROM PAMPHLETS TO PODCASTS
An Institute for Thomas Paine Studies Series
Nora Slonimsky and Mark Boonshoft, Editors

CREATING AN INFORMED CITIZENRY

Knowledge and Democracy in the
Early American Republic

GEORGE D. OBERLE III

UNIVERSITY OF VIRGINIA PRESS
Charlottesville and London

Published in association with the
Institute for Thomas Paine Studies at Iona University

The University of Virginia Press is situated on the traditional lands of the Monacan Nation, and the Commonwealth of Virginia was and is home to many other Indigenous people. We pay our respect to all of them, past and present. We also honor the enslaved African and African American people who built the University of Virginia, and we recognize their descendants. We commit to fostering voices from these communities through our publications and to deepening our collective understanding of their histories and contributions.

University of Virginia Press
© 2025 by the Rector and Visitors of the University of Virginia
All rights reserved
Printed in the United States of America on acid-free paper

First published 2025

9 8 7 6 5 4 3 2 1

Library of Congress Cataloging-in-Publication data is available for this title.

ISBN 978-0-8139-5415-8 (hardback)
ISBN 978-0-8139-5416-5 (paperback)
ISBN 978-0-8139-5417-2 (ebook)

Cover art: The Exhumation of the Mastodon, Charles Willson Peale, ca. 1807 (courtesy of the Maryland Center for History and Culture, BCLM-MA.5911, Baltimore City Life Museum Collection); plow, from *Catalogue of the Mount Airy Agricultural Institute*, 1849 (courtesy of Penn State University Libraries/HathiTrust); paper, thongdeekhieo/vecteezy.com
Cover design: Cecilia Sorochin

To Heather, Mason, and Linda

CONTENTS

Acknowledgments	ix
Introduction	1
1. A National University: The American Founders' Vision for the Creation and Dissemination of Knowledge in a Republic	11
2. A National Academy: The Politicization of Knowledge	37
3. A National Museum? Disseminating Knowledge in the Early Republic	64
4. National Agricultural Institutions: Democratizing Authority over Knowledge	91
5. A National Research Institution: Citizen Science and Controlling the Information Revolution	116
Conclusion	141
Notes	149
Bibliography	191
Index	225

ACKNOWLEDGMENTS

When I started this work, I had no idea how many debts I would rack up by the time I completed it.

I owe an intellectual debt to so many of my teachers at George Mason University. I transferred from the Northern Virginia Community College to George Mason in the fall of 1994 because it was the only public university in the area. Little did I know that I would spend the bulk of my adult life at this institution. This was in large part because of the amazing teachers and scholars in the Department of History and Art History. The first two history classes I took were Jack R. Censer's Introduction to Historical Methods and a course taught by the renowned philosophy professor Thelma Z. Levine. Later Jeffrey Stewart, Marion Deshmukh, James Piffner, Timothy Conlan, Dina Copelman, Martin Cohen, and Lloyd Duck all helped me learn what it meant to be a serious student. I am grateful to them.

This book is based on my 2016 dissertation, which I completed under the guidance of my advisor, Rosemarie Zagarri, and a committee of scholars that included Jane Turner Censer and Paula Petrik. Rosie provided outstanding guidance and encouragement throughout the dissertation process. She helped me focus and taught me how to manage the work while still being true to the "meta questions" I was trying to engage with. I am very thankful of her friendship and ongoing support of my work. Jane provided exceptional questions and feedback for me to consider as I turned away from the dissertation and started working on the book. Finally, Paula, who is no longer with us, was a good friend who constantly pushed me to be better. I am sure she would have been disappointed that I did not include zoos in this book, but I think she would have been happy otherwise.

Being a librarian has been critical to my scholarly pursuits outlined in this book. While studying at the College of Library and Information Studies at the University of Maryland, I learned about information sciences from Bruce Ambacher, Bruce Dearstyne, and Michael Kurtz. I had the good fortune to work full time for the George Mason University Libraries in various roles beginning in 1999. My colleagues taught me how to assist patrons in finding and using sources and stimulated my curiosity about how information is structured and presented. Colleagues such as Kevin Simons, James B. Young, Scott Breivold, Amy Pearce, Miriam Bridges, Sharon Hybki Kerr, Craig Gibson, Lara Bushallow, Jessica Bowdoin, John Walsh, Jamie Coniglio, Theresa Calcagno, Allison O'Connor, John Zenelis, Wally Grotophorst, and Bridget Euliano all have influenced my thinking about the dissemination of knowledge.

Since becoming a faculty member the Department of History and Art History in 2017, I have benefited from the help of many colleagues and friends, as well as from much-needed financial assistance to help pay for the rights to use the images included in this book. Brian Platt, Joan Bristol, Sam Lebovic, Randolph Scully, James Ambuske, and Zachary Schrag all read sections of this book and provided useful comments and kind encouragement. And I learn from my students every day.

I also want to acknowledge the spiritual connections forged while working on this book with Benedict Carton and Wendi Manuel-Scott. Our work on the Enslaved People of George Mason Memorial and our creation of the Center for Mason Legacies (CML) has been a life-changing experience. Alyssa Fahringer has been an important intellectual touchstone for me at CML. I am grateful for her friendship and her feedback on this work.

Many people and organizations beyond George Mason University helped make this work possible. Johann Neem generously commented on many iterations of the manuscript and introduced me to several colleagues who have improved it. Among the most meaningful connections has been with my friend Mark Boonshoft, who provided many useful comments on my explorations into the meaning of an educated and informed citizenry. Fellow panelists Lindsay Schakenbach Regele and David McKenzie helped introduce to me to new colleagues at SECOLAS where we presented on Joel Poinsett in March of 2000. I also benefited from a fellowship at the International Center of Jefferson Studies (ICJS) at Monticello. There I met Frank Cogliano and John Ragosta, who introduced me to other fellows and staff. Anna Berkes and Enrina Tay, the outstanding librarians at ICJS, were particularly helpful in providing sources and guidance to their collections. I also benefited from participating in the American Philosophical Society's symposium "Networks: The Creation and Circulation of Knowledge from Franklin to Facebook." Additionally, archivists and librarians from across the country helped me find and get access to important content, especially during the COVID-19 pandemic. Archivists at the Lily Library, the New York Historical Society, the Academy of Natural Sciences, the Maryland Historical Society, the Library of Virginia, the American Philosophical Society, the Library of Congress, the National Archives, the British Museum, and the Smithsonian Institution's archives all provided exceptional assistance.

Cynthia Kierner, professor of history at George Mason University, deserves special acknowledgment. Cindy read almost every iteration of every chapter. She did so with a keen eye for analytical points and with a sense of humor. Without her encouragement I might never have finished this book. Similarly, UVA Press editor Nadine Zimmerli showed an unflagging commitment to me and to this work. Even while she was managing many other projects, she always had time for me and helped make my work better. Nadine also gave us two cats she had rescued. They have been a joy to our household.

I am also grateful to the professionals at the University of Virginia Press, who through their sound editorial interventions and their artistic skill have made this a much better book. Andy Edwards was particularly helpful in assuring that all the deadlines in the production of this work were met. I especially want to acknowledge Joanne Allen's meticulous editorial skill and patience in reviewing the manuscript. I also am grateful for Rebecca McCorkle's exceptional skill in providing a useful index for the book. Thank you.

Finally, I thank the people who have made this life as a scholar possible: my family. They bring joy to my life and have sacrificed so much for me. My father, George, my deceased mother, Judith, and my stepmother, Hwa Kyoung Choe Oberle, raised me in a safe environment despite how difficult I made that for them. My brother has always shown an interest in the work I do. My dear friends Jeff Somer and Debbie Delaney, who were as close as family, were very caring and always wanted to know what I was working on even when I didn't have a good answer. My family in Florida were wonderful to see when I needed to get away from work to see the Mouse and his friends in Orlando. My Aunt Linda gave me a stable place to find myself as I floundered after my high school years. Most important, my dear son, Mason, and my bride, Heather, both provide me with hope and comfort. I am grateful for all that you have done to help me finish this work.

CREATING AN INFORMED CITIZENRY

INTRODUCTION

On Saturday, May 1, 1847, numerous public officials gathered together in Washington, DC, for a public ceremony to lay the cornerstone for the newly established Smithsonian Institution. The *Baltimore Sun* declared it a "memorable day" and a "glorious jubilee." A grand procession began at City Hall. It consisted of the mayor of Washington, William Seaton, and several lodges of Freemasons from the city of Washington itself, Virginia, Maryland, and Pennsylvania. A large contingent of the Independent Order of Odd Fellows accompanied the renowned Washington light infantry, popularly known as the "National Blues," adding to the pageantry. Reportedly, the "exceedingly rich regalia, splendid banners, and other paraphernalia rendered the procession grand and imposing."[1] After advancing past the president's mansion and the Capitol, where President James Polk, his cabinet, and members of Congress and the judiciary joined the celebration, the parade ended at the public square designated for the new building on the mall. Several dignitaries then addressed the crowd of thousands, with George Dallas, vice president of the United States and chancellor of the Smithsonian, delivering the keynote address. He recounted the congressionally sanctioned purpose of the Smithsonian, which he described as a national institution that served "not a chosen or designated class, not the followers of a particular sage or sect, not the favorites of fortune, nor the lifted of rank, but . . . men of every condition, of every school, of every faith, of every nativity! Men!"[2]

The celebration marking the founding of the Smithsonian Institution was the culmination of a decades-long debate over what type of knowledge institution ought to collect and disseminate information in the early American republic. Indeed, a radical transformation, an information revolution, occurred between the American Revolution and the Civil War, with an emphasis on the ideal of the public's widespread engagement in the creation of useful knowledge—represented by the dream of a national university, which the founding generation hoped to build in the 1790s—giving way to deference to credentialed experts whose work constituted authentic knowledge, as embodied by the scholars who founded the Smithsonian Institution in the late 1840s. This change in vision, away from a national university designed to promote universal knowledge, came about as ever more learned societies sprang up and proliferated across the young republic. This diverse array of organizations, ranging from military academies, museums, lyceums, and libraries to learned societies of all types, profoundly altered the ways in which Americans participated in the creation and dissemination of knowledge. While initially, in the late 1700s, Americans desperately sought to create institutions to help promote the creation and dissemination of knowledge populated by the new nation's elite thinkers, by the 1840s they saw an excessive proliferation of institutions populated by a broad citizenry that had no national leadership or vision for scientific progress. These new institutional platforms offered opportunities for a growing population to contribute to the process of learning, creating, and disseminating knowledge in the United States. This process, in turn, shaped the way American citizens viewed their ability to engage in the creation of knowledge and ultimately how they participated in a democratic polity.

From the earliest days of the republic, its leaders presumed that American citizens would be educated and informed; after all, in a government that derived its power from the people, every citizen needed to be knowledgeable about history, politics, and science, ensuring the success of the republican experiment. George Washington himself called for the establishment of a great national university designed to forge enlightened leaders who could direct the future path of the country. This institution would teach the nation's youth the privileges and duties of citizenship in their nascent republic.

Despite political leaders' widespread belief in the need for an educated and well-informed citizenry and their general agreement on the usefulness of this kind of institution, profound questions emerged over the appropriateness of the new federal government to lead this effort. As American leaders debated a national university, their discussions began to revolve around more complex questions: What constituted the appropriate epistemology of knowledge for future leaders, and who ought to participate in the process of creating knowledge in a republican society? While the American founders believed that an informed citizenry was essential to the success of their republic, they also worried that a revolutionary expansion of information to commoners could result in chaos and hinder the development of the nation. Most leaders accepted that a participatory government rested its fortunes on the expertise of its citizens. Yet how inclusive could this information revolution be? How could information circulating in the public sphere be verified? How should institutions be developed to promote that learning? Should there be a focus on the universal nature of knowledge or on specialized knowledge? Would one be better for a large, diffused populace in a society that emphasized democratic values? What systems could be developed to assure that the ways in which knowledge was created, disseminated, and consumed could help bind the nation together—or rip it apart?

The expansive print world of books, periodicals, and newspapers spreading across the nascent republic documented these crucial debates over the appropriate characteristics of these institutions within government circles, among the cultural elites, and across the growing middling classes. In the end, as this book shows, instead of a single centralized institution designed to promote a common vision for a homogenous citizenry, as dreamed of by Washington, several heterogenous institutions developed to represent a plethora of specialized interests, each designed to fulfill the information needs of its distinctive community.

Although America's national university never materialized, an opportunity to establish a national institution for the promotion and dissemination of knowledge arose when in 1835 the US government learned that an unlikely clause in the 1829 last will and testament of the wealthy Englishman James Smithson had kicked into effect. After Smithson's nephew died without an heir, his estate was given to the United States of America for the purpose of founding "at Washington, under the name of the Smithsonian Institution, an establishment for the increase and diffusion of knowledge."[3] This bequest removed the economic excuses marshaled against a national university in the 1790s and brought into focus the real question: What type of institution ought to serve as a national institution for the promotion of knowledge, and who should participate in that institution?

In the intervening decades, a host of organizations expressly designed to promote an engaged and active citizenry had emerged across the country. Civic societies produced a vibrant and active culture of participation among newly minted Americans committed to improvement and self-making. Local communities and states established schools and military academies to help the nation's youth learn critical skills and made considerable investments in adult learning by opening libraries, museums, and lyceums so that residents could achieve their personal goals of self-improvement. Indeed, between 1790 and 1840 several thousand social libraries were established to collect and disseminate the thousands of magazines and newspapers published across the country. Museums also proliferated as scores of new institutions opened previously closed cabinets to wider audiences, who came to admire the natural wonders that abounded in their halls. Lyceums and other civic organizations hosted hundreds of thousands of Americans who came to hear lectures about diverse ideas of scientific advancement. Meanwhile, the newly established post office ensured that citizen-scholars could share their publications and correspond with like-minded people across the young country.

At the same time, a revolution of printed content spread across the United States as more people consumed and created new information. In 1804 alone a *Catalogue of All the Books Printed in the United States,* published in Boston, listed 1,105 new titles.[4] This number represented the approximate total number of books published in the country up to that point. The number of books published in a year increased regularly. In the 1830s the *Booksellers' Advertiser,* an early trade magazine for publishers, showed that in the years 1833–35 approximately 1,030 original books and 854 reprints were published.[5] Newspapers and magazines also proliferated. By 1840 there were at least 1,631 newspapers and magazines nationwide.[6] Astoundingly, the number of newspapers alone went from 37 in 1776 to 1,403 by 1840.[7] Each community had its own printers and access to a growing network of knowledge produced and spread via the US mail. As a result, local institutions sprang up to direct and filter this new knowledge by promoting what their communities believed was useful knowledge. In a way, this was a self-enforcing cycle: an expanding number of organizations led to an increase in print, which in turn increased memberships in societies.

The core objectives and questions animating this growth never changed: What was the best way to ensure that there was an active and engaged American citizenry and that the population had access to useful knowledge? How would these institutions be organized, who could participate in them, and most importantly, who would decide what constituted useful knowledge? Credentialed elites only or a broad range of American citizens? Most participants in the debates agreed that the country needed a way to promote and disseminate scientific learning to ensure the security and advancement of a republic dedicated to a vision of "progress" through the advancement of "civilization." Yet what form an institutional answer would take and who among the American populace would participate in creating and receiving knowledge were hotly contested for decades, only to be worked out in the 1840s.

In fact, the debates over the purpose of the Smithsonian resembled the discussions decades prior over the need to establish a national university and encountered much of the same resistance. Eventually, the Smithsonian's creation involved a compromise designed to appease diverse constituents. The legislators who designed the Smithsonian wanted it to acquire and disseminate various forms of knowledge; however, once the institution was launched, its leaders decided to focus on a particular type of scientific knowledge that changed the breadth of its mission. The legislators hoped that the Smithsonian Institution would serve the diverse information needs of the American citizenry. Instead its leaders focused on promoting a scientific research agenda designed for a limited number of experts, and they developed public programming that encouraged visitors to marvel at the extensive collections accumulated by the federal government—especially during the celebration of the nation's centennial in 1876—but not to participate as citizen-scholars themselves. Yet, as this book makes clear, who ultimately would participate in knowledge creation and dissemination in the American republic was not a foregone conclusion but rather the culmination of decades-long debates and alternative visions.

To understand these competing visions, I analyze Americans' expanding access to knowledge by looking at organizations with national ambitions that I call knowledge institutions. These organizations, ranging from learned societies, museums, and lyceums to agricultural societies and libraries, emerged in the early republic to both collect and disseminate new knowledge to Americans who were both eager to learn and enthusiastic to engage in producing new scientific information themselves. My analysis of the rise and multilayered functions of these knowledge institutions benefits from the rich scholarship on print culture, citizenship, nation building, and scientific advancements laid out below, but my primary interest is in documenting the connections between these organizations and highlighting that their proliferation constituted a veritable information revolution in the nascent United States that over half a century did broaden Americans' access to knowledge but ultimately restricted who could produce it.

The expansion of print culture—and the information revolution it made possible—was both a cause and a consequence of the American Revolution, which provided a space for a broader community of people to openly engage with policy and political debates within the public sphere, and they often did so in writing.[8] The many newly created newspapers were run by ambitious editors who transformed their labor from a mechanical into an intellectual endeavor. Their publications helped link disparate parts of the country together within evolving political networks.[9] In addition, large groups of people celebrated the ideals of the Revolution, thereby participating in the public sphere and shaping the contours of an evolving nation.[10]

Scholars have long highlighted the significance of an informed and actively engaged citizenry to the success of a republic after the Revolution, connecting citizens who were capable of "exercising their civic responsibilities wisely" to their widespread civic engagement in institutions promoting the diffusion of knowledge.[11] These scholars have documented the importance of the printed word and the rich print culture that emerged in the United States after the American Revolution.[12] As mentioned above, elites promoted access to an ever expanding number of publications by creating a communication infrastructure via a network of post offices and the US mail.[13] Historians have also investigated the plans for a grand national university to be constructed in the federal city designed to forge future leaders dedicated to the promotion of republican principles, and they have analyzed the series of debates in the first decades of the republic over the nature and the purpose of education.[14] I now add to these insights by tracing the arc from the failed national university to the successful creation of the Smithsonian Institution by investigating various visions for an actively engaged citizenry that both engaged with new scientific knowledge and sought to actively create it.

The existing scholarly literature also shows how postrevolutionary Americans joined together to build a host of institutions to support their learning needs as adults. A robust civic society formed as a result of like-minded Americans joining together to create the abundant knowledge institutions I analyze in this book. Privately funded and mostly locally organized, these institutions collected and disseminated research designed to serve their individual communities; each also developed connections to other organizations, thereby creating wide-ranging networks dedicated to promoting useful knowledge in the young country.[15] Thus far, scholars have studied these various knowledge institutions in isolation, whereas I now examine them holistically, which allows me to retrace the active conversation early Americans engaged in with one another over what type of institution could best serve the information needs of the citizenry in the new United States.

In addition, the rich body of work on the history of science and technology offers critical insights into Americans' desire for broad participation in the promotion of scientific knowledge. Early historical scholarship focused on documenting the existence of scientific work in the United States despite the lack of centrally funded scientific infrastructure. These scholars also explored the emergence of the professional scientific apparatus that evolved in the late nineteenth century.[16] These projects often foregrounded the people, military explorations, and emerging scientific organizations that conducted expeditions and other scientific work across the continent.[17] More recently, scholars have looked to earlier eras and focused on connecting the central drive of the European imperialistic missions in establishing their colonial enterprises to the development of scientific knowledge throughout the world. Colonies became the tools of empires to create wealth, with colonists exploiting Indigenous resources and knowledge for the benefit of the metropole.[18] Many of these works on the American context detail the importance of engineers who were trained at the US Military Academy at West Point and led or were significant contributors to scientific expeditions.[19] Indeed, military academies proliferated across the country, including in the South, and became hubs for promoting knowledge to both elites and the middling classes.[20]

The debates over the establishment of the Military Academy at West Point are especially instructive to my own work since they focused the attention of American elites on the critical need for developing a scientifically focused curriculum. This resulted in an intellectual struggle between those who believed that education required a specific type of practice focused on understanding and deploying rhetoric in any context and those who championed the acquisition of specialized knowledge.[21] Lastly, the fracture between the newly independent United States and Great Britain severed ties to traditional institutions. This break forced Americans to construct their own scientific and technological infrastructure, designed to ensure the nation's economic and cultural independence.[22]

The need to construct this new infrastructure developed amid a broad cultural and intellectual revolution of ideas that some scholars call an information revolution, which I follow here.[23] This revolution is evident in the wide variety of knowledge institutions that Americans established, which, although generally limited to white men, proliferated in great numbers across the nation and proved to be critical to promoting interest in "useful knowledge" in the United States. Rather than chronicling an intellectually limited postcolonial space in which there was little advancement in science and technology, these scholars point to the emergence of a vibrant culture of pragmatic experimentation in the early republic that helped to expand American productivity, markets, and trade.[24] This book builds on these insights and argues that the diversity of institutions that developed in the United States modeled a culture of participation in knowledge creation that mirrored the expanding political participation.

Despite the increasing political participation by white men in the American polity and a near-universal agreement among elites that a well-functioning participatory republic required a well-educated citizenry, many worried about the appropriateness of a strong central government's role in education and diffusion of knowledge. Political historians have detected these problematic concerns throughout the first political party systems, and my work demonstrates that these anxieties underlay many political debates over the influence national knowledge institutions could have on the citizenry. Fear of foreign influence, fear of elite domination, fear of mob rule, and fear of the spread of misinformation all permeated the early republic from the founding to the midcentury crisis leading to the Civil War. This political fight over the dissemination of knowledge was directly connected to the fear of centralized power in relation to a variety of contemporary issues. Over and over, from the founding into the antebellum period, the question was who ought to be able to participate in the creation and dissemination of new knowledge within a participatory democratic society.[25]

This book chronicles the emergence of a variety of knowledge institutions created by people with differing types of national ambitions. Chapter 1 examines the early calls for the establishment of a national university to serve the new country. I argue that Federalists hoped to establish a single institution to train future leaders, while Jeffersonians resisted this impulse despite agreeing that there was a need to create an informed American citizenry. Although the United States never founded a national university, this debate set the tone and terms of discussion over who could access and who could produce knowledge for the next fifty years. Chapter 2 examines the connection between the scholarly activities within learned societies and the federal government's role in establishing the Military Academy at West Point. I argue that the applied scientific curriculum became a model for fusing learning and scientific research in the United States. Importantly, this chapter explores the growing divide between the proponents of two distinct and competing systems of knowledge, one focusing on the traditions of the past and elevating established authorities and one looking to the future and championing broader access to knowledge.

The third chapter explores the rise of museums as institutions that introduced an expanding number of people to natural-history resources. Museums filled the needs of a young country with only a limited scientific infrastructure. They provided a space where experts could study scientific specimens and the curious could learn about new scientific understandings of the world. Chapter 4 focuses on the development of a national scientific infrastructure by examining the ways in which interest in agricultural knowledge spread throughout the country through regional societies. I argue that the widespread interest in experimentation led to an actively engaged group of citizen-scientists, but this resulted in a crucial divide. On one side, these citizen-scientists seized the opportunity to explore and disseminate a wide range of ideas, leading to an increase in the number of charlatans and ill-informed pseudo scholars dominating public discourse. On the other side, credentialed scientists began to argue that a national scientific agenda with centralized resources in the federal city was critical for US success in the wider world.

Finally, the fifth chapter explores the political debates that led to the establishment of the Smithsonian Institution and examines its foundational years, in the 1840s and 1850s. I argue that the institution emerged from the chaotic and competitive environment outlined in chapter 4. The builders of the Smithsonian embraced the ideal of modern scientific expertise—in essence the practices then emerging in the German research universities to ensure that information was authoritative and reliable—to bring order to the chaos. In doing so they rejected both the civic impulses of George Washington and his vision for a national university and the more democratic impulses of the museums and lyceums. Ironically, this meant that they embraced a form of elite knowledge that failed to create national coherence.

Ultimately, this book chronicles the rich scientific information landscape that emerged in the United States after the Revolution. By focusing on various types of knowledge institutions and their connections to one another, I show that the participation of the American populace in creating and using new knowledge institutions offered a chaotic opportunity for experimentation that encouraged creativity and new ways of promoting access to information to a broader community of participants. This was a messy process, and despite the celebrations and messages promoting the progress for all "mankind" promised by the founders of the Smithsonian, the results were mixed. Instead of serving as a space in which all Americans were active participants in creating knowledge, the Smithsonian focused on promoting a research agenda created by the elites, pursuing only what they defined as scholarship.

CHAPTER 1

A NATIONAL UNIVERSITY

The American Founders' Vision for the Creation and Dissemination of Knowledge in a Republic

In his last will and testament, George Washington stated that one of his most profound regrets was that the new nation had sent its young men "to foreign Countries for the purpose of Education, often before their minds were formed." He and many other founders worried that impressionable youths had not yet "imbibed any adequate ideas of the happiness of their own; contracting, too frequently, not only habits of dissipation & extravagance," but had developed "principles unfriendly to Republican Governmt and to the true & genuine liberties of Mankind." Washington hoped that a new, national institution would be designed to promote knowledge "on a liberal scale, which would have a tendency to sprd systemactic ideas through all parts of this rising Empire, thereby to do away [with] local attachments and State prejudices." To help pay for this new "UNIVERSITY to be established within the limits of the District of Columbia, under the auspices of the General Government," Washington established an endowment funded by fifty shares in the Potomac Company given to him by the state of Virginia for his service to the country.[1]

Washington's endowment for the creation of a university under federal oversight reflected his belief that a national center of higher education ought to serve as a tool to centralize learning and promote a common education for the next generation of republican citizens. As reflected in his will, this national university would help diminish factional and sectional differences by encouraging the creation of fraternal bonds among the new nation's youth through a universal framework of knowledge. Yet despite the dedication of his political capital calling for the creation of this institution, his gift of fifty shares in the

Potomac Company was never used; the shares ultimately became worthless, and his national university never materialized.[2]

Previous scholarship on the push for a national university blamed its failure on short-sighted and petty partisan debates and a stingy Congress that failed to pay for planned building projects. The opposition faction feared the university would be a "federal Trojan horse" used to enhance federal power as well as to appropriate overwhelming authority for the national government. Overall, these scholars tended to view the failure to build a national university as a missed opportunity to establish the country's first research university long before Johns Hopkins was founded in 1876.[3]

Of course, Washington did not offer a prescient vision for a new type of educational institution, and his was far from the only idea for promoting education in the new United States. As various scholars have shown, there were persistent calls for designing the right system of education for the young nation. Thomas Jefferson's well-known plan in his Bill 79, *A Bill for the More General Diffusion of Knowledge,* which sought to create a three-level educational system for the state of Virginia, remained unfulfilled. In 1795 the American Philosophical Society, the oldest learned society in the country, sponsored a cash prize for an essay designing "the best system of liberal education, and literacy instruction, adapted to the genius of the government" in the United States, a system "best calculated to promote the general welfare" of the country, and "also, a plan instituting and conducting public schools in this country on principles of the most extensive utility."[4] The two co-winners both included a national university in their model of a system of education.[5]

These various plans for education in the country rested on the important need for widespread access to information to create an educated and informed citizenry. As one historian has suggested, American thinkers hoped to implement a means of enlightenment that secured both public and private happiness, with government providing "a way of life that serenely balanced the intellectual and moral faculties" of American citizens. Importantly, education also became a critical means for reasserting and ensuring elite rule via newly established private academies that would proliferate across the country. The debate over who ought to be educated and where institutions of education should be established was really about who should rule in a republic. Even before the establishment of the new constitution, the Northwest Ordinances of 1785 and 1787 provided that one of every thirty-six parcels of land in the western territories was to be set aside for common schools. This dedicated land was to be rented to pay for the education of children in the region. Even though this demonstrates a clear interest by those in the early government to support education in the areas that it controlled, this strategy had limited success because of widespread mismanagement and the policy's limited scope for the education of children. At the heart of these debates were questions about what constituted the most important forms of information in a republican polity, who should have access to this knowledge, and how to disseminate information among the public.[6]

Unlike Alexander Hamilton's Bank of the United States, which caused deep political rifts, the debates about a national university offer a more subtle opportunity to understand widening political divisions among America's founders. Most agreed that a national university was useful and would promote national progress, yet they could not agree on the details. An in-depth exploration of the proposals and calls for a national university provides key insights into how the young nation's leaders envisioned the construction of a republican society and how they thought to weave the legacy of the American Revolution into the fabric of the newly established republic. As I argue, the debates over where a national university should be founded and what should be taught revealed how different political factions viewed the meaning of the American Revolution. Washington's vision for a national university focused on the goal to promote a homogenous leadership class trained in America. Washington's opponents worried that if successful, this institution would train a new aristocracy to promote their personal interests instead of an independent-minded republican citizenry.

The call for a national university emerged in the Confederation period and served in large part as a rebuke to the existing colleges across the United States. These colonial-era colleges were often viewed as provincial and ill-equipped to provide the advanced training needed for men to produce scientific knowledge, and they lacked the resources or imagination to transform themselves into institutions offering the type of education that matched the needs of a republican society. Instead, most of these colleges remained true to their traditional religious inspirations and remained committed to educating only the current and future gentry.[7]

In this landscape the founders, including Alexander Hamilton, Benjamin Rush, and Thomas Jefferson, committed to the idea of an expansive system of higher education. However, conflict emerged when Federalists and Jeffersonian Republicans staked out political sides over what constituted an appropriate type of curriculum and the best type of knowledge for citizens. While Federalists saw an existential crisis for the new country since it still relied significantly on European institutions for new scientific knowledge and hoped to construct similar institutions in the United States, Jeffersonian Republicans worried that a strong federal government would reproduce older aristocratic educational institutions and believed that a new, modern curriculum focused only on knowledge that would be "useful" and scientifically driven would ensure prosperity, security, and enlightenment. These debates and the divisions that emerged around them resulted in clear ideological differences about the purpose of a national university. The Federalists saw a university providing classical knowledge to the elite, while the Republicans imagined a university that offered opportunities to a broader citizenry to explore the natural and social sciences.[8]

Calls for a National University

Advocacy for a national university emerged at the same time that many sought to create a strong federal government to help solve the challenges Americans had experienced during the chaotic Confederation period. Among the earliest public advocates for a centralized federal university was a person who took on the pseudonym Nestor. The name came from Greek mythology; Nestor was the wise king of Pylos, known for providing sound advice. In an essay published on June 3, 1786, in Philadelphia's *Independent Gazette* and then promptly reprinted in several other newspapers Nestor argued that Americans needed to acquire sufficient knowledge, especially in the science of government, to ensure that "the principles, morals, and manners of our citizens" were prepared so that their "forms of government" could be "brought to perfection." Nestor argued that although the "American War" had ended, this was "far from being the case with the American revolution." Even though states had established governments, they had been formed in "unfavourable circumstances," emerging from "a corrupted monarchy." The only way to avoid "tyranny" was to "guard against the effects of our own ignorance and licentiousness." Nestor's solution was to establish a federal city, and he wrote that Congress "should appropriate" resources for "founding a FEDERAL UNIVERSITY." This university would allow advanced study *after* a student's training at local colleges, and it would focus on all subjects connected with government, including history, all facets of law, commerce, economics, and the military sciences. Nestor recommended that one of the students or the professors should receive funds to "visit all the nations of Europe and transmit . . . all the discoveries and improvements in agriculture and manufactures." The investment of the public in this sojourner would secure new knowledge for the American people.⁹

Nestor called his fellow citizens to action and reminded them that they could not rest after the Revolution because "every man in a republic is public property. His time and talents—his youth—his manhood—his old age—nay more life; *all* belong to his country." Nestor concluded the essay with the exhortation "Patriots of 1774, 1775, 1776—Heroes of 1778, 1779, and 1780—come forward! Your country *demands* your services.—Philosophers and friends to mankind, come forward! Your country demands your studies and speculations." In Nestor's view, individuals' developing and utilizing their minds for the good of the people would result in public happiness.¹⁰

Nestor was not alone. Americans throughout the country discussed issues in the periodical press related to education. While the Constitutional Convention was wrapping up in Philadelphia in 1787, Eleazer Oswald's *Independent Gazetteer* published a series of twenty-nine essays from August 6 to October 2 designed to cultivate "FEDERAL SENTIMENTS" by promoting bonds across the diverse republic. A significant section of one essay, penned by Nicholas Collin, referred to Nestor's call for a federal university and argued that this institution would be needed to help promote national unity. A federal university, Collin wrote, would help form new citizens and inculcate them with the qualities needed to lead the republic; it would produce alumni who would help bind the new federal nation together.¹¹ Oswald as editor and educational advocates such as Benjamin Rush sought to establish an effective educational system that would encourage civic virtue and "convert men into republican machines."¹²

Rush engaged on education with transatlantic correspondents such as the English philosopher and nonconformist preacher Richard Price, who believed the purpose of education was to teach people how to think critically. In his political tract *Observations on the Importance of the American Revolution,* Price included a section on education, in which he emphasized the need to "teach *how* to think, rather than *what* to think; or to lead into the best way of searching for truth, rather than to instruct in truth itself." To Price, the spread of knowledge and information created opportunities for improvements to the human condition. He believed that public education was crucial for this progress and ought to be expanded, yet the right method and the right people were needed. Price observed that while many readily sought to teach, they were unprepared to teach in the right way; he believed that "it is better to teach nothing, than to teach what they hold out for truth."¹³

In private correspondence, Rush urged Price in 1786 to engage directly on the issue of education in the United States because the American Revolution would remain incomplete until the people received "*knowledge* as well as virtue." Rush proposed that the "common people" provide a "good English education" to their children and that there be "colleges in each of the states, and one federal university under the patronage of Congress" for advanced studies. Rush begged Price to submit a pamphlet to the Confederation Congress and state legislatures supporting this plan since "this plan alone will render the American Revolution a blessing to mankind."[14] There is no extant record of Price fulfilling this request, yet he did publish a sermon delivered the following year emphasizing the need for "the nature of improvement to increase" among mankind via the "discoveries" of the sciences.[15]

Rush's sweeping ideas on education included women. He published several pamphlets, including the 1787 *Thoughts upon Female Education*, which argued that "the education of young ladies, in this country should be conducted upon principles very different from what it is in Great Britain . . . when we were part of a monarchical empire."[16] A woman's role as "mistress of a family" made it critical for women to be well educated. Rush and Noah Webster both developed a set of skills that were critical for "female education" in the early republic, yet they could not imagine this to extend beyond the work of a mother in the home. Importantly, however, their proposed curriculum included a broad education that went beyond the domestic arts. Even so, Rush remained fundamentally conservative in his thinking about women's education, seeing their primary role as supporting the household of men, particularly their husbands. Alternatively, women such as Eliza Harriot advocated for women's role as political actors in their own right. In the end, Rush's limited view of women's role in society forced women to have separate academies in their communities; a federal plan advanced by Rush did not include women.[17]

Rush shared some important ideas for establishing a national university with fellow Philadelphian Nicholas Collin. Both believed that the institution would promote an American social order that relied on the notion of self-improvement through learning. Ending reliance on Europe was crucial for both, and they argued for expanding knowledge domestically instead of relying on Europeans for advanced education and scientific breakthroughs. Americans' concern about the influence of foreign education upon the nation's youth permeated educational proposals and even made its way into legislation. Georgia, for example, passed a law stipulating that any student who had studied in a foreign country would be considered an alien and ineligible for civil or military office for a period of time equal to the time they had spent abroad. Thomas Jefferson, although a great admirer of the scientific knowledge being produced in Europe, worried that American students abroad were in danger of learning bad habits and having their morals corrupted. Noah Webster also worried that the wrong kind of education could be a source of corruption. Webster associated foreign education with training in classics, ornamental studies such as dance and music, and rhetoric, which were not needed in America and a detriment to moral improvement. These forms of education emphasized monarchical traditions and institutions, which would degrade the republic.[18]

Rush was a tireless advocate for the enhancement of free comprehensive education and learning in the United States. His first *Plan for the Establishment of Public Schools* focused on a program in his home state of Pennsylvania. Published in 1786, it outlined a program for the proper education for the citizens of a republic. Rush specifically insisted that "one general and uniform system of education will render the mass of the people more homogeneous," which would help promote patriotism and cleanse the former colonies of the corruption of monarchies."[19] Rush presented education as a moral duty for all citizens and stated that the government itself was responsible for public education. Rush was not alone in viewing public education as a core baseline for citizens, who now played active roles in governing and therefore needed to be well informed in order to fulfill their public duties, but free, state-sponsored public education turned out to be a complicated issue for many. Some state legislators balked at the notion of raising tax revenue for educational purposes since it benefitted individuals. Yet citizens increasingly looked to the state to provide appropriate educational institutions.[20]

Rush expanded on his thoughts over the course of the next few years as he called for a new institution for national knowledge. In his first publicly signed statement, published in the *American Museum* in January 1787, Rush solicited support for substantial changes to the structure of the American government at the upcoming Constitutional Convention. His essay "Address to the People of the United States" argued that "THE REVOLUTION IS NOT OVER!" and stressed that "to conform the principles, morals, and manners of our citizens to our republican forms of government it is absolutely necessary that knowledge of every kind, should be disseminated through every part of the united states." Here, Rush put his finger on a significant problem for those who sought to create a culturally independent and self-reliant nation: the United States lacked the appropriate institution. Yet Rush believed that once such an institution was established, after completing their studies in their "respective states" the best students would attend this national university, and then "the honours and offices of the united states should be confined to persons who had imbibed federal and republican ideas in this university."[21] This institution would provide advanced study in the sciences, which in that period included courses on government and the economy, all taught in the proper way for the future leaders of the republic.

In October 1788, Rush wrote a pseudonymous communication for the *Federal Gazette* (Philadelphia) that was widely reprinted in several newspapers, including the *American Museum*.[22] Rush sent at least one copy of the plan to his longtime correspondent in New England, Jeremey Belknap, asking that it be published in papers across the region if he deemed it "proper."[23] Widely published in New England, it spelled out a full proposal for the establishment of an institution that would encourage a broad liberal education with an emphasis on natural philosophy and natural history. He also advocated for the establishment of a great museum and garden to support this educational enterprise.[24] His new organization would serve as a home base for missions of exploration both to the Old World and within the United States.

Rush argued that this was common in Europe and in countries such as Sweden, Denmark, and Russia, which relied on the "discoveries made by young gentleman employed for these purposes [to extend] their manufactures and commerce, so as to rival . . . the oldest nations in Europe." These young American men would return to the university with their collections and organize and classify their findings "for the benefit of our country." In Rush's view, a national university would also serve as a vetting ground for the future leadership of the country. He argued that Congress should establish a law that prevented people from serving in either elected or appointed positions in the national government without first acquiring a degree from the university. As he put it, "We require certain qualifications in lawyers, physicians and clergymen before we commit our property, lives or our souls to their care . . . why then should we commit our country . . . to men who cannot produce vouchers of their qualifications for the important trust?" Further, since the "degrees conferred in this university" would themselves be new, they should "receive a new name, that shall designate the design of an education for civil and public life." This means of control was seen as a way to keep inappropriate people out of positions of importance and to ensure that new systems of knowledge were used in order to promote the proper types of republican citizens to leadership roles in the United States.[25]

Rush's justifications for a national university presented a need for a new institution designed to centralize power and promote the concentration of knowledge in the hands of a few while also promoting the idea that knowledge offered a means of self-improvement. These calls by the elite for expanding participation in learning were revolutionary in acknowledging that their new model of government required a citizenry devoted to self-improvement. Nevertheless, these same proposals recognized that the citizenry had to be transformed to hold a common set of ideals that fit their understanding of the existing social structure. In the end, these tensions were at the heart of these early calls for a national university and mirrored the social and political environment of the revolutionary era.

Washington's National University

It is likely that Washington first heard of these proposals for a national university while he was in Philadelphia for the Constitutional Convention. He may already have been familiar with Rush's writings on the matter, but as president of the Constitutional Convention he certainly became aware of the proposals put forth by James Madison and Charles Pinckney for the establishment of this type of national educational institution.[26] In Madison's original proposal, dated August 18, 1787, the power to establish a national university was one of nine powers to be granted to the federal legislature, along with the power to "encourage by premiums and provisions, the advancement of useful knowledge and discoveries."[27] Pinckney introduced his own version, which also empowered Congress to "establish seminaries for the promotion of literature and the arts and sciences."[28] These proposals were forwarded to the Committee on Detail.

Then, on September 14, 1787, Pinckney and Madison submitted a compromise draft that gave Congress the authority to, among other things, establish a national university in the federal district. James Wilson, of Pennsylvania, supported the measure, while other members of the Convention, such as Gouverneur Morris, of New York, opposed the proposal as unnecessary. Morris argued that Congress would already have exclusive jurisdiction over the federal district. Six states—New Hampshire, Massachusetts, New Jersey, Delaware, Maryland, and Georgia—were against adding this power, leaving Pennsylvania, Virginia, North Carolina, and South Carolina in favor while Connecticut was divided. Ultimately, the state delegations split over the issue. With only three days left in the session, many may have agreed with Morris that it was an irrelevant issue and did not need a vote by the membership. Roger Sherman, of Connecticut, went on record as opposed to the measure during the Convention, declaring that the proposal in the Convention was voted down because these powers "should be exercised by the states in their separate capacity."[29] This suggests that the issue of a national university became wrapped up in larger debates about the proper role of the national government, which was not lost on George Washington.[30]

After his election as president of the United States, George Washington became the leading champion for the creation of a national university. As president, Washington was cognizant of the need for an educated citizenry and saw the importance of supporting and spreading useful knowledge in the new republic. He was also concerned that the next generation of leaders might be misled and degenerate into worldly sophisticates, corrupted by the influences of monarchical decadence and idleness because of European influences. In 1790, Secretary of War Henry Knox provided a report to Washington to aid in the writing of his annual message to Congress. The report included a section about the need to establish a national institution of learning to assist "in diffusing light and knowledge," which would serve the new country by "cementing the several states of this extended Republic, and preventing a practice of sending American youth to different parts of Europe for their education."[31] As secretary of war, Knox regarded this institution as a matter of national security and a public good for the long-term viability of the military. Subsequently, Washington clearly expressed his public support for the expansion of knowledge and learning in his first message to Congress, on January 8, 1790. Washington stated that there was "nothing, which can better deserve your patrionage [sic], than the promotion of Science and Literature. Knowledge is in every Country the surest basis of public happiness. . . . Whether this desirable object will be best promoted by affording aids to Seminaries of Learning already established—by the institution of a national University—or by any other expedients, will be well worthy of a place in the deliberations of the Legislature."[32] Washington, who was always cautious in his public pronouncements, sought to avoid giving an impression of usurping power from Congress, yet this call for a national university was clear and seemed uncontroversial.

Congress acknowledged Washington's message a few days later and confirmed the value of learning by stating, "Literature and science are essential to the preservation of a free constitution; the measures of Government should therefore be calculated to strengthen the confidence that is due to that important truth."³³ Yet Congress did not, in fact, act on these sentiments. In May 1790, William Loughton Smith, of South Carolina, made a motion in the House of Representatives to act on the part of the president's speech that promoted the encouragement of science and literature, and he asked that the matter be sent to committee for consideration. Debate ensued. Some believed that the power to establishing institutions of higher education belonged to the states. This point was made by Michael Stone, of Maryland, who argued that no prescribed power existed for Congress to take part in these affairs. He further explained that Congress had already passed laws to promote knowledge, which were within its purview, as specified in article 1, section 8, of the Constitution, "To promote the Progress of Science and useful Arts, by securing for limited Times to Authors and Inventors the exclusive Right to their respective Writings and Discoveries."³⁴ Stone argued that this had been done and stated, "We have encouraged learning by giving authors an exclusive privilege of vending their works."³⁵ His line of reasoning suggests that some legislators believed that knowledge was akin to property and that the proper role of the federal government was to secure the rights to that property. Others, such as the aforementioned Roger Sherman, believed that the states needed to develop their own institutions of learning. In the end, the measure received no action, and the fate of the national university remained unaddressed on the national level for several years.

Despite legislative inaction, the push for a national university continued in the public sphere. Key administration supporters published their approval of a national university in newspapers. The Federalist publisher John Fenno wrote a supportive article in the *Massachusetts Centinel* (Boston) only days after Washington's first annual message in 1790 entitled "Importance of a Proper SYSTEM of EDUCATION—Establishment of a FEDERAL UNIVERSITY RECOMMENDED." Fenno reiterated the arguments of Rush and Collin and added that "no country is more indebted to the cause of learning than America." He recommended erecting a university in a "central situation of the Union" where "students graduating" at the colleges throughout the states would "finish their education," studying "the political interests of their country" and securing their "freedom and independence for which they so nobly fought."³⁶

Washington never formally developed his ideas on what constituted an appropriate curriculum of study at a university. This was likely owing in part to his never having received a formal education, a fact about which Washington remained self-conscious throughout his life.[37] Washington greatly valued the type of education he had not received, and he relied on college-educated trusted advisors such as Alexander Hamilton and James Madison to help him navigate questions when he lacked the necessary expertise.[38] Although contemporaries acknowledged that "Washington was not a scholar," they recognized his formidable mind and regarded him as "a man of the highest natural talents."[39] In addition to his determined support for the establishment of a national university, he wrote frequently on the importance of education in his correspondence. In 1784, after receiving a copy of *A Treatise on Education* from the author George Chapman, Washington thanked him and shared that "my sentiments are perfectly in unison with yours sir, that the best means of forming a manly, virtuous and happy people, will be found in the right education of youth."[40] Chapman espoused a systematic classical education for a young boy, which would "smooth his way to the science . . . when he is sent to prosecute his studies at the university."[41] Later, in a letter to his nineteen-year-old nephew, George Steptoe Washington, who was a student at the University of Pennsylvania along with his brother Laurence, Washington encouraged them to use their time wisely and complete their studies and dedicate themselves to developing "good moral character [since it was] the first essential" quality of a man. Washington insisted that it was "highly important that you should endeavor not only to be learned but virtuous."[42] In other words, mastering a domain of knowledge was significant, but self-making through self-discipline made a future leader.[43]

Washington's personal library held at least thirty-one titles on education, ranging from curriculum suggestions to works on geography, works on manners, and works about specific institutions. He added to those books over time, and at the time of his death he owned more than twelve hundred books.[44] Washington also made liberal use of association libraries wherever he resided, such as the Library Company of Philadelphia when he attended the Constitutional Convention.[45] Washington also made use of the New York Society Library, and he checked out at least two books during the short period in which the Federal government resided in New York City.[46] In 1791 Washington received a letter from William Rawle notifying him that he and the members of Congress "shall have the free Use of the Books in the Library in as full and ample Manner as if they were Members of the Company."[47] As a member of the American Philosophical Society, Washington also had access to the society's extensive collections. The use of these collections allowed Washington to work on his own moral development while acquiring information he needed as a plantation owner and general. Yet individual efforts alone would not replace formal education, which he remained convinced offered the best way to secure the future of his legacy to the fledgling nation.[48]

Therefore, Washington was pleased whenever he heard news of new establishments for promoting the education of the country's youth. In 1789, for example, he acknowledged the honorary doctor of laws degree he received from Washington College in Maryland. The college was the first chartered in the United States upon its becoming a sovereign nation. In his letter to the college, Washington emphasized the importance of "the prosperity of Colleges and Seminaries of learning" in "civilized Societies" since they promoted the "welfare of the State and happiness of the People," and he stated that he longed for the "encrease of our Seminaries of Learning through this extensive country."[49] There is an irony in that Washington's doctoral certificate was inscribed in Latin, a language he had never formally studied and in which he could use only a few phrases.[50]

Although discussions about a national university waned as Congress focused on other legislative matters, Washington utilized his authority as president to establish the groundwork for positive legislative action in favor of one. As president, Washington had significant latitude to plan the details of the new national capital, and he appointed commissioners for public buildings for the federal district who promoted his agenda.

The commissioners conducted much of the business of planning and building the early District of Columbia, and Washington participated in extensive private correspondence with them.[51] While the actors changed over time, Washington remained at the center of the planning process. Samuel Blodget, who contemporaries knew as a "great Speculator" and whose reputation for success "would answer well their selfish and temporary views," became a leading advocate for the university within Washington's administration.[52] One of the first to purchase a lot in the city, Blodget had an ambitious plan to develop a street with a hotel and other properties. He tried several schemes, including a lottery, to raise money for a national university and to fund the other building projects in the city. Blodget marked out a site for the university on one of his properties and hoped that a lottery to sell a grand hotel in a strategic area would bring in the resources needed to build the federal city.[53] Washington and the commissioners were unconvinced and directed him to refrain from advertising a lottery. When he went ahead, the commissioners were "surprized

FIG. 1. Portrait of Samuel Blodget Jr. by John Trumbull, ca. 1784. This portrait shows Blodget as a man of financial expertise. In his hands are financial papers, and a merchant ship is clearly visible in the background. (Courtesy National Portrait Gallery, Smithsonian Institution)

and concerned that Mr Blodget should have proceeded in a new Lottery, not only without our Consent but after a contrary Explanation which took place with him a little before he left this place."[54] One of Washington's advisors for DC matters, Thomas Johnson, reported to him that Blodget's entrepreneurial schemes were concerning, that the commissioners did not think Blodget's aid should be retained, and that he "will not be useful in the Affairs of the City."[55] Washington concurred. He wrote to Johnson that Blodget's conduct had begun to demonstrate his inadequacy for assisting in their planning for the new federal city; "it appears evidently enough now, that speculation has been his primary object from the beginning."[56] Blodget's schemes and his failure to secure investors resulted in his losing Washington's favor. Blodget later went to debtor's prison, but he remained committed to building Washington's national university even after the president's death.[57]

Washington and his supporters saw a national university in the federal city as a way to create a leadership class for the new country. They hoped that it would give future leaders the necessary knowledge and skills to effectively govern the populace in a republican society. They also hoped that this institution would bring the best men among the elite class across the country together at an early age so that they would develop bonds of mutual affection and reduce the chances of factions and sectionalism. Others worried that this looked painfully similar to the British system of government they had just fought a revolution to escape and wondered if there might be a new way to focus on knowledge for future leaders.

Jefferson's Gambit

Thomas Jefferson worried that Washington and his administration and the Federalists were promoting an aristocratic government. Jefferson hoped for a broader educational agenda and saw the Federalist's ideas as better suited to Europeans.[58] Yet despite his many efforts to promote wider access to education, at least for white children in his home state of Virginia, Jefferson's plans failed. Further, his ideas for promoting education at the federal level became embroiled in broader political battles between the Federalists and his own republican faction. These two groups of elites disagreed about what constituted useful knowledge and who that knowledge was destined to serve. Jefferson's ideas on establishing a graduated public education system are well known, yet he struggled to reconcile his belief in one's ability to improve oneself with his lived experience that certain kinds of learning promoted an aristocracy. Jefferson hoped for an entirely different kind of education based on scientific knowledge instead of classical and ornamental training. This struggle became clear when Jefferson directly entered the discussion over establishing a national university through his advocacy of a first-class university staffed with renowned scientific experts from Europe who were identified as being sympathetic to the leveling spirit of the revolutionary age.[59]

By 1795, Congress still had not acted on the idea of establishing a national university, yet an opportunity to transplant the faculty of the University of Geneva to America might have instantaneously provided the United States with some of the leading scientific experts in the world to staff their planned university. Jefferson wrote a calculated letter to Washington dated February 23, 1795, in which he told the president of an imminent opportunity to secure a group of faculty sympathetic toward republican government who were considered as one of the "two eyes of Europe in matters of science."[60] Jefferson emphasized the expertise and knowledge of these learned men, and he urged Washington to move quickly to secure them and make the fledgling country an intellectual powerhouse.[61]

By 1795 Jefferson had resigned from Washington's cabinet. The distrust Jefferson felt toward the administration was pervasive. Many worried that Washington was being led to support nationalistic policies that were aristocratic in their implementation and took power away from local American communities.[62] Jefferson's letter to Washington left out crucial details of the Geneva scheme because Jefferson wanted to maneuver Washington away from the idea of establishing a national university in the federal city; Jefferson believed that such a central, federally funded university would corrupt students' morals just as central universities did in European capital cities. Even more importantly, Jefferson worried that centralizing power in the federal government for institutions like a national university constituted a threat to the republic, especially if that power was concentrated in a single place like Washington, DC. Jefferson slipped in his grand maneuver near the conclusion of the letter to Washington when he said that "a question would arise as to the place of the establishment. As far as I can learn, it is thought just that the state which gives the revenue should be most considered in the uses to which it is appropriated."[63] Jefferson thought the institution should be located in Virginia because the Commonwealth of Virginia had paid for the fifty shares in the Potomac Canal Company intended to honor Washington's service to the country during the Revolution.[64]

Washington was deeply skeptical of Jefferson's motives and resisted his attempt to "dazzle" him "with the brilliance of the Geneva faculty."[65] Additionally, Jefferson did not know that Washington was well informed of Jefferson's scheme to bring the faculty to Virginia thanks to conversations with his dutiful vice president, John Adams. Washington was concerned at the prospect of the "transplanting of an *entire* Seminary of *foreigners,* who may not understand our language" and would likely retain their "language, habits & principles (good or bad) which they bring with them," which would retard their ability to be "assimilated to our customs, manners and laws: in a word, soon become one people."[66] Since they would be teachers of the future American leaders, this concerned Washington and his Federalist allies. Further, Washington was likely advised by Edmund Randolph, who had succeeded Jefferson as secretary of state after Jefferson resigned in 1793, that nothing could be done by the federal government to support the move of the faculty since many would call it "an aristocratic establishment."[67] Even so, Randolph offered his support for a national university, thinking it should be established in the federal city.[68]

Washington replied to Jefferson in March 1795 indicating that he had already promised the commissioners of the District of Columbia the shares from the Potomac Canal Company to endow a national university. Washington was adamant that the federal district should house this institution. He countered Jefferson's concerns about youths being corrupted, writing that "this seminary is contemplated for the *completion* of education, and study of the sciences (not for boys in their rudiments)."[69] Washington also noted that his primary purpose for supporting a national university was to eliminate the need of sending youth abroad for education and to bring together the leaders of the new republic so that they could develop friendships that would diminish the factional and sectional divisions that he observed in the republic. Bringing foreign faculty to American shores seemed at odds with his goals.

Overall, the views on education of Washington and his supporters and Jefferson differed with regard to much more than where to locate a national university. They disagreed about the very purpose of knowledge dissemination in the republic. Washington and his supporters viewed the need to create a leadership class of young men from across the republic who were free from foreign interference. In essence, they considered teaching them to become leaders of men to be the purpose of a national university. Jefferson imagined a university with a different purpose: to give the best young minds in the new republic an opportunity to acquire specialized scientific knowledge and become the most learned men in the latest scientific disciplines. Such a national university would emphasize a curriculum to promote self-improvement, and the pupils would be taught by the best professors in scientific learning. Thus, while both Washington and Jefferson envisioned a national university for an elite group, they differed in their views of how knowledge should be disseminated.

Polysophic Institution

The distrust between Washington and the emerging Federalists and Jefferson and his emerging Republicans rested on a clear difference in how they saw the world.[70] In short, Federalists resented new ideas and pretenders who claimed a scientific authority that the Federalists deemed undeserved. Federalists relied on traditional education paradigms that embraced the two core tenants "ancients and axioms."[71] These leaders embraced the "axioms of Christianity" to assure leaders' good moral character and trusted the ancients to provide a solid background for writing and speaking well. Students need not become experts in a disciplinary set of knowledge if they understood how to read and speak about the topic in a refined fashion. Thus, to Federalists, orators, with their training in grammar, rhetoric, and logic, were superior to the philosopher who focused on the acquisition of specialized knowledge about the human and natural worlds.[72] This grounding—as emphasized by the British system of education—would ensure that youths matured and acquired the proper mental framework to take their place in the public sphere.

Jefferson instead encouraged the study of "every branch of science."[73] He and many of his supporters viewed the national institutions that embraced modern scientific learning established in revolutionary France as a modern, forward-thinking option. Jefferson, along with many Republicans, viewed science as paramount and advocated moving away from the traditional curriculum taught in America's colleges toward the applied sciences needed in a modern world.

Jefferson's leadership on the issue of creating new educational institutions and disseminating information represented a key point of departure within the broader public debate over the nature and location of learned institutions in the early American republic. Jefferson's promotion of disciplinary knowledge is critical to the changes in knowledge creation in the early republic. Jefferson saw the value of having leading scientific practitioners associated with teaching and learning. The faculty from Geneva actively participated in the domains of knowledge that they were teaching. They were actively engaged in learned societies and advancing new knowledge, not merely teaching the same staid curriculum that had been the norm in places like his own College of William and Mary. Further he continued to want to design a program of study for a broader audience of people rather than just the elites. Still, there were conflicts over the mission of education: would the population be better served by the past curriculum or by a new revolutionary form of knowledge?[74] Jefferson wanted to hear fresh ideas, especially if they were focused on scientific learning.[75]

In 1796, William Thornton, who was a graduate of the renowned medical program at the University of Edinburgh[76] and served as one of Washington's loyal DC commissioners, wrote an excited letter to Jefferson about a new idea from the distinguished French philosopher Volney. The idea, which Volney thought would be useful to the people of the United States, was that the government should create a new institution in the federal city. This institution would incorporate "in the University a Philosophical Society, upon an extensive Scale," which would centralize the knowledge-creating institution of the republic.[77] Thornton saw American education as being exceptional since "we have no fetters to the human genius" thanks to the freedom bestowed (on male, white Americans) by the Revolution and because Americans "combine the various nations whence we come and mutually adopt . . . whatever our particular circumstances require." In an unpublished essay titled "On National Education," Thornton focused on philosophers and the promotion of knowledge in the arts and sciences. Thornton asserted that education and the advancement of individual knowledge were a "national benefit" and that learning needed to be directly relevant to "the real concerns of life," not just disconnected "scholastic learning." Thornton lamented that the founders of educational institutions in the United States focused on curricula that "have been too abstracted in their pursuits, and by too distant a recession from the common avocations" of people and their needs. Thornton remained committed to the idea of a national university, though apparently one focused on promoting a mission more in line with Jefferson's priorities than with Washington's. Years later Thorton's participation became critical to the establishment of a science-focused learned society in the federal city.[78]

Washington, for his part, made a last major push for his national university near the end of his administration, when he corresponded intensively with Alexander Hamilton as they worked on both his Farewell Address and his final annual message to Congress. In a letter to Hamilton dated September 1, 1796, Washington defined his ideas on learning: "I mean Education *generally* as one of the surest means of enlightening & givg. just ways of thinkg to our Citizens." Here Washington espoused the idea that the citizenry needed a particular kind of training by which the elite "Youth from *all parts* of the United States might receive the polish of Erudition in the Arts, Sciences & Belle Letters." Washington saw these young men as the future leaders of the country and believed that among these men "those who were disposed to run a political course, might not only be instructed in the theory & principles"; "this Seminary being at the Seat of the General Government," these students would see the legislature in action. Washington's vision for a national university and its curriculum remained specifically focused on the elite and on a traditional way of learning.[79]

Washington's ideas on education can also be detected in his correspondence with his nephews and other young charges. He counseled them in lengthy letters about the need to secure friends of high moral character and to develop good habits. Additionally, he advised them to master the material in assigned books, and he paid for their training in music, while demanding that they be industrious in their studies.[80] The virtuous man needed to become a gentleman who would be mindful of his obligations while also learning to manage his self-indulgent nature through proper training. Founders like Washington focused on the need for young elites to secure an education in the "polite arts," which included learning how to dance and to speak foreign languages, which served to display their refinement and status. In the end, Washington hoped that those who were the best men, as measured by their erudition, would be prepared to lead the next stage of the republic.[81]

Others believed that education offered a means to accomplish the true goal of the American Revolution, which in their view was equality, at least among white men. In March 1791, Robert Coram, a thirty-year-old teacher, librarian, and newspaper editor who had served in the navy during the Revolutionary War, sent his newly published work, *Political Inquiries: To Which Is Added, a Plan for the General Establishment of Schools Throughout the United States*, to George Washington. In a letter accompanying the 109-page pamphlet he wrote, "I take the liberty herewith to request your acceptance of a Small Pamphlet which I have wrote on the Subject of Education[.] I wrote it chiefly with a design of being useful to my country."[82] This in and of itself was a revolutionary act, in that he believed that he had an important contribution that he could, and should, offer to his country.[83]

Coram's primary message was that in order to be free, men needed property. This property could take the form of real estate or training in a trade. Education ought to provide the means to acquire property, yet he believed that the elites were trained in schools so "that part only of the citizens should be sent to colleges and universities to learn to cheat the rest of their liberties." Coram sought a public system of education for all to replace the system of private academies promoted by many of the Federalists. Coram wrote that "by Education I mean instruction in arts as well as sciences," and he said that it should be for "every class of citizens."[84] Education in a republic should promote knowledge and thus economic and civic prosperity. It had to be led by the government and could not rely on the discretion of parents. Coram also pointed to what he viewed as the wretched state of education throughout the country and the fact that "the teachers are generally foreigners shamefully deficient in every quality necessary to convey instruction to youth."[85] Additionally, Coram lamented that the curriculum taught included "modes of faith, systems of manners," and even "foreign or dead languages" to train the natural aristocrats. Although institutions of education in the new United States ought to offer a means to transform society, academies in the early republic were often still modeled upon European examples and served as a "justification for *unnatural* inequality."[86] Coram's message was clear: the United States needed broader participation in education directed by the government to promote enlightened progress in the new country.

There is no evidence that Washington replied to Coram's letter nor that it changed his mind about establishing an institution for the best in the nation to learn how to govern, yet Washington and Coram did agree on one thing: foreign influence on the minds of America's youth was a danger to the future of the republic. Coram also sent his pamphlet and a letter to Thomas Jefferson at around the same time: "In conformity to an act of Congress for the encouragement of Learning I herewith send you a Copy of a Pamphlet which I have lately published."[87] Jefferson too never responded. In the end, Coram promoted a more egalitarian and universal system of education than either founder envisioned, pointing toward the fact that Americans from a variety of backgrounds thought seriously about education in the 1790s and were aware of and espoused a wide variety of educational paths for the young nation.[88]

Washington's commitment to a national university, as mentioned earlier, was demonstrated in his months-long correspondence with Hamilton beginning in September 1796, culminating in his final address to Congress on December 7, 1796. In that address, Washington reiterated the need for a national university and articulated a vision for an institution focused on the need to inculcate students from across the United States with a shared knowledge in order to help them forge relationships to bridge their differences. Importantly, his vision emphasized the need for the future leaders of the republic to receive a uniform education to ensure "our prospect of permanent union."[89] The response from Congress was mixed. The Senate responded with unanimous approval on December 10.[90] Senators agreed that the time had come to finally pass this legislation. Unlike the Senate, however, the House saw a protracted debate over its response to the president's proposal.

In addition to the president's call for the establishment of a national university the House received a memorial from Washington's DC commissioners on Wednesday, December 21, 1796. They informed Congress that in the course of carrying out his duties in managing the land designated for the federal city the president had already appropriate land, and they reaffirmed their commitment to the goal of the university. They also requested the creation of a corporation to manage funds collected for the creation of a national university. Washington's commissioners worked hard to help fulfill his goal for a national university. William Thornton, one of the commissioners, affirmed their commitment to the success of the proposal and recommended that they promote the potential success of their shared goals through an "appropriation for the express use of the university."[91] This appropriation included "nineteen acres, one road and twenty-one perches . . . for the site of a national university."[92] Washington had already announced that he would provide an endowment in the form of fifty shares in the Potomac Company. This action taken by the commissioners was a show of their firm commitment and support for the proposal.[93]

Further, the commissioners' memorial argued that the new national university should promote a set of core values to the future leaders of America. These values emphasized the need for an American education system focused on a useful and virtuous body of knowledge in order to promote national unity. This stance was firmly within the goals articulated by Washington. The commissioners also seemed politically astute, anticipating some political resistance to the measure, as evidenced by the proposal's lack of a request for federal appropriation of monies to endow the new institution. Instead, the memorial called for the establishment of an organization that would receive private donations from the community.[94]

Alexander White, one of the commissioners, wrote to James Madison asking that he help shepherd the measure through an increasingly factious Congress. Madison, a longtime friend and confidant of Washington's, had recently experienced a strained relationship with his old friend because of their increasing political differences. One reason was Washington's distaste for the emerging opposition in the form of the democratic societies that he blamed for the Whiskey Rebellion.[95] More significantly, the serious tensions over the Jay Treaty caused a major divide between them. Nevertheless, Madison decided to help the outgoing president meet his unfulfilled objective.[96]

The proposal was sent to a committee led by the leader of the congressional Republicans, James Madison. The committee, which also included Washington's friend William Craik, a Federalist representative from Maryland, and Chauncy Goodrich, a Federalist from Connecticut, returned the proposal a few days later with no changes.[97] After extensive debates in the House, there was clear opposition to the establishment of a national university. The arguments against the university varied, but most of the extant record show a concern over who would pay for the institution.[98] This surprised many supporters, such as Federalist Maryland representative William Murray, who protested that "not a single shilling is asked" from the Treasury. His colleague William Craik also indicated his surprise, stating that "some gentlemen who opposed the report yesterday conceived there was some secret poison lurking within it—some dangerous principle not to be discovered on its face, which would some time produce baneful influences—this has been insinuated though not directly said."[99]

Supporters of the university proposal could not quell the Jeffersonian Republicans' mistrust of the Federalist administration. Proponents of a university tried to frame the issue not in terms of Congress creating a national institution but rather in terms of local governance establishing an institution for the citizens of the District. This strategy was not successful. Members opposed to a national university explicitly cited the granting of the federal land by Washington and his commissioners as evidence of the great subterfuge that was being perpetrated on Congress. Edward Livingston, of New York, had argued that the commissioners' job was to lay out public lands for public use and not to give away lands for private enterprises. "Such institutions are not public, but private concerns," he said.[100] In the two days of debate there was little substance about the types of subjects that would be taught in the proposed national university, but the Jeffersonian Republicans were convinced that the institution aimed to establish a new aristocratic elite led by their Federalist opponents. Ultimately, the debate ended in a close, 37–36 vote to postpone the matter. That is where the issue died in Congress.

A map published in an 1802 traveler's directory (Fig. 2) shows the grounds for the planned university, in a key spot near the President's House. William Thornton persuaded the president that this site for the university would "add much to the grandeur of the city."[101] The map showed a spot overlooking the Potomac. The site contained "Braddock's Rock" and was commonly called the "key of all keys" because of its strategic location as a reference point for surveyors. Now this site is near the Kennedy Center. The reportedly massive stone, which allowed ships to be secured at the site, was later mined and utilized for the fabrication of some federal buildings. Now only a small stone at the base of a well with a memorial plaque remains near a busy road, but at the time it was a site that everyone in the city knew. This map is evidence that Washington and the commissioners did try to utilize what authority they had to secure a future for the university they envisioned to provide America's future leaders.[102]

After Washington's death, the nation mourned its leader, and newspapers across the republic published his will. People must have wondered what would happen to the shares he had left as a gift to the people of the United States for the establishment of a national university. Samuel Blodget added resources to

FIG. 2. Map of Washington, DC, 1802. A location is reserved for a national university overlooking the river two blocks from the President's House. (Courtesy American Antiquarian Society)

Washington's endowment, claiming in his 1803 memorial to Congress on the proposed national university to represent more than "one thousand subscribers to the same object, whose respectable names accompany this memorial." He also stated that public calls for an equestrian statue of Washington ought to be combined with the national university to serve as a monument to Washington. The *Annals of Congress* reports that Blodget's request was accompanied by a plan including an "Equestrian Statue of Washington, surrounded by halls and colleges regularly arranged, the whole to be styled the Monument to Washington."[103] Further, the memorial proposed that Washington's tomb be placed in the center of the complex, making the entire campus similar to the Timoleonton of Syracuse, as described in Plutarch. After a vote of 42 to 27, the proposal was submitted to a select committee. John Peter Van Ness, a representative from New York, was selected to chair the committee. He later became mayor of Washington, DC, and a leader in the Washington Monument Society. Yet Congress never took any concrete action on Blodget's proposal, and the memorial to Congress with the drawing seems to have disappeared. It seems that Washington's dream of a national university died with him.

As the years passed, the details surrounding the debate over a national university began to fade, but fragments of memories of the bequest left by

Washington remained. Many thought the stock had been overlooked during the internal improvement booms and busts of the early nineteenth century and lost forever. Some suggested that the US Treasury held the stock at the time of the British Conflagration in Washington in 1814. Others speculated that the funds had been included as part of an endowment for the Columbian College, which would eventually become George Washington University. The reality is that the stock simply lost value over time and ultimately became worthless when the Potomac Company was forced to give up its charter due to heavy debts to the Chesapeake and Ohio Canal Company in 1828.[104]

As Washington's dream faded, others began to promote a different vision for the university. Joel Barlow, a friend of Jefferson's and a radical freethinker, wrote to Jefferson from Paris in September 1800 that he had seen Washington's will. Barlow suggested that Washington's memory be made use of to create "an institution of much more extensive and various utility than anything of the kind that has hitherto existed." Barlow's detailed letter to Jefferson identified the deficiencies of the colleges and universities in the United States and pointed to the superiority of European learning institutions. Barlow made the case that the new university needed to be one in which "the twofold object of collecting and disseminating knowledge should be wrought into the system, the Institution to be called the Polysophic Society, or some such comprehensive name by which the variety of its labors should be designated."[105]

This vision was similar to what William Thornton had described to Jefferson in May 1796, although Barlow's proposal was more detailed. Importantly, Barlow did not point to the need for students to develop a sense of brotherhood to minimize factionalism. His focus was on the collection and dissemination of knowledge, which he believed would yield better inventions and productive citizens, which in turn would expand US commerce and security. Jefferson was interested in learning more about knowledge institutions, and he continued to correspond and discuss the idea of a university with Barlow for many years. Yet ultimately, Jefferson chose a different route, preferring to establish a university in and for his home state of Virginia rather than for the nation as a whole.

Washington envisioned a national institution that would provide the necessary knowledge—which included training to become a learned gentleman who excelled in politics, morals, and the classics—to the future leaders of the republic. A national university would ensure that the youth of the nation, or at least its elite male offspring, became a unified, homogenous citizenry. This plan offered an opportunity for early leaders to create and disseminate knowledge for citizens to consume. However, this vision was irreconcilable with the vision of many of the Jeffersonian Republicans and those who sought a broader, participatory education system for the benefit of their new republic. The opposition, led by Thomas Jefferson, favored new kinds of institutions dedicated to expanding specialized knowledge in the arts and sciences. In the end, arguments about the nature of what constituted useful knowledge and who should control that knowledge doomed one of Washington's most cherished ideas.

CHAPTER 2

A NATIONAL ACADEMY

The Politicization of Knowledge

Shortly after it became clear that Thomas Jefferson had lost his 1796 bid for the presidency of the United States and had resolved to perform his duty in Philadelphia as vice president to John Adams, he received a letter from the secretaries of the American Philosophical Society (APS), the oldest learned society in the United States, telling him that that he had been "chosen President of that respectable Institution." The secretaries wrote that although the membership of the APS still mourned the death of their second president, David Rittenhouse, "they look forward with this consoling Reflection, That, in the same Chair, from which two American Philosophers have, successively, instructed *them*, and *the World*, a Third is now seated; by whose Genius and Knowledge, our National Name will preserve a distinguished Place in the Annals of Science."[1] Jefferson's friend the noted scholar and physician Benjamin Rush had informed him a few days earlier of the APS's plan and congratulated Jefferson on his "*escape* of the Office of President" of the United States; now the APS looked forward to his presiding over their meetings.[2]

Jefferson's deferential reply indicated that he longed to be taken seriously as a man of learning and science. The news of his election by the APS, whose "suffrage of a body which comprehends whatever the American world has of distinction in philosophy and science, in general," was to him "the most flattering incident of my life." Jefferson assured his colleagues that despite feeling "no qualification for this distinguished post but a sincere zeal for all the objects of our institution," he would work diligently to "see knowlege [*sic*] so disseminated through the mass of mankind that it may at length reach even the extremes of society, beggars and kings."[3]

Despite these radical statements, the differences between Jefferson's APS and the Federalist organizations were not clear at first. John Adams, newly elected US president in 1797, served as the president of the American Academy of Arts and Sciences (AAAS) in Boston from 1791 to 1814. Adams had worked hard to establish the AAAS as an alternative to the Philadelphia-based APS. Adams tired of hearing how laudable the work of that Philadelphia institution was from learned men of Europe and sought to bring attention to the New England men of renown.[4] Adams and sixty-one other elite men joined together in 1780, in the midst of the American Revolution, to found their learned society dedicated to the ideal that "the Arts and Sciences are the Foundation and Support of Agriculture, Manufactures, and Commerce," which were needed for "Wealth, Peace, Independence, and Happiness of a people." Their goal was to bring together "Men of Genius and Learning into Public Societies" for the benefit of the people of the country.[5] Scholars have agreed that the gentleman societies focused on a universal approach to knowledge were the norm and that few imagined these organizations as anything more than a place for the elite to participate in advancing scientific learning.[6]

Thomas Jefferson and others who saw a need for a broader participatory culture of scientific learning saw opportunities for new kinds of learned societies dedicated to specialized studies. Some of these men urged learned societies to embrace educational curricula and direct applied learning in the field in order to develop the scientific knowledge the new country needed. A new epistemological framework promoting hands-on fieldwork and direct engagement through the sharing of findings was seen as the key to learning. Upon being elected president of the United States in 1801, four years after becoming president of the APS, Jefferson seized his opportunity to put forth a new, more specialized path to knowledge. Specifically, he utilized the need for reconstituting the leadership of the army to train republican soldiers in a new way.[7] The fusion of the work of the military and the work of learned societies transformed how Americans gathered, vetted, processed, and disseminated information. A model for a specialized learned society that moved beyond the traditional universal learned societies filled with gentleman scholars, such as the APS and the AAAS, and was instead open to all who practiced a certain profession emerged in the early 1800s. This chapter explores the development of this model by charting how the United States Military Academy—a small, underfunded school—transformed its educational curriculum to become a catalyst for growth and national expansion in the empire of liberty.[8] The result was a major epistemological shift in the creation and dissemination of specialized knowledge that inaugurated a new intellectual infrastructure in the United States.

Some scholars see learned societies in the United States within the context of the emerging spirit of "cultural nationalism" built around the promotion of scientific learning in the revolutionary era.[9] These learned societies promoted the efficient collection, organization, and dissemination of information.[10] Traditional elites as well as government officials and military officers, plus a growing number of professionals, both demanded and created ever more specialized information, feeding into an expanding information cycle.[11] However, much of this activity was ad hoc, and the United States failed to create a centralized scientific policy because most American politicians at the time thought the federal government ought to play a limited role in this work. The only thing most founders agreed on was the establishment of a series of copyright and patent monopolies that protected creators and allowed them to profit from their writing or inventions.

Importantly, ideological differences began to manifest in the types of scholarship the members of various early American learned societies pursued. Federalists, such as Adams, worried incessantly over the emergence of demagogues and charlatans who claimed to be the voice of the people. As Linda Kerber shows in her book *Federalists in Dissent,* the Federalists feared "that an ordered world was disintegrating; that a cherished civilization was imperiled" by the Jeffersonians, who rejected classical learning and focused on what the Federalists viewed to be the wrong types of scientific endeavors.[12] Jeffersonian Republicans, meanwhile, believed that the "new empire of liberty" needed more men at all levels of society and especially government trained in the new sciences to promote progress.[13] The acrimony developing between the two political parties became evident in the halls of America's emerging learned societies even as their members desired to demonstrate national unity to European observers and correspondents.

This fundamental clash between the Federalists and the Jeffersonian Republicans demonstrates the interconnection between the creation of scientific knowledge and the authority of leaders in the republic. Who ought to be able to participate in the creation of knowledge and how that knowledge was disseminated was deeply contested as there were fundamental differences between the ways these groups viewed the proper nature of learning and who were bona fide participants in the public sphere. The conflict centered on a clear distinction between traditional pedagogical models focused on lectures, on the one hand, and close reading of texts commonly used for studying classical languages, basic mathematics, rhetoric and logic, and moral disciplines, including ethics. In contrast to this classical epistemological framework, a new model of learning focused on an expansive view of what should be learned and how it should be taught. The promotion of disciplinary knowledge offered an opportunity for broader participation in what became known as useful knowledge.[14]

Many believed that to achieve lasting independence the United States needed the wherewithal to produce scientific knowledge. This became evident during the Revolutionary War, when the Continental army relied on foreign engineers and other experts for assistance in effectively utilizing modern artillery as well as mapping and engineering. Critical among these scientific advances through applied sciences was a well-trained officer corps well versed not only in the latest leadership strategies but also in the latest military engineering. Following the American Revolution, most leaders agreed that the military sciences needed to be expanded domestically. Federalists looked increasingly to the British model of training soldiers, while Republicans looked to the European powers for the latest military know-how.[15]

There were stark differences. Americans looking toward the Continent found that the French, rather than following the traditional tutorial method used by the British, emphasized new mathematics, modern foreign languages, and natural history, creating officers versed in the new sciences ready to serve the French nation-state. European nation-states also increasingly established military schools, scaling up instruction to ensure that more students received expert training. This transformation represented a move away from a tutorial tradition and toward an emphasis on institutional learning focused on science and engineering.[16] Americans came to see mathematics and statistical analysis as an antidote to what Jeffersonian Republicans regarded as the effeminate study of belles lettres and classical learning, whose emphasis on rhetoric encouraged the perpetuation of the established leadership class and the elite throughout the United States.

French mathematicians especially became renowned for creating more precise maps and better fortifications. Their mathematics required new approaches to calculating and honing the "judgment of young officers and orient[ing] their approach to practical problem-solving."[17] The new methods of study required a discipline to produce engineers who collected, organized, and displayed information with exactitude.[18] The British, however, were playing catch-up to the French and the Germans, and they struggled for many years to develop a new curriculum based on the liberal-education strategies being deployed elsewhere.[19]

This new, practical way of thinking about problems as military officers encountered them in the field was well suited to educating the soldiers that made up the large armies of the emerging nation-states. For example, Napoleon's Commission des Sciences et des Arts (Commission of Science and Arts), a scientific corps of 151 people—including eighty-four who had technical qualifications and ten others with medical expertise—accompanied his expeditionary force in Egypt from 1798 to 1801. In August 1798 they established the Institut d'Égypte, or Egyptian Scientific Institute, which held more than sixty meetings during the two years of French occupation.[20] News of the scientific work of the the Institut d'Égypte, composed of the "wise men whom Buonaparte carried with him," spread in American periodicals. At the center of the reporting were the pragmatic security problems that these scientific men sought to solve, such as "the establishment of mills and the making of gun-powder." Readers in America also learned that their officers were exploring important scientific questions related to governance of provinces and to the availability of natural resources, as well as various "optical phenomen[a] by which distinct objects are represented in the sky." Further, the commission established a journal, *La decade egyptienne*, which was published every ten days and "confined to subjects of science and literature."[21] This news was reprinted across the United States and whetted Jefferson's appetite.[22] The news and work of the French military scientific society also was spread through the publications of memoirs by participants, which also were advertised in newspapers.[23]

Jefferson also received news about the Egyptian expeditions from other correspondents, including the renowned Constantine Volney, who in addition to reporting news of the expedition promised to send a "geometric relief model of the Great Pyramid of Egypt," which Jefferson later displayed in his entrance hall at Monticello.[24] Also Jefferson's frequent correspondence with Joel Barlow and Pierre Samuel Du Pont de Nemours on the French model for a national institution of scientific knowledge was likely on his mind as he thought about the exciting synergies for Americans if they only modeled their own institutions after that of the French.[25]

There were other Jeffersonian Republicans who acknowledged the importance of the scientific military education breakthroughs of the French. In an

1803 letter Horatio Gates wrote to Robert Livingston that he wished his former aide during the Revolutionary War and relation by marriage to Livingston, John Armstrong's son Horatio, had

> gone with you to Paris, and been put to the best Military School there during your Embassy; He would then have known what was the Foundation of the 1st Consuls Fame, & through a Similar Education, have rais'd himself to Eminence here; you know, that without being perfect in the French Language; it is in Vain to attempt being of the First Consequence in the Bustle of this Modern World; & you have known for a long time, what a Scientific Engineer would have been worth; in our Contest with England; for until the French Army came, we had no such Man.[26]

Gates loathed the idea that Armstong's son was being educated by a "Clergyman [whose] Head is of course well stuffed with Greek, & Latin" because he viewed this as simply useless knowledge. Instead, Gates believed that Napoleon had established the best military and raised himself to his high station because of the advancement of scientific knowledge in France. Many believed this all pointed to a real need to reduce what many perceived as a deficiency that added to American anxieties over their standing in the "civilized" world. Washington solicited advice from his generals about the proper establishment of a military in peacetime. All worries about the establishment of a permanent standing army acknowledged the need for a core of learned men with specialized military training and that these men needed to be Americans. George Washington wrote to the French military engineer that he had recommended that "Congress should form Military Academies & Manufactories, [and] should this Idea be adopted, and the Plan carried into execution; it will doubtless, be necessary for us to retain some of the French Engineers now in America, for the first beginning of the Institution." Washington ended the letter by assuring his comrade that he was "persuaded that none will be more agreeable [to serve as instructors] than those Gentlemen of your Corps who have distinguished themselves in our Service with so much Ability & Satisfaction."[27] Washington was willing to accept French assistance, but only from those who had served during the American Revolution. Americans' lack of military expertise was universally seen as a shortcoming that many political leaders believed needed to be addressed immediately.[28]

Yet not all agreed that Napoleon's scientific enterprise was of value. Two Federalist papers, the *Connecticut Gazette* and the *American Mercury*, introduced the news of the formation of the National Institute with a snarky edge, calling the group "a kind of institute" and characterizing their work as "trifling discussion not quite suitable to the present doubtful state of their affairs."[29] Likewise, the preface of a book of translated copies of "original letters from the army of General Bonaparte in Egypt" captured by Admiral Nelson's fleet indicated to its American readers that the goal of the expedition was to plunder and likened it to the "conquests of Cortes and Pizarro." Napoleon took with him the "artists of all kinds, chymists, botanists, members of the pro-technical school in prodigious numbers" only to "promote the farce" that the expedition was for more than seeking to satiate their avarice, not to reorganize the county using the best information available.[30] Yet these Federalist objections paled in comparison with the veneration in which Jeffersonian Republicans held the expedition.

Indeed, the collections gathered by Napoleon's institute were substantial, resulting in numerous publications and crates of scientifically preserved specimens. The first edition of the multivolume work on the French army's Egyptian sojourn contained rich narrative descriptions of Egypt's population, plants, minerals, and animals complete with tables, musical compositions, and illustrations.[31] Numerous works in English, including detailed descriptions of the formation and work of the Institut d'Égypte, documented Napoleon's scientific endeavors.[32] These made clear that the large-scale scientific endeavors attached to the scientifically trained military units served as a means to secure wealth for the nation-state and the materials needed to promote technological progress.

These scientific endeavors excited Jefferson and his fellow Republicans, who realized that their own American officer corps needed to be transformed if they were to "provide for the common defense." This required a purging of the existing officer corps, whom Jefferson viewed as men filled with aristocratic tendencies, in favor of a new cadre of citizen-soldiers with republican virtues taught to appreciate new scientific knowledge. This pivot necessitated the creation of a new curriculum for a new military academy that would emphasize different priorities from those at existing colleges. Jefferson's idea to use the United States Military Academy at West Point to disseminate scientific knowledge to a large number of students, who would then return to their home states as military and civic leaders, was crucial for realizing his goal to create a group of republican, scientifically educated American citizens. However, Jefferson was not blind to the power of national institutions like the US Military

Academy, especially in light of Napoleon's rise from a military education system in France and his subsequent betrayal of the French Republic.[33]

The construction of the US Military Academy merged the traditional work of a university with the work of a learned society to create a new American curriculum. This new curriculum focused on practical and applied knowledge and emphasized learning by doing. Experimentation through applied fieldwork became critical for serious scientific scholars. Expertise in specialized subjects became critical for modern military engineers, who helped ensure that the United States could project its power across its emerging empire.

American Learned Societies and the Politics of Knowledge

Learned societies became sites of political and social discourse in the early years of the republic. These institutions, modeled on European societies, offered ways for the elite to participate in a community built around adult learning and the creation and diffusion of new knowledge. Election to a learned society provided a gateway into the leadership ranks of civil society. Elites used learned societies to control access to information and to legitimize those involved in knowledge production. These societies pondered new objects or scientific questions, founded journals, and published their transactions after vetting their content. Traditionally, learned societies in Europe elected gentleman scholars to membership, often after a sustained career in the public sphere. American learned societies initially modeled their own membership on European models, requiring elite social status and significant economic means of those who would conduct the work of a gentleman scholar.

European societies such as the Royal Society in London and the National Institute of Sciences and Arts in France became models for the American Philosophical Society in Philadelphia, the American Academy of Arts and Sciences in Boston, and the Connecticut Academy of Arts and Sciences in New Haven. These three institutions represented the pinnacle of scholarly authority in the early years of the republic, and they served as the key place for adult, elite men to continue learning. Nevertheless, they struggled in the earliest years to produce enough content to fill a publication. Once they published their own volumes, however, these societies began to develop stronger relationships across state lines with similar institutions and to share their content with the others. This offered a way to build library collections without having to secure the money required to buy the transactions of other learned societies. Being able to produce its own proceedings also showed that a society was a serious organization with authority over knowledge production.[34]

As this system expanded, Federalists became uncomfortable. They were concerned that people who had not been properly trained were participating in the domain meant for the learned. Conflicts over who should be able to speak for the public played out in debates over the impact of the revolutionary changes that helped to take the scepter of knowledge from the learned clergymen trained in established colleges and turn it over to the masses of "ambitious men eager to develop their talents and contribute to the progress of the arts and science, agriculture and commerce, jurisprudence and civil policy."[35] Rapidly diversifying types of knowledge and the eagerness of ever more Americans to participate in knowledge creation and dissemination led the Federalists to fear a cacophony of voices that would lead to discords and the destruction of society.[36]

The Federalists dominated the AAAS, which tended to stress mathematics and astronomy and viewed with skepticism the Republican-dominated APS, which emphasized the pursuits of botany, geology, and paleontology.[37] In 1803, John Adams, while president of the AAAS, warned friend F. A. Van de Kemp to avoid submitting natural-history content for publication with the AAAS since "Jefferson and Buffon have no weight with me" and "neither of these illustrious Personages is held in much Veneration among our New England Philosophers."[38] The affiliation with Jefferson politicized certain types of knowledge, and Federalists resented new ideas and pretenders who claimed a scientific authority that the Federalists deemed undeserved.[39] Nevertheless, the subjects now known as biology and geology came to dominate the American scientific landscape in just a few decades.

Scientific production abounded during the republican administrations of Thomas Jefferson and James Madison, and scientists and explorers sought the patronage of the government through individual pleas to these leaders of the republic.[40] For example, Jefferson's report *An Account of Louisiana*, submitted to Congress in 1803, represented a synthesis of several types of reports that emphasized natural history and resources to be exploited for the benefit of the new country.[41] It clearly shows a need for further research and establishes a scientific agenda to be fulfilled by expeditions like that of Lewis and Clark, which began in the same year. The precursor proposal had been laid out ten years earlier in the APS instructions for an expedition led by George Rogers Clark and Andre Michaux to "explore the country along the Missouri, and thence Westwardly to the Pacific ocean."[42] The plan to fund Michaux's expedition, spearheaded by Jefferson, included the support of seventy-five subscribers, approximately thirty-nine of whom were members of the APS.[43] Jefferson wrote the instructions for the expedition on behalf of the APS, which proved similar to those issued later to Lewis and Clark, with the chief objective being "to find the shortest and most convenient route of communication between the US. and the Pacific ocean, . . . and to learn such particulars as can be obtained of the country through which it passes, it's productions, inhabitants and other interesting circumstances."[44]

The instructions pointed out that finding a water route to the Pacific via the Missouri River offered a means of communication and expanded commerce. The explorers were directed to "take notice of the country you pass through, it's general face, soil, rivers, mountains, it's productions animal, vegetable, and mineral so far as they may be new to us and may also be useful or very curious." The instructions urged the party to avoid undue risk since their scientific mission would enhance the lives "of the inhabitants of the US. in particular, to whom your Report will open new fields and subjects of Commerce, Intercourse, and Observation." [45] Like earlier attempts to commission expeditions to the West, the expedition failed to get enough resources, yet it became the model for all US scientific expeditions in the first half century once Jefferson was able to commit government resources to them.

The Federalist-dominated AAAS sponsored different kinds of research and expeditions as well. At its third meeting, on August 30, 1780, the academy and Harvard University agreed to cosponsor an expedition to Penobscot Bay in present-day Maine. The Harvard professor and academy fellow Reverend Samuel Williams led the expedition to observe a solar eclipse in British-occupied territory. Eventually published in the *Memoirs of the American Academy of Arts and Sciences*, the expedition's findings showcased Williams's recordings of "beads of sunlight," which later were shown to be the effect of the "uneven surface of the moon."[46] Although the academy's charter stated that it also sought to "promote and encourage the knowledge of the antiquities of America," it did not sponsor any major expeditions in the West.[47]

By contrast, Thomas Jefferson believed that the trans-Appalachian West offered the American people the only realistic opportunity to maintain their republican society. Historians have noted that Jefferson was the "most expansion-minded president in American history."[48] Although many associate Jefferson's westward expansion with his effort to encourage a society built on yeoman farmers, it is important to see it as a means to promote acquisitions of wealth through scientific exploration and the belief that new knowledge would lead to progress in society. In addition, it established a pattern for public-private partnerships between learned societies and the federal government, which were tightly bound together by the presence of scientific experts trained by the military. Explorations conducted by John Sibley in 1803, William Dunbar and George Hunter in 1804, and Zebulon Pike's 1806 expedition, continuing through to Stephen Long's expedition in 1819 all utilized the expertise of members of the APS and the American military.[49]

Many Federalists scoffed at these expeditions' findings and wrote satirical responses to the work of these men, whom they viewed as charlatans. While some scholars point to this as evidence of the evolving nature of the political landscape, it is important to recognize that Federalists worried about a shift away from the expertise of a disciplined mind toward scientific knowledge that required deep expertise, which Republicans increasingly championed. This concern remained prevalent throughout the Jeffersonian era, with Federalists worrying more about the research agenda of Jefferson's administration, as conducted by the members of the APS, than about the content of the scholarship that Republicans produced.[50] These satirical pieces offer important insights into how the Federalists portrayed their antagonists.

The publications of early American learned societies show the types of knowledge their members privileged, as well as their expertise. The APS published twice as much content focused on natural history as the AAAS. However, the APS also published a significant amount of work on natural philosophy and the natural sciences, which were fields privileged by the Federalists in the AAAS. That said, the APS's total output surpassed that of both the American Academy of Arts and Sciences and the Connecticut Academy of Arts and Sciences (CAAS), so it is not surprising that its members occasionally also published on the natural sciences; through 1810 the APS published close to 487 essays, while the AAAS put out 158, and the CAAS only 17.[51] The size of each institution's membership is also important to note. Membership lists from the three institutions through 1815 show that the APS elected 812 members, while the AAAS elected 345 members, and the CAAS 111 members. Even though both the APS and the AAAS had several elected members die since they had been in existence longer, these figures do demonstrate a significant difference in the size of the three organizations.

Of the 487 articles published by the *Transactions of the American Philosophical Society*, 107 (22%) were on natural history and 87 (18%) were on natural philosophy. On the other hand, of the 158 articles published by the *Memoirs of the American Academy of Arts and Sciences (MAAAS)*, 40 (25%) were on natural history and 65 (41%) were on natural philosophy. This suggests that the AAAS members were not necessarily opposed to publishing natural history and indicates that the content published in the *MAAAS* was less diverse.

Including the *Memoirs of the Connecticut Academy of Arts and Sciences (MCAAS)* then makes clear that natural history and natural philosophy were both very important to all three groups and that they were less interested in most other forms of knowledge. What we now think of as scientific discourse was the most essential form of knowledge represented in all these publications. Of the 17 *MCAAS* articles, 8 (47%) were on natural philosophy and 4 (23%) were on natural history. Together the 12 articles represented 70% of the content. Still, there were distinct differences between these groups.

What is most interesting is that the APS's priority shifted toward an understanding of the natural history and the natural resources of North America. Westward exploration had become a critical research agenda for the APS by 1792, when members of the society were actively discussing the possibility of funding expeditions to the West, and they used their close ties with members of government to promote their own research agenda and position as the de facto learned society for the country. Some leaders hoped for an official national society that would emulate those in Europe and be closely tied with education. William Short, a diplomat and leading Virginian politician whom Jefferson called his "adoptive son," sent Jefferson a report on the plan of public instruction before the National Assembly in France in 1791.[52] In 1796 the renowned architect William Thornton, who was an avid proponent of establishing a national university, described to Jefferson a conversation that he had had with the renowned Comte de Volney regarding the plan to develop a national university in the federal capital. Volney, a French political philosopher and anthropologist, adamantly opposed the special privileges of the nobility and the dogmatic teachings of the church. He was also an early supporter of Napoleon. Like many intellectuals, he believed that supporting Napoleon would protect freedom.[53] Thornton reported that Volney supported the idea of establishing a national university in the United States; moreover, the "thought of incorporating in the University a Philosophical Society, upon an extensive Scale, and of having in its Bosom a Select Committee is much approved of by Mr. Volney."[54]

Thornton also indicated to Jefferson that Volney had discussed with him a new French institution, the newly established National Institute of Arts and

Sciences. Alexandre Lerebours, a French scientist elected into the American Philosophical Society in April 1796, also reported this news in a letter to Jefferson.[55] The new institution aimed to remove the aristocratic privilege associated with the acquisition and creation of scientific knowledge and be an institution for the wider French public. It would educate the "best students selected from the lower echelons of the system and . . . oversee the continued progress of letters, sciences, and the arts."[56] The National Institute's well-developed and well-maintained infrastructure included laboratories, libraries, museums, botanical gardens, communication networks, and the other apparatus needed to expand the arts and sciences. The institution also was a place where the authority of information was established and maintained.[57]

Yet since the United States was unable to establish a national institution of learning, the APS served as the core knowledge institution for pursuing westward exploration, housed institutional archives, and produced new scholarship and scholars. To the Federalists, however, the APS looked more like a means for Jefferson to promote his own interests rather than a learned society designed for promoting the national good. To leading Federalists, the APS's institutional apparatus became a site for political intrigue by people only interested in filling their purses by spinning sensational yarns through a corruption of knowledge. In the minds of Federalists, no one represented this corruption more than Thomas Jefferson. They saw the president's excessive curiosity and inventiveness and his scattered interests as evidence of an unsound mind. These men were concerned that Jefferson's interests in natural history would result in a spirit of leveling within the halls of scientific institutions. They worried that as president of the United States he would use APS-sponsored scientific expeditions to promote his own interests.[58]

Federalists targeted Jefferson and his APS colleagues in satirical pieces that portrayed his lifelong study of natural history and his interest in studying bones from the time of his youth as evidence of mental illness and their fascination with natural history as unsuitable for an institution designed for the universal diffusion of knowledge. In the twelfth iteration of Josiah Quincy's devastating series titled "Climenole," in which he attacked Jefferson and his colleagues at the APS, he consistently compared the publications in the *Transactions of the American Philosophical Society* to children's stories. In this article Quincy focused on the fourth volume of the *Transactions*, ridiculing the works of several APS members, including Jefferson, John Heckelwelder, Dr. Benjamin Smith Barton, and Charles Willson Peale. Quincy suggested that their work was better described as "three penny gifts for children" and said that their minds were fixated on filling their "purses" by selling their "celebrated *philosophical transactions,*" which ought to be circulated under the names "Jack the Giant Killer, Mother Gooses's Melody and other high-sounding titles."[59] Quincy continued his acerbic assault by insisting that the "heroic hunt" conducted by Barton and Peale seeking "*frozen rattlesnakes in the winter* all for the sake of science and of *memoir-writing* . . . is so entirely *that species of philosophy,* in which children's fancies delight, that I have never known them tired with its perusal." Quincy added that these men had the "happy talent at description, and that *rare accomplishment of amplification in* details, which has enabled him [Jefferson] to spin out an account of a very trifling pursuit into a story of twenty quarto pages in length, are doubtless the causes of that preference, which these young philosophers show for his labours." This assault was designed to denigrate their ability to discern what was important knowledge and how they reveled over trivial facts and descriptions of everyday occurrences fit only to amuse an untrained child. It is hard to imagine a more biting criticism that this one, and Quincy's essay abounded with examples of how he and other Federalists viewed their Republican-dominated sister society in Philadelphia. Although they resisted the idea of the type of knowledge being privileged by the APS, they could not deny the institution's de facto status as the leading organization in the new republic.

Jefferson and his fellow natural-history scholars served as a scientific and educational institutional nexus for the western expeditions meant to explore North America. One historian explains that "the Society in those early years of the republic often served as national library, museum, and academy of sciences."[60] The Lewis and Clark expedition is well known, but two other expeditions explored the Red River basin region and the Washita country. These were major scientific expeditions that ventured into the unknown parts of the continent and relied on military leadership and soldiers. Officers did not always have the scientific training needed to do the work assigned to them, however. Additionally, no other scientific institutions had the resources to prepare men for this type of mission. The APS provided the much-needed scientific expertise for those officers commissioned to undertake these early western explorations. It was crucial for them to learn astronomy, mathematics, surveying, and advanced mapmaking from APS member Andrew Ellicott. In addition, they learned natural history and preservation strategies from Charles Willson Peale and Benjamin Smith Barton. It is also noteworthy that the APS was the only group at the time that brought together experts in North America to conduct a serious study of Native Americans. The American government thus relied on the institution to help train both the leaders of and the participants in these expeditions.[61] The planning of these expeditions provided evidence of the specialized knowledge needed by the country's officers while Jefferson's newly established military academy at West Point began to take shape. This new institution would finally promote a national scientific agenda unified under a common banner for scientific progress.

The United States Military Philosophical Society and the Specialization of Knowledge

The military served as critical creators and consumers of specialized knowledge, and the US Military Academy at West Point became a model for many colleges in the United States to emulate in the nineteenth century. Importantly, the curriculum of the academy became closely tied to applied practical research. The academy emphasized specialization in math, foreign languages, and natural history and other subject-matter expertise to impart knowledge that would be most useful to an American populace dedicated to westward expansion. Jefferson believed that the academy should function as a training facility to prepare American military officers for defending the republic and participating in the scientific exploration of the country. The need for scientifically trained officers offered a particular challenge to Jefferson since he had inherited an army filled with Federalists, who despised the political philosophy of his administration. A transformation in West Point's curriculum was key to enacting Jefferson's long-term policy goals. Also important was replacing the Federalist-dominated military leadership.

Most scholarship examining the military and the founding of West Point has focused on the debates between Federalists and Republicans over the need for a standing army. As the historian Max Edling has demonstrated, as a compromise the legislators proposed a small standing army of "about 3,000 men. Part of the force would be made up of a corps of engineers. . . . Attached to the corps of engineers would be instructors in mathematics, chemistry, natural philosophy, and civil architecture." Some also believed it was necessary to ensure future military capacity by preserving the "military skills and traditions acquired by the Continental Army."[62] Nevertheless, Republicans worried that the nation was too poor to support that type of institution. They hoped instead that the development of a small core of educated officers would serve as a means to prevent American dependence on foreign expertise and promote the scientific knowledge needed for the defense of the new country.[63] This work required the right type of leader.

Jonathan Williams (1750–1815) exemplified the new scientifically minded officer that Jefferson sought to promote. Williams was a man of specialized scientific learning, not a battle-hardened soldier. A grandnephew of Benjamin Franklin, Williams earned membership in the APS through his extensive writing on natural history, fortifications, and engineering.[64] The APS elected Jonathan Williams in 1787, and he remained an active member throughout his life. He was elected secretary four times in a span of six years, and a councilor six times in fifteen years. His tenure culminated with an appointment as vice president of the organization in 1815, shortly before his death at the age of sixty-five. Williams submitted several essays to the APS for consideration, and he published translations of key military works from French. Williams and Jefferson corresponded frequently on "philosophical" topics; in one letter Williams even referred to how he had benefited from Jefferson's "Experience" from his "Indulgence in many Conversations" related to science.[65]

Williams's elected roles in the APS afforded him ties to leading men of learning across the country. His role as inspector of fortifications kept him busy and away from the academy. His fieldwork provided him the opportunity to allow students to participate in a scientific laboratory through practical work. The model of the APS encouraged specialized knowledge through the development of committees of experts in specific fields of knowledge. For example, a committee made up of Thomas Jefferson, James Wilkinson, Caspar Wistar, Adam Sebert, Charles Willson Peale, and Jonathan Williams was formed by the APS in 1799 to solicit, collect, and study "information relative to American Antiquities."[66] These antiquities included natural history and the history of America's Indigenous populations. Jefferson's fascination with the history of American Indians has been well documented by scholars, but it is critical to understand this scholarly interest within the context of the emerging expertise in natural history and the mysteries of the ancient past of the Americas.[67]

In 1798, as the APS marveled over Jefferson's presentation of "a Bone of the Mammoth some time ago found in Virginia" they worked together "to devise the best methods of preserving Fossil Bones" because word had been sent that a new find in the "western Territory" had been made of the "American Incognitum."[68] Further, the minutes abound with reports of natural curiosities, including the "tooth of a large non descript animal," and studies of materials sent to the society, such as an "analysis of the materials composing supposed ancient wall in N. Carolina."[69] All these items were referred to a small number of people in the APS with instructions to review them. In other words, the APS came to serve as a hub for requests to explain the mysteries of the world to the new nation.

The APS received donations from members and nonmembers across the country. Its connections to the government and to government officials ensured their access to diverse natural resources wherever the American military or other government officials visited. In 1798 Jonathan Williams reported that the APS had received a donation from General James Wilkinson, chief of the Western Army, of "thrre [sic] barrels" of "Bones and Fragments of the Bones of nondescript animals." This led to an examination of the contents and a report on them in the minutes and in the curator's records. Additionally, Wilkinson sent "Two Meteorological Journals" that he had kept while at Detroit and on his voyage by canoe to "Michilimacanac on the Lakes" for the members to utilize. Williams later asked that the APS send the bones to Charles Willson Peale for his museum.[70] Williams had quickly become well known to the members for his knowledge of surveying and natural history, making him an ideal candidate for a place in Jefferson's military academy.

Jefferson appointed Williams as inspector of fortifications and superintendent of the military post at West Point on December 14, 1801. Just under a year after his appointment, Williams wrote to Jefferson of his proposal for "Gentleman composing the Corps of Engineers" who believed that they would best serve their country by forming a group to collect and preserve information of "military science" from across the country and share it with "our Citizens in any Walk of Life" to promote "a Character distinguished in the Republic of Science."[71] This new learned society, named the United States Military Philosophical Society (USMPS), sought to promote scholarly communication both inside and outside the Military Academy.[72] This group was critical to redirecting the focus of West Point's curriculum toward specialized scientific knowledge; by the 1820s the curriculum would be renowned across the country as a new, progressive educational model.[73]

The emerging framework established strong and deep ties between the APS and the USMPS. In fact, Williams modeled the USMPS on the APS, and a significant number of its early members also belonged to the Philadelphia group.[74] The USMPS, founded in 1802, included all members of the Corps of

Engineers and "Officers and Cadets" retaining "membership of right" as long as they served on active duty. This tied a central group of officers together through the auspices of the United States Army. Linking the learned society to the federal government provided crucial resources and credibility to the fledgling institution. The society could also invite into membership "any gentleman" elected by three-fourths of the members present, as long as he was a citizen of the United States "whether a military man or not."[75] The membership rolls of the society included many of the top intellectuals of the period, such as John Quincy Adams, Joel Barlow, George Clinton, DeWitt Clinton, Robert Fulton, Thomas Jefferson, James Madison, and James Monroe, to name a few. Some of these men actively introduced Williams to other learned men, including Charles C. Pinckney, who became the vice president of the organization in 1807.[76] One scholar has noted that by 1809 there were about 219 members, only about 40 percent of whom were active-duty military officers.[77]

The USMPS served as a critical incubator for scientific knowledge for the early members of the Military Academy, and they set an applied scientific research agenda for the new institution. Williams argued that all branches of scientific content were relevant for study. Members of the USMPS shared a common purpose, to enhance the study of all aspects of military science. To help reduce the possibility of political friction, the constitution of the organization ordered that the "Society will never give their judgement or opinion upon any literary performance"; the hope was to avoid members' involvement in the civil war of the belles lettres and keep the corps focused on scientific endeavors.[78] In an address to the society in 1808 Williams told his fellow members that the society had never been intended to become a "political engine to aid any sect or party"; rather, it had been "founded on patriotism of the purest kind."[79] Williams called science the most useful expression of knowledge, and to him, all specialized disciplines intersected: "Astronomy, geography, and mathematics" as well as "Chymistry and mineralogy are inseperable," and "military science embraces all these branches, it therefore has as good a claim to the title of philosophical as any other."[80]

Williams and his colleagues quickly established an official motto for the society: *Scientia in Bello Pax* (Science in war is the guarantee of peace). Mottoes expressed both the aspirational ideals and the core purpose of many early American institutions, and the USMPS's seal and certificate of membership were important symbols designed to convey its new expression of knowledge for the world to see. In 1805, Williams began to create a seal and a certificate of membership. The discussion around these is illustrative of how the members viewed information and knowledge. Williams and Francis de Masson, the first instructor of drawing and French at West Point, created a first draft of the group's symbols. Williams asked for feedback from Jefferson on their appearance because he wanted to avoid criticism from the society's Federalist political enemies. Jefferson suggested that Joel Barlow would be better suited to comment on the matter and recused himself. Barlow provided extensive feedback and criticism of the original proposal, which was a complex mix of figures from classical mythology with images of scientific warfare. Barlow believed that the imagery was confusing and did not accurately convey the society's basic tenets. Others in the society objected to the imagery because of the emphasis on classicism. Louis Simond, a member of the society and a renowned artist from New York, asserted, "Mythology and its Allegories have been in use so long that they are some what threadbare."[81] Simond preferred an alternative version set forward by Professor de Masson that emphasized Archimedes and his inventions.

Ultimately the members reached a compromise. The seal placed on the certificate used the classical imagery of "Minerva causing an olive branch to start from the ground by the touch of her spear the goddess of Science in full armour produces peace from the very lance with which she is prepared for battle." The choice of Minerva was important since she was the Roman goddess of wisdom and the "protector of intellectual and manual skills."[82] Further, Williams selected Minerva because she represented useful knowledge, which he saw as the marriage of science with art. The distinctions that now separate art from science were immaterial to those at the time. They viewed science to be concerned with theoretical truth and art to be concerned with methods to achieve a result.[83] Benjamin Henry Latrobe told Johann Mathias Reich that the seal he had engraved "has given me so much genuine pleasure" that he had

FIG. 3. Seal of the United States Military Philosophical Society (1 7/8" diameter) from a USMPS certificate, 1805. (Courtesy New York Historical Society)

to write and share his "most heartfelt and sincere approval." Latrobe saw the perfection captured in "the attitude of Minerva" and Reich's ability to "combine perfect and classical knowledge" for all to admire.[84] This combination showed that universal knowledge based upon empiricism and application would result in truth. Therefore, the sigil of the institution served as a rallying banner for those who sought unified knowledge.

As part of the compromise, while the seal drew from Roman mythology, the certificate utilized modern imagery. The artwork on the certificate of membership includes a broad array of symbols drawn from both military science and traditional knowledge. The certificate is an intricately crafted work, 18 × 23 inches, printed on high-quality paper. At the top of the certificate is an image of the harbor of the city of Syracuse. The Roman fleet in the harbor has been set ablaze by the mirror of Archimedes, which reflected sunlight and created a burning death ray. Framing this picture are many representations of weapons of war, including cannons, mortars, muskets, pikes, halberds, and spears. Amid these familiar weapons sit a book, gold coins, a map, a compass and carpenter's square, a sextant, a snake, and an artist's palette with brushes. These instruments of knowledge and science were crucial to the execution of war. The certificate also demonstrates the complexity with which these men of learning viewed the world of knowledge.

The USMPS was more than a collection of images, however; it was a means for Williams to exert his authority over the academy and designed to be a keystone to Jefferson's plan for reinventing the army. The learned society served as a core component of the activities of the Military Academy itself. Members met twice a month to discuss scientific issues and to present papers or ideas for the good of the army.[85] The society devoted its attention to the study of military sciences. Williams defined military sciences broadly, stating, "Science is in its own nature so diffuse, that it is almost impossible to designate any dividing lines."[86] Williams also sought to include members from outside the military. First and foremost was Jefferson himself, who acknowledged the honor of membership and gave his approval of the society's goals to advance scientific knowledge.[87]

Williams set the standard for scholarly production by publishing a book titled *Thermometrical Navigation*, which was used for several decades by sailors to safely navigate the coast, as well as several reports on fortifications and different military construction projects. Newspapers reported that the USMPS had been instituted "under the auspices of that scientific officer, Colonel Jonathan Williams, commanding the United States corps of Engineers at West

FIG. 4. Certificate of membership for the United States Military Philosophical Society, showing the society's motto, *Scientia in Bello Pax*. (Courtesy American Philosophical Society)

Point."[88] Williams often translated important scientific works into English, allowing excerpts to be published in American periodicals, such as a selection from the Marquis of Montalembert's ten-volume *La fortification perpendiculaire*. Williams proudly declared that the set had "not yet appeared in English and the copy from which the foregoing was translated, is probably the only one in American hands. They were imported for the use of the Military Academy."[89] He was proud of the expert resources being developed in the collection of the Military Academy and wanted everyone to know that he and his fellow engineers were learned men of science.[90]

Williams's expertise was widely recognized by leading scientist of the period, such as Samuel Mitchill, who wrote in a letter published widely of his support of the work Williams performed while he designed and oversaw the erection of the fortifications in New York harbor, calling him a "learned and ingenious director of the military academy."[91] These fortifications, dubbed "Castle Williams," stood as an effective part of New York's harbor defense through the 1830s and were used as a barracks and prison throughout the remainder of the nineteenth century.[92]

Williams encouraged several other members to give papers and publish works, which further enhanced the reputation of both the USMPS and West Point. Extracts from the minutes of the 1806 meeting show that after Professor de Masson presented a "memoir on the *Fuzil a Clapet* of Montlanbert" demonstrating the superiority of this type of rifled canon, the members resolved to make one "at the Society's expense to serve as a model and to be used in experiments."[93] Further, the newly installed professor of mathematics, Swiss-born Ferdinand Hassler, delivered a report stressing the urgent need for a national coastal survey. In 1832 his recommendations were realized, and Hassler served as the head of the US Coast Survey.[94]

Williams and his engineers often learned by performing fieldwork and then presenting and publishing their geographic observations to the USMPS. For example, at the meeting on October 6, 1806, four different officers provided fourteen charts and drawings of coastal regions and forts for the consideration of the members. Importantly, whenever they were sent on duty to the West, they were expected to provide reports. At the same meeting Williams donated to the society "A collection of Geographical, and Astronomical Observations" made while traveling from "Fort Niagara ... to Wilkinson, near the junction of the Ohio with the Mississippi."[95] The work of these members provided significant knowledge and signaled a pedagogical shift for the students and teachers by focusing students' attention on applied scientific methods.

The prolific works of Williams and his compatriots gave the society instant credibility. The expanding membership of the society brought with it a growing archive, library, and museum, making it an international center for the study of military sciences. The society received reports and collections from across the world, thanks to its leaders and outside patrons. Williams and the other faculty members used the opportunities to work in the field during their assigned postings to expand on their classroom instruction. They collected a variety of materials and used them as practical experiments in the pursuit of new knowledge.[96] Outside discussion groups and the library and classroom environments, the society engaged with the latest practical military engineering. They discussed suggestions for new technology, such as *A Memoir on a New Construction of a Gun Boat or a Floating Battery*, as well as mathematical experiments using locally modified artillery, practical examples of trigonometry, and "notes taken at West Point during an eclipse of the sun by William Partridge, liet. Of engineers."[97] Williams and his fellow members believed that the purpose of the society was to gather all military knowledge for the benefit of the nation. The publications and the society's expansion allowed the group to hold occasional meetings in other cities, including at New York City's City Hall and the War Department offices at Washington, DC. The transition to holding meetings outside West Point occurred because of Williams's travel schedule and the deployment of the members of the engineering corps throughout the country. Although the permanent home of the society and the engineers was at West Point, only the junior officers or cadets remained there. The engineers were actively engaged in fieldwork across the United States.

Explorers and leaders of westward expeditions were members of the USMPS, and the camaraderie of their body engendered lasting loyalty. In 1810 Major Zebulon M. Pike addressed the 504-page proceedings of his expeditions in western Louisiana in the years 1805–7 to "The President and Members of the U.S.M.P.S." He presented the work to them and hoped they "would plead in my favor" the value of the work since the institution was "formed for the promotion of military knowledge." Pike hoped they would accept his work with "approbation of your honorable institution" and signed it as a member of the USMP Society.[98]

Jefferson's intention to create a science-centered academy appeared to be successful. Still the Military Academy and the Military Philosophical Society resided in the hinterlands of New York. Consequently, in the minds of some these institutions lacked the resources to fulfill the needs of the nation. In 1808, Williams submitted a report on military readiness that sought to enhance the security of the United States. In it, he articulated the limitations of the academy, "barely existing among the mountains and nurtured at a distance out of sight and almost unknown to its legitimate parents" residing in the nation's capital.[99] Williams outlined a new plan for an expanded institution, which would grow from a small number of officially sanctioned professors to a well-endowed institution. The enlarged faculty would include a new professor in natural and experimental philosophy, two additional mathematics professors, and three specialists to teach astronomy, geography, and navigation. Williams also wished to add an engineering professor specializing in the building of fortifications and canals, as well as professors for drawing, French and German, architecture, chemistry, and mineralogy, and finally a riding master and a sword instructor. The plan envisioned building a worthy physical plant with the auxiliary services and instruments needed to support scientific education. Central to this was an enhanced library and scientific apparatus needed to perform research and scholarship.[100] This report most likely represented Jefferson's vision and approval, since Williams submitted it to him as a draft for comments before the final submission to Congress.[101]

In submitting Williams's report to Congress, Jefferson recounted concerns about the cadets' lack of scientific knowledge and recognized that the "scale on which the Military Academy at West Point was originally established is become too limited to furnish the number of well instructed subjects . . . which the public service calls for." Jefferson told Congress that the readiness of the military required officers with advanced training in mathematics, sciences, and foreign languages. Jefferson further commented that Williams's proposal to move the academy to Washington was "worthy of attention" since it offered the opportunity to place the institution "under the immediate eye of the Government."[102] He also saw an advantage in sharing a location with the Navy Department and other departments of the federal government. Jefferson believed that the scientific mission of the USMPS and the academy was crucial to the work of the republic since many of the instructors and officers would leave the academy to oversee the construction of fortifications and other construction projects at inopportune times.

Yet despite both Williams's and Jefferson's emphasis on these needs, many political leaders in both parties opposed the proposal. The published debates provide only slight clues to the rationale behind the congressional decisions to reject the proposal first submitted in March 1809. Josiah Masters, a Republican representative from New York, opposed the proposals and succeeded in having the legislation tabled. Masters reasoned that West Point was a better location for the academy and that the expense of relocating it would be too great. He added that the owners of private property in the West Point area would be "injured by the removal." Meanwhile, Joseph Lewis, a Federalist representative from Virginia, stood in favor of the relocation, arguing that as a "national institution the propriety of its being under the immediate superintendence of the head of the War Department" was a critical advantage and that the academy belonged near the capital.¹⁰³ Lewis tried to bring the measure to relocate the academy to the floor of the House at least four times, but he failed to receive a majority of supporters, and in the end the measure to relocate the academy did not resurface.¹⁰⁴ Once again, Congress had stymied a measure that would have brought a national center of higher learning to the US capital. As a result, this effort to create a national institution focused on a broad range of knowledge for the military sciences based in the federal city became yet another failed attempt to fulfill Washington's vision, but with a Jeffersonian twist.

Williams's influence began to fade when Jefferson retired to Monticello. He resigned from the army for a second time in July 1812 and served as brigadier general of militia for New York responsible for defending New York Harbor. He was greatly offended at not being given command over his masterpiece, Castle Williams. In the meantime, Williams's science-focused agenda continued under the leadership of Joseph Gardner Swift, the academy's first graduate and Williams's protégé. In April 1813 Swift added Andrew Ellicott as professor of mathematics. Ellicott, who while in the APS had trained Meriwether Lewis to make maps, brought even more expertise to the society and the academy. Swift formalized many aspects of the curriculum begun under Williams, assuring their longevity.¹⁰⁵ After the War of 1812 concluded, Williams was elected to the House of Representatives, but he did not serve long, dying in 1815. In addition, because of the increasingly dispersed membership it became impossible for the USMPS to meet. In 1817, it transferred its remaining funds and collections to the New York Lyceum of Natural History.¹⁰⁶

Federalists were not sad to see it go. Some believed that the USMPS had become an arm of the Democratic-Republican Party. After all, it had many members in common with the APS, the Federalists' nemesis.¹⁰⁷ Although Williams asserted that the Military Philosophical Society was apolitical, clearly some disagreed. Timothy Dwight and Noah Webster were among the most outspoken opponents of the scientific progress the society emphasized. Dwight in particular challenged the notion that material progress led to moral progress. The connections between the Jacobin scientific associations in revolutionary France and individual liberty seemed to Dwight to be antithetical to republican liberty.¹⁰⁸ The *New-England Palladium* outright associated the societies formed in Philadelphia and New York with the Jacobin societies in France. One article stated: "Taught by France, the democrats established similar societies here, and they now exist in Connecticut under the imposing name of Republican Societies."[109] The fear that the Republicans would overturn sensible governing was rampant among the Federalists. Fundamentally, as scholars have shown, neither political party recognized the legitimacy of the other. Thus, despite Jefferson's support for a military academy and the promotion of scientific knowledge among the officer corps, his opponents remained convinced that the kind of knowledge he promoted was dangerous to the country's stability and future.[110]

Nevertheless, the military academy's revamped curriculum became well received across the country within a few short years. John Adams, the retired Federalist president and former leader of the AAAS, addressed a group of two hundred young West Point cadets in the summer of 1821, congratulating them for acquiring exceptional knowledge in the arts and sciences, which "well qualify you for any course of Life you may choose to pursue."[111] Adams wrote to Jefferson of the growing renown of the Military Academy and gave credit to the administrations of "Jefferson Madison and Monroe," who had promoted the development of "military Science" and seen it through to "a considerable degree of perfection."[112]

Joseph Swift, the academy's first graduate, assumed the role of chief engineer and superintendent of the Military Academy in 1812 from his mentor, Jonathan Williams, and he continued the work of constructing fortifications on the Atlantic coast until 1817, when the role of chief engineer and superintendent was split into two positions. Swift became head of the Corps of Engineers, while Alden Partridge took the leadership role at the academy. All these men benefited from West Point's scientific educational curriculum and were actively engaged in the work of specialized learned societies, which they learned from their experiences at the USMPS. Many of the members of the USMPS would eventually be elected to the APS, yet their intellectual home remained the army. The lasting influence of the USMPS was owing to the way applied scientific work became infused with the curriculum of the academy. The graduates of the academy all continued to utilize the standards learned under Williams and from the USMPS.

In 1817, West Point officially formalized its curriculum under Colonel Sylvanus Thayer. In one of his first actions upon assuming command of the academy Thayer "directed the principal of each Department of instruction to draw up a programme for his department."[113] This formal curriculum included the branches of study introduced by Williams years before, and now standardized examinations ensured that republican officers would emerge from the nation's military academy.[114] The military academy's curriculum would be well received across the country within a few short years. No one, not even John Adams, questioned the usefulness of the specialized training received from the men that led scientific expeditions into the West accumulating specimens and knowledge for the emerging scientific establishment, and in the antebellum era military academies flourished throughout the country.

The Military Academy at West Point was an unlikely site for a new amalgamation of applied sciences that offered opportunities for students to directly engage in the activities of a learned society. Bringing together the work of the university and the work of the learned society offered opportunities for specialization of knowledge through members' experimentation. Despite the real ideological and political differences between Federalists and Jeffersonians, a radical transformation in the curriculum of the Military Academy led to the acceptance of a new type of knowledge within a generation. The new model of learning, based on the model of the French military sciences, provided an opportunity for more people to participate in creating new scientific knowledge in the United States. The officer corps took these models with them to their posts across the new country; this became a critical way of promoting new ways for Americans to spread and use scientific knowledge in the early republic.

CHAPTER 3

A NATIONAL MUSEUM?

Disseminating Knowledge in the Early Republic

The founding generation agreed on one thing: citizens in a republic needed access to the latest scientific information to ensure American cultural independence from European centers of learning and to ensure American economic progress. Yet as these leaders failed to fund and build national institutions, and as no federal scientific infrastructure emerged, new institutions began to compete in a marketplace of ideas. A further complicating factor was the ongoing struggle between mainly Federalists, who believed that a good education focused on rhetoric, and Jeffersonian Republicans, who championed the acquisition of specialized knowledge. Thus, one person's informed citizen might be another person's ignorant dolt. It remained unclear what kind of organization could fulfill the needs of a fledgling republic forged during an information revolution.[1]

In the abstract, American elites imagined an idealized citizenry whose interest in scientific knowledge and technological innovations would spur advancements across the new republic. For example, in 1784 Francis Hopkinson delivered an address to the American Philosophical Society in which he underlined that "philosophical pursuits" were widespread and that "the door of knowledge seems to be wider open than ever it was: the authority of the schools is daily giving way to the authority of nature."[2] To him, reading books written in dead languages was not the way to advance a republican society; instead, "the great book of nature is open to all—all may read therin."[3] Elite men like Hopkinson invited the broader American populace to participate in scientific work, especially when it came to collecting specimens of what was then called natural history, which encompassed diverse fields, from archeology, to anthropology, to biology, and even history itself.

This call for public participation in scientific learning and experimentation legitimized untrained people's participation in work previously open only to learned elites. In other words, Americans who lacked a classical college education now had the opportunity to develop scientific expertise. The resulting widespread dissemination of new scientific knowledge via commercial and scientific expeditions persuaded Americans that scientific endeavors enhanced the well-being of their community through the promotion of the ideal of humanity's progress and advancement of learning and technological improvements. It was not lost on them that these scientific advancements also provided opportunities for increasing their personal fortunes and status.[4]

In the absence of strong traditional or national institutions of authority over scientific knowledge, diverse approaches championed by individuals and organizations alike presented themselves as the providers of authentic knowledge about the natural world. As a result, the early republic saw a proliferation of new institutions offering ever more Americans—who were fascinated by the world around them and wanted to engage with leading thinkers and with all kinds of curiosities—ways to learn about the world. These new institutions evolved to meet Americans' demand for new knowledge, each one promoting arguments about its importance to a republican government. Some saw natural history as a means to promote patriotism, nationalism, and public service. Others hoped to secure American access to wealth in distant lands, especially Asia. Still others hoped to create truly democratic institutions that encouraged a broadly inclusive membership, for white men of all stations at least, so that ever more participants could be brought into the process of cultivating knowledge through scientific research. And some saw opportunities for participation in more limited terms, encouraging hobby collectors to report their findings and submit samples from far-off places so that trained scientists could perform their work. What they all had in common was reliance on a diverse network of people to secure the collections they needed for their research.[5]

Importantly, the proliferation of these collections provided an opportunity for early Americans to reframe what constituted knowledge, who should have access to it, who would create it for consumption, and what type of institution could best diffuse that knowledge. The debates on these questions, which once more evolved along partisan political lines, led to more types of individuals seeking to take part in the educational process; founders of museums—a new kind of institution created specifically for knowledge dissemination—epitomized this transformation.[6] Groups of roving natural scientists formed museums and learned societies, assembling collections in the eastern cities but also in the new cities and towns of the American West. As this chapter shows, these museums became ever more important sites for Americans to tell compelling stories of resources and riches waiting to be mined.

These new museums were fueled by the various expeditions to collect items for businessmen and scientists alike, who worked in tandem to expand the country and to promote the United States as a member of the world's learned nations. American explorers told stories of newfound scientific wonders to eager museumgoers, crafting a national story of scientific progress through American exceptionalism. In particular, Charles Willson Peale revolutionized museums as public institutions designed to promote broader educational experiences for a clientele that extended beyond only the richest in society. He also encouraged the use of museums to promote national identity. In fact, donating to collections became a patriotic act to promote the expansion of American knowledge.

In addition, early exploratory missions such as the 1804–6 expedition of William Dunbar and George Hunter, the Lewis and Clark expeditions during those same two years, the voyages of members of the Salem East India Marine Society in the first quarter of the nineteenth century, the Academy of Natural Science's 1817 collecting trip to Florida, and the Stephen Long expedition to the Rocky Mountains in 1819 all provided rich collections for their sponsoring institutions. By analyzing both Peale's efforts and the activities of newly emerging learned societies such as the Salem East India Marine Society and the Academy of Natural Sciences, this chapter explores the politics of collecting and disseminating knowledge to an evolving American public and demonstrates the increasingly participatory nature of collecting knowledge that came about through the creation of museums in the early republic.[7]

Developing a Museum and Encouraging Patriotic Donors

Charles Willson Peale epitomized the modern collector, whose dedication to scientific classification and desire to promote knowledge allowed him to refashion himself from an artisan as a man of learning. Peale's rise to national prominence is well known; however, few scholars have recognized the mistrust that existed between many learned men and new men of science like Peale, whom they disparagingly called "philosophers." An active member of Philadelphia's republican circles, Peale had served as a militia captain during the Revolutionary War. He had also served as an agent for the confiscation of Loyalist estates and helped organize large political demonstrations, including one in 1780 when Philadelphia citizens burned Benedict Arnold in effigy after a parade through the streets.[8]

After the Revolution, he converted his painting gallery into the first scientifically organized museum of natural history in the United States. Peale envisioned his museum as a republican school where all people could learn about the natural world and improve themselves through the acquisition and application of useful knowledge. Many scholars forget his radical, egalitarian roots as they focus on his work as an artist or a museum proprietor, but it is important to recognize that for Peale the purpose of a museum directly reflected his democratic ideals.[9] Peale did benefit from the patronage and support of men of status; however, he saw himself as someone who could bridge the gap between the elites and the new citizen. In fact, his ambition was typical in an age dedicated to promoting economic progress in the newly constituted country via enhanced knowledge institutions and through enterprise.[10]

Peale's experiences had placed him in the company of the country's greatest men. Benjamin Franklin, George Washington, and Thomas Jefferson, together with other members of Philadelphia's American Philosophical Society, were among his greatest supporters, and the APS president David Rittenhouse and member Dr. Robert Patterson encouraged Peale to establish a museum. Patterson, a professor of mathematics at the College of Philadelphia, donated a paddlefish caught in the Allegheny River in 1785, which Peale acknowledged as the first gift to his museum.[11] Subsequently, paddlefish by paddlefish, he developed the museum into an information system and mechanism for framing knowledge for large communities.

Peale believed that the ideal expression of knowledge was embedded in nature and thus required a combination of philosophy and practical application. Critical to communicating Peale's vision was to place his preserved specimens in natural settings through the use of habitat dioramas to establish complete representations of life. Verbal and printed representations simply could not convey the complexity and marvels of a living creature. Peale painstakingly produced naturalistic backgrounds and refined the skills that he had long utilized in his portrait paintings to place animals within authentic American landscapes. His work was so accurate that many of the drawings in Alexander Wilson's landmark work, *American Ornithology, or, The Natural History of the Birds of the United States*, published in nine volumes from 1808 to 1814, were created from the backgrounds and dioramas that Peale manufactured for the specimens in his museum displays. Peale also carefully positioned birds "in Various attitudes on (an) Artificial ponds. Some Birds & Beasts on trees and some Birds suspended as flying."[12] Ironically, mid-nineteenth-century museum professionals frowned upon these techniques and preferred that specimens be displayed within taxonomic order inside cabinets rather than providing a naturalistic background to produce a virtual representation of the environment. Later, however, the profession would silently adopt Peale's method of using dioramas and other techniques, including textual placards to help interpret exhibits.[13]

Peale relied on gifts from his allies in the APS, which he secured by demonstrating his mastery of the practice of preservation.[14] Peale secured many gifts from Washington and Jefferson over the years, such as rare Chinese pheasants given to Washington as a gift by the French revolutionary hero the Marquis de Lafayette from King Louis XVI's aviary. Peale longed to add these rare birds to his collection once they had died, and he gave specific instructions to Washington on how to pack them so that "such beautiful and rare things should not be wholly lost and which [happens] too often, even when undertaken to be preserved by persons not sufficiently skilled in the manner of preserving."[15] It is likely that he learned of these rare birds through newspaper accounts covering the French gift.[16] Washington in turn told Peale that if he "wish[ed] to possess any bird, or Annimals, which you may at any time send to preserve the form, please to inform me, and I will most chearfully do my best to serve you."[17] Washington followed through and sent the birds to Peale when they died, and Peale did successfully preserve these specimens, which he proudly displayed in his museum, as announced in the March 1, 1787, issue of the *Pennsylvania Packet*. Peale's announcement mentioned not only the beauty of the birds but also the story associated with Lafayette's gift to "His Excellency General Washington."[18] In addition to enabling him to secure collections, Peale's friendships were critical to asserting the scientific authority of his collections. These preserved specimens remain in the collections at Harvard's Museum of Comparative Zoology, a testament to his preservation skills.[19]

Peale was also masterful at using newspapers to promote his work and to enhance his networks of patronage. In his first advertisement, Peale announced on July 7, 1786, in the *Pennsylvania Packet* that he would "make part of his House a Repository for Natural Curiosities" for the public to experience "the sight of many of the Wonderful Works of Nature . . . now closeted." Peale's advertisement indicated that the "Articles will be classes and arranged according to their several species" and to help the "Curious . . . each piece will be inscribed the place whence it came, and the name of the Donor."[20] By providing the donor information, Peale sought to increase his network of supporters while also promoting his new enterprise to the public. Acknowledging the donors provided not only provenance information to the viewer but also recognition to the donor, and it made visible his vast global network of supporters.

Peale solicited his correspondents to help build collections. In October 1786, for example, he asked David Ramsay, of Maryland, for any of the curiosities secured from the Carolinas, including the "stuffed skin of an Alligator."[21] Peale also worked with his friend Christopher Richmond, the auditor of Maryland, to procure information about the quality of a collection of birds offered for sale in Annapolis.[22] Richmond placed an advertisement in several issues of the *Maryland Gazette*, as early as 2 November 1786, asking that "The gentlemen or ladies of Maryland, who are will to encourage Mr. Peale . . . are informed that Mr. Richmond of Annapolis willing receive and forward to Mr. Peale any thing which may be offered to him" for his museum.[23] On April 29, 1787, Peale wrote to Richmond thanking him for "his favors," which included donations received through him from Maryland.[24] In this manner, Peale's core collections came from his network of friends and patrons.

In addition to relying on the benevolence of his friends and patrons, Peale also made direct appeals in newspapers to encourage donations from across the new country. Peale informed "The curious" in an August 1788 article published in the *Pennsylvania Mercury, and Universal Advertiser* that his collections were from around the world and his "MUSEUM . . . has been enriched" by "valuable donations from his generous friends."[25] Newspapers listed the items given to Peale and the names of donors in the hope that others would also want to be recognized for supporting his efforts to build a collection of national importance and international note by donating items. This strategy worked. His appeals resulted in gifts such as the one from Elias Derby, a merchant from Salem, Massachusetts, of "a particular sheep sent me as a present from Russia as a curiosity"; Derby hoped "it might be acceptable" to add to Peale's museum.[26]

These stories were often reprinted in newspapers across the country, as was customary at the time. In 1788 both the September 22 issue of the *State Gazette of South-Carolina* and the December 31 edition of the *Massachusetts Centinel* carried the news to those interested in knowing about "the . . . CURIOSITIES . . . recently presented to Mr. Peale's American Museum in Philadelphia." The announcement listed a wide variety of items, several species of snakes, plants, "fine specimens of cloathing made of bark by the inhabitants of the Islands in the South Seas," and "curious fish-hooks used by them and a spear of fine workmanship," along with "a Mandarin dress . . . the silver pheasant of China; a Chinese lady's shoes, . . . specimens of minerals and fossils . . . a tyger-cat from South America," and the donors' names were included for all.[27] Peale strategically named donors from Great Britain, France, Maryland, Georgia, and Pennsylvania in this advertisement placed in a New England paper, which was designed to demonstrate the geographic diversity of his supporters.

Peale cultivated a rich network of contributors who were engaged with international relations and trade. Among these elites were well-known persons such as Benjamin Franklin, the French consul Chevalier D'Anmour, the merchant Benjamin Laming, and the merchant and financier Robert Morris and his wife, as well as lesser-known individuals such as the young merchant George Harrison, who sailed on the "federal frigate *Alliance*" and achieved the status of "supercargo."[28] A supercargo was a business agent who managed all the investments, cargo sales and purchases, and other financial dealings overseas. Usually, the ship captain took care of this, but as voyages became more and more complicated (sometimes sending up to $100,000 in specie from multiple investors), merchants wanted a business agent on board. Supercargos were often merchants or ship captains themselves who were experienced in Asian trade. They usually received a commission on the profit turned by the ship. Harrison's position as "Navy Agent in Philadelphia" positioned him to provide gifts to Peale from the Pacific and across the world for decades.[29]

These newspaper articles were updated periodically. For example, the *Massachusetts Centinel*'s edition of September 2, 1789, printed "Sundry Late Communications to Mr. Peale's MUSEUM," which identified such new items of interest as a "War Cap and Cloak made of feathers" and "The bow of an African Prince which was given by the patriotick *Mrs. Motte.*"[30] Peale's goal was for his work to be seen as an international enterprise carried out by dedicated Americans while he managed, preserved, and curated the collections for his Philadelphia audience.

Peale emphasized the scientific quality of his collections when he utilized newspapers to encourage visitors to his museum. The earliest advertisement in the *Freeman's Journal; or, The North-American Intelligencer,* on August 27, 1788, provided readers with a short explanation of the holdings of the facility. Peale's museum contained "the Portraits of Illustrious Personages, distinguished in

FIG. 5. Eighteenth-century Hawaiian mahiole (crested helmet), a gift from Captain Robert Gray to President George Washington. Washington gave it to Charles Willson Peale for his museum. (Courtesy Peabody Museum of Archaeology and Ethnology)

the late Revolution of America" and "a Collection of preserved Beasts, Birds, Fish, Ruptiles, Insects, Fossils, Minerals, Petrefactins, and other curious Objects, natural and artificial." The advertisement also indicated that since "this *Museum* is in its Infancy, Mr. Peale will thankfully receive the assistance of the curious."[31] Peale frequently placed these types of advertisements in the Philadelphia papers, often sending them to at least two papers, and they would then be reprinted by other papers throughout the expansive republic.[32] Peale also added nuanced and intriguing details to the entries, such as "Birds Nests, very costly, which made into Soop is much esteemed in China," a "Coatimundi (alive) a very good humored, playful animal from South America" and "a Grotto for receiving marine subjects and a number of rare birds are added."[33] Peale's advertisements were designed to entice visitors from all walks of life to come and experience nature in his controlled environment.

Importantly, Peale's organizing his items for display in a scientific manner distinguished his well-ordered collection from the "magpies nest of historical and scientific rarities" typified by earlier collectors such as Pierre Eugène Du Simitière.[34] Once the preservation challenges were overcome, Peale turned to the work of producing a scientifically organized catalog, which, when published, would allow the curious to peruse his museum from afar before making a visit to view his "Temple of Wisdom" in Philadelphia, America's capital city of scientific endeavors.[35] The fifty-six-page museum catalog published in 1796 was cowritten by Peale's fellow APS member the internationally renowned botanist A. M. F. J. Beauvois. Titled *A Scientific and Descriptive Catalogue of Peale's Museum*, the work was groundbreaking; it was the first known catalog of specimens in a natural history collection in the nation. Peale and Beauvois followed the latest scientific standards and placed items into proper Linnaean order. Further, they defined the classifications so that all readers could understand how the system distinguished animal from vegetable from mineral. After reading the catalog descriptions of the physical characteristics of the specimens, a visitor could wander through the museum and view them. Peale's work was recognized with his election to the APS on July 23, 1786, for his mastery of natural history.[36]

In 1805 Peale followed up with a new, shorter work titled *Guide to the Philadelphia Museum*, which opened with a quote from Milton, "Here undisturb'd, By noisy Folly and discordant Vice, On Nature muse with us and Nature's GOD!"[37] The idea that everyone could appreciate the knowledge displayed in Peale's museum—which was the first to use descriptive placards and set specimens within habitat dioramas—was revolutionary, although customers had to pay for access.[38] Strategies and tools like these publications made these collections accessible to a broader set of consumers hungry to learn about a world that many would never get to see in person. Peale's museum offered a democratic space for those who could pay to enter.

Peale hoped that his museum would become the new country's prime repository of scientific knowledge and promote the collective good. In 1792 he issued a call to the "Citizens of the United States of America" to create a national museum, as published in Philadelphia's *Claypoole's Daily Advertiser*. Peale promised to cultivate the value of his institution "until it shall grow into full maturity and become a NATIONAL MUSEUM."[39] His plan included selecting prominent men from the nation to be board members for his museum. Most of the twenty-seven were members of the APS. Three members of Washington's cabinet, Thomas Jefferson, Alexander Hamilton, and Edmund Randolph, also served on the board. Peale hoped that this group would shepherd his call for federal or state support. Despite the affinity many had with Peale and the admiration many had for his skillful applied knowledge, the support Peale hoped for failed to materialize. Thus Peale continued to try to find ways to demonstrate that his museum was a public good that deserved federal support.

On November 16, 1799, as part of his agenda to promote his museum as a national museum, Peale delivered his "Introduction to a Course of Lectures on Natural History" at the University of Pennsylvania. This lecture was the first in a series of forty-two lectures outlining the importance of natural history and providing a description of the animals in his museum. He asserted that "natural history is not only interesting to the individual, it ought to become a NATIONAL CONCERN, since it is a NATIONAL GOOD."[40] Peale built his case for the importance of a national museum by citing European examples such as Sweden's use of the scientific advances of Carl Linnaeus to institute systematic changes in medical practices that resulted in the saving of their shipping industry. Peale also stressed the importance of natural history to a diverse set of occupations and all citizens. Peale wrote, "The very sinews of government are made strong by a diffused knowledge of this science—of this, agriculture, the mechanic arts, religion, are striking evidences."[41] Using his museum catalog as his guide, Peale delivered lectures that advocated the study of natural history as a means to spread universal harmony.[42] In fact he told his audience that science rose above faction, which was why he had given up his political career for the "peaceful studies of the fine arts: When the merit of each was put in the balance, The peaceful muse outweighed political warfare—and since that period I have been scarcely so much as a common observer of the political world."[43] Of course nothing was further from the truth, as knowledge became deeply politicized in this period.

Thomas Jefferson, the newly elected president of the United States, remained one of Peale's greatest patrons and allies for many years. This is best exemplified by their long and voluminous exchanges of letters and their joint support for various projects, such as the excavation of the mammoth in New York during the summer of 1801.[44] Peale wrote two letters to Jefferson announcing that he had secured access to a pit with well-preserved bones of a complete mammoth.[45] Jefferson wrote to Peale on 29 July 1801 "to congratulate" him on his prospect of "obtaining a compleat skeleton of the great incognitum," and he believed that Peale was the person "at the critical moment of the discovery" who had "zeal enough to devote himself to the recovery of these great animal monuments."[46] In the same letter Jefferson assured Peale that the US Navy agent in New York would loan him a pump used on frigates to remove water from the excavation site. Jefferson had encouraged Peale's work for many years by donating items to his collections. Because of Jefferson's power and position, Peale was certain that his own hopes for a national museum that provided widespread access to knowledge for all Americans would be realized.

The following year, Peale requested guidance from Jefferson on the fate of his museum in a letter dated January 12, 1802, that included a draft address calling for government aid. In the letter Peale asked whether he should send the application to the state of Pennsylvania or could expect that his work "would be crowned in a National Establishment of my Museum."[47] By this time

Jefferson had decided that no hope existed for a national institution like the one Peale had proposed. He assured Peale of the importance of his work but told him that their endeavor had little hope of obtaining enough support to purchase Peale's collections for the country. Jefferson wrote that he wished that the museum could be used for the national interest; however, he did not want to give Peale false hope that Jefferson could publicly support the establishment of a national museum since "those who hold them to the enumeration, have always denied that Congress have any power to establish a National academy." Jefferson continued, "if there were an union of opinion that Congress already possessed the right, I am persuaded the purchase of your museum would be the first object on which it would be exercised."[48] In the end, Jefferson encouraged Peale to continue his efforts and to focus on obtaining funding from the state of Pennsylvania.[49]

Although he did not receive federal funding for a museum, Peale continued to benefit from his relationship with Jefferson, receiving numerous donations from federally funded expeditions to the West. While president, Jefferson resolved to investigate the West and exert control over the vast American interior through scientific exploration. The objects gathered on these expeditions and later displayed served as a symbol of the United States' newfound scientific prowess and were testaments to the cultural and scientific power of their own citizenry. Jefferson gifted many specimens gathered on federally funded expeditions to Peale, as evidenced in their frequent correspondence and in "Documents Relating to the Peale Museum" in the Peale Family Papers.[50] On October 6, 1805, for example, Jefferson sent items including "the skeletons of the white hare, badger, antelopes and a skeleton of the small or burrowing wolf of the prairies," as well as a "living burrowing squirrel of the prairies, a living magpie," and animals that never had "been found out of Europe."[51] The new finds from these federally funded explorations, including valuable artifacts from the many Native American peoples obtained by the Lewis and Clark expedition, were critical for the growth of Peale's collections.

Increasingly, Peale's collections included live specimens, adding complexity to his goal to construct a world in miniature. Newspapers publicized the addition of live specimens, such as "two living Rattle Vipers, from North Carolina," about which it was reported that "a mouse . . . introduced to one of them . . . expired in five minutes after being struck by it."[52] Peale added that these creatures were "well secured with wove wire and glass," so visitors could view them in

FIG. 6. Charles Willson Peale, *Exhumation of the Mastodon*, ca. 1806–8, oil on canvas, 49 × 61 1/2 in. Maryland Historical Society, Baltimore City Life Museum Collection, gift of Bertha White in memory of her husband, Harry White, BCLM-MA.5911. (Courtesy Maryland Historical Society)

safety. Among many live animals collected by Peale were grizzly bears secured by the explorer Captain Zebulon Pike. Pike sent "two cubs of Grisly Bear taken from the Rio Bravo," along the border with Mexico.[53] These bears, like most of the live animals he kept, eventually needed to be killed, whereupon they were preserved by Peale for posterity in his museum.[54] These specimens promoted the idea of a rich western lands waiting to be exploited for the expansion of the nation and offered a dream of progress for American citizens. In the words of one historian, Peale "displayed the expanding nation to itself" via these animals, minerals, and anthropological artifacts gathered by new national heroes who explored what was to them the great unknown. By making the unknown visible to a broad swath of visitors to his museum, Peale spurred the imaginations of early Americans.

The Limits of Democratic Knowledge

Peale managed to expand his museum because he capitalized on the curiosity of Americans who wanted to know more about the world around them. Yet he did not foresee that his scientific work would be at the center of a political attack on his greatest advocate when Federalists took aim at Jefferson via Peale and scrutinized the duo's interest and endeavors in natural history to question their intellectual authority. Previously, Jefferson and his only book-length work, *Notes on the State of Virginia,* first published in 1785, had come under repeated attack by Federalists, who paid special attention to parts of the work on natural history. In pamphlets and periodicals, Federalists such as Washington Irving, Josiah Quincy, Clement Clarke Moore, Samuel Ewing, and Joseph Dennie attacked Jefferson and then all general interest in natural history as a peculiar mental deficiency.[55] During the mammoth excavation, Joseph Dennie, the Federalist publisher of the famous high-brow magazine *The Port-Folio,* mocked the endeavor as an example of the intellectual corruption of Americans. On July 18, 1801, Dennie wrote an extensive criticism of American society, indicating that many had turned their back on the virtues of the Revolution in favor of self-promotion. As an example, he claimed that members of the "American philosophical society" longed for "these bony treasures" to be secured and for "Mr. P." to "put together a complete skeleton for the museum." Dennie wrote that once the skeleton was completed, "We presume this *idol* will be set up and worshipped by our first consul" and revered by modern philosophers.[56] This reference to the first consul was to obliquely disparage Thomas Jefferson and his modern philosophers friends from the APS.

Dennie's warning must have still been ringing in readers' ears when news of a farewell dinner for Peale's son Rembrandt aroused the ire of Federalists a few months later. The Federalist critics read in horror as newspapers reported a scene in mid-February 1802 in which thirteen men joined in this farewell dinner underneath the skeleton of a mammoth that the younger Peale was taking on tour with him to Europe. The men sat underneath the thorax of the extinct beast and offered a series of ten toasts celebrating mankind's advancement of scientific knowledge and understanding of nature. The first two toasts, celebrating mankind and the American people, were followed by toasts to agriculture and the "Constitution of the United States" that included important symbolic connections between nature and the American republic. The men in the room believed that their new scientific way of understanding the world was superior to others, and they even toasted "the brains of freemen—may they never be so barricaded by the jack-ass bones of opposition as to crush their native energy."[57] The point of this toast was to emphasize the American spirit of knowledge and learning as exemplified by the dedication to natural history and men like the self-taught Peale, who were not slaves to older forms of knowledge and learning.

Newspapers across the country reported the story and the toasts, and the mammoth became an instant symbol of American pride to many across the nation. Americans reveled in how this ancient extinct beast's great size demonstrated that a flawed European argument of American degeneration, famously espoused by the French natural history scholar Comte de Buffon, that had dominated natural-history intellectual debates for decades was flawed. These men celebrated the overturning of this natural-history paradigm that held that the American continents were filled with weak and inferior creatures. They desired to demonstrate that the Americas and those who inhabited those continents were not biologically inferior to Europeans but were every bit as capable of performing intellectual work as their counterparts in Europe. In fact the desire to prove this encouraged a large number of Americans to participate in natural history and added to the patriotic ideals expressed by Peale and his work in the museum. This participation by Americans was viewed by Peale and his comrades as a foil to European arguments of American degeneration. Others, of Federalist persuasions, saw this dinner as evidence that the country was led by a bunch of frauds and needed to awaken from its reverie.[58]

The response from the Federalists came quickly. Samuel Ewing immediately responded to this story by producing a satirical poem mocking the banquet, the mammoth, and Peale. Ewing's poem provided an unpleasant description of the scene that grossly intermingled imagined aromas and ghastly sights of the foods mixed with the tools of Peale's trade. The work referenced literature dating back to antiquity and included Dante's *Paradise Lost* to demonstrate Peale's failure to attain the training necessary to be a gentleman.[59] Ewing's vivid ridicule focused on all who rejected classical knowledge in favor of the modern philosopher's hunt for truths within fossils found in the wilderness. Federalists believed these men had deserted their "moral and religious obligations in their search for scientific artifacts and skeletons."[60] Furthermore, these men, whom classically educated elites like Ewing believed to be misguided, had wormed their way into the company of good people. In the eyes of Federalists, men like Peale focused on individual self-interests and entertainment, which these elites believed to lead to social decline and the republic's doom.[61] In the end, the division between elites in the form of the Federalists, who saw themselves as preservers of intellectual traditions, and those who sought to promote a meritocracy based on expansive opportunities increased dramatically. The elites retreated to their colleges and emphasized classical aspects of learning that included the study of Latin, while more average people visited museums and sparked their intellectual curiosity while also being amused in this setting.

Despite some Federalists' opinion that museums were institutions of amusement, other Americans sought to emulate Peale's endeavors by establishing their own museums to showcase their curiosities. Daniel Bowen established the Columbian Museum in Boston as early as 1791. A 1798 broadside advertised portraits depicting historical people and events from history and literature, as well as "Figures of Wax-Work (large as Life)."[62] The following year a broadside advertised that Bowen's Columbian Museum contained "WAX-FIGURES, Paintings, Curiosities &c.," including representations in wax of important American and international figures. The museum included representations of President John Adams, George Washington, and Benjamin Franklin sitting with Ezra Stiles. Also depicted were several tableaus of the bloody events during the French Revolution, such as the assassination of Marat and "The Guillotine, and a man beheaded with the executioner holding up the head to public view." Near the bottom of the page the advertisement announced that the museum also included a "large Collection of Natural & Artificial CURIOSITIES." The scientific curiosities seemed secondary within the overall collection of "very entertaining" items for those who could afford "HALF A DOLLAR." Unlike at Peale's museum, scientific knowledge for the masses was a secondary part of the Columbian Museum collection; instead, this new museum in Boston featured story-based attractions that focused on moral tales.[63]

Peale was not the only innovative museum operator and creator. John Scudder's American Museum in New York was an important example of an institution that offered a counter to traditional forms of knowledge dissemination to the community. Both Peale and John Scudder, a contemporary of Peale's, used published guides to their collections to entice visitors and to orient visitors within their museums. Peale's 8-page guide from 1805 outlined the history of the museum and described the spaces and collections within the museum.[64] Peale continued to solicit donations from "Gentlemen travelling into foreign countries" whose specimens "are rendered valuable in the collective view but otherwise lost to the public, and of little value to the possessors."[65] Scudder's

103-page guide to his museum, titled *A Companion to the American Museum*, included the rules for access and descriptive information about the bulk of the collections. In addition to requiring that each visitor pay twenty-five cents upon admission, there were no "coloured people admitted in the evening, except servants with their masters."[66] This implied that Black Americans could peruse the museum, at least in the daytime hours, if they could pay the entrance fee. Although Black people and Indigenous people were often portrayed in a negative light, the fact that they could attend these institutions does suggest that there was an opportunity for engagement with these natural-history specimens for all people who could pay. It was the kind of access to knowledge that was often prevented in many colleges and universities during the period. While at the museum, they might have encountered an African American man, Moses Williams, who made silhouettes using Peale's machine, called a physiognotrace, as souvenirs of their visit. Williams was so successful that he was able to marry Peale's white cook and purchase a two-story house, where they had a family. By using the guide to these collections, visitors could engage with the collections directly as long as specific rules were followed. Each display case in the Scudder's museum was numbered, and the *Companion* directed the user through the museum, taking them from one display case to another; the visitor was asked to "commence as he enters the museum, with case No.1 and follow all the numbers" so that they would see everything in turn. Still this was an opportunity for a visitor to choose their own adventure into a world curated for them to see faraway lands and the creatures who lived in them.

Scudder used techniques similar to Peale's and delivered lectures on the accuracy of the display of the specimens. He also had several natural-science apparatuses, including an "Electrical Machine" that he operated "for the gratification of visitors, and for medical purposes."[67] To some scholars, Scudder's museum seemed to be a "museum for the masses" and less part of the educational mission that Peale championed, yet these two museums were very similar in layout, approach, and mission. However, Scudder did add the notion that museum curators were obliged to present collections that fit the popular taste, which was why he responded to the desires of the public.[68]

Many admired Scudder's museum, and some scientific leaders, such as a leading natural-history expert from New York, David Hosack, met with Peale in 1817 to urge that the two museums be combined to form a national museum if Peale received no answer from the state about public funding.[69] Yet Scudder's premature death in 1821 left the museum in the hands of a group of five trustees and eventually Scudder's son. The museum fell into disrepair without the creative dynamism of Scudder, and without the ability to secure new collections the museum's status deteriorated. Eventually, after two decades of mediocrity, the museum was purchased by P. T. Barnum. Unlike Peale's, Scudder's operation was not designed to grow, and apparently his son, John Jr., was not as well trained in the model that Scudder and Peale had perfected.[70]

While Peale kept expanding his collection, the subscription lists of those who could afford admission to his museum reveal that middle- and upper-class men were the main viewers of those objects. On July 18, 1810, Peale boasted that his collection held "upwards of one hundred thousand Interesting Articles of NATURE AND ART." The "MAMMOTH SKELETON" remained a big draw and was exhibited along with "a great variety of other Skeletons and Bones," which were now available to view for twenty-five cents. This was half of the total fifty-cent entry fee "to defray the enourmous expence of procuring the skeleton."[71] Peale also tried to secure public affiliates by selling tickets for annual admission. The price of an annual admission ticket in 1788 was one dollar; in 1802 it was six dollars, and by 1819 it was ten dollars. Sixty-two percent of annual ticket holders in 1794 held public office or were occupied in commerce, reflecting Peale's patronage network.[72] But a significant number of ticket holders were mechanics and manufacturers who worked with their hands. Yet despite Peale's democratic call to open the book of nature to all, women and the unskilled labor force in Philadelphia, both white and Black, were mostly left outside the museum doors.[73] Thus, while Peale had managed to democratize access to scientific knowledge somewhat, his revolutionary plans for democratizing access to knowledge about nature had limited success because he failed to secure direct patronage from the national government. Although Peale needed the museum to succeed for financial reasons, it was more important as a means of centralizing the efforts of collecting and presenting natural-history knowledge. Peale desperately appealed to his friends for support so that they could achieve their dream of a widely accessible means of presenting science to a broad swath of people.

Although he was nominally successful, Peale's frustration with the various levels of government and the lack of official financial support continued throughout his life, and he resolved in a letter to Jefferson in 1815 that if support were not forthcoming, "the Museum must be sold, for if it is not disposed of, before my death, a division of it will be its distruction."[74] He listed the many political problems he had had securing public assistance. In the end, despite

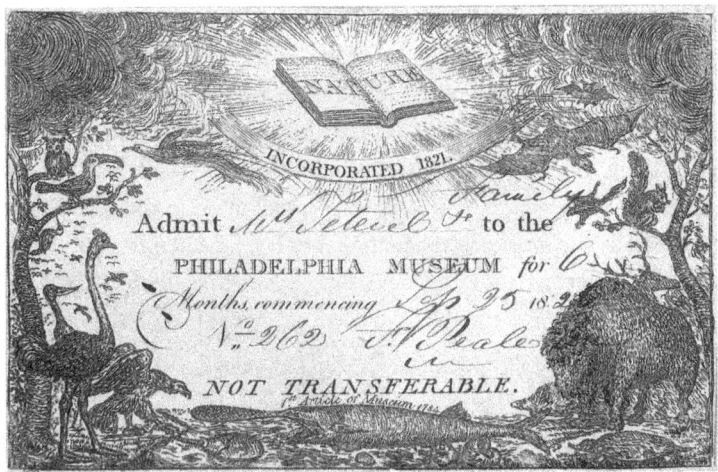

FIG. 7. Admission ticket to Peale's Museum in Philadelphia, 1822. American Philosophical Society, Peale-Sellers Family Collection, Mss.B.P31. (Courtesy American Philosophical Society)

his years of efforts to secure government patronage, the museum remained a private institution that Peale passed along to his sons, who opened companion museums in Baltimore and New York.[75] Peale's fruitless appeals to state and federal government officials reveal that there were significant concerns over who these institutions should be for and, just as important, who should run them. Much as with a national university, some worried that since people in South Carolina or Kentucky might never be able to see a national museum, it would not directly benefit them. Still others were skeptical that a man like Peale, who had not been educated in a traditional college or university, could lead this kind of institution. Few saw a need for such an institution at the state level, much less at the national level.

Still, ultimately Peale's work as a museum proprietor helped to promote collaborative collection development among a diverse and diffused citizenry. The self-educated artist and scientist successfully leveraged his contacts with the country's elites to create "a world in miniature" through his "ardent love of collecting" and presented the "scientifically arranged" contents to his visitors.[76] He consistently emphasized his private enterprise as a public good worthy of public support since it promoted scientific advances. Finally, Peale believed showing the collective effort made across the expansive republic would advance an agenda of scientific learning for the larger society. Peale's museum was a place where those interested in self-improvement could explore the wonders of the world even if these visitors, like him, had never attended a college or university. In this way, Peale's attempts to create a national museum offered opportunities for a broader set of the people in the United States to learn about sciences while also encouraging them to participate in building access to knowledge. It instituted a sense of pride that Americans were capable of engaging with the latest scientific theories and could be participants in the advancement of the ideals of learning and self-improvement in their republican experiment.

Specialized Learned Societies

Taking inspiration from Peale's work, specialized learned societies such as the Salem East India Marine Society (SEIMS) began to collect information needed by their members to perform their work.[77] They were particularly interested in promoting a better understanding of Asia by collecting curiosities and displaying them for members and their community. SEIMS is a useful example of the new learned societies that sprang up across the early republic, which emerged to meet the information needs of their membership while also serving the needs of their broader community. The SEIMS established a collection of resources including the journals from voyages of their members as well as a "Museum of natural and artificial curiosities, particularly such as are to be found beyond the Cape of Good Hope and Cape Horn."[78]

The society was originally established in 1799 for the mutual benefit of those "who shall have actually navigated the Seas near the Cape of Good Hope or Cape Horn, either as Master or Commander, . . . as Factor or Supercargo of any vessel belonging to Salem."[79] The items in its collections came from both members and friends of members, such as John Fitzpatrick Jefferie, who had heard about the society's "formation of a museum, into which you readily admitted any curiosities collected by travelers: and received such information as they could give relative to the productions, manners and customs of different Countries and People."[80] An 1804 article in the *Salem Register* indicated that Peale's museum was a useful model for the society's museum by invoking his use of a separate room "assigned for models of useful machinery" and that a visitor to Salem's museum had been "much pleased that a specimen of the kind appeared in our own museum."[81] The SEIMS museum quickly became a site of note and regional pride, filled with valuable collections for consultation and use by the local community.

The growth of the collections was impressive, and the merchant group quickly outgrew their facilities. Within three years they needed to expand their hall, and by 1804 they had moved to a new building. The items on display provided tangible evidence of adventures and exploits of their American members, who brought back to Salem scientific specimens and treasures from around the world for all to see. In 1821 the society published a catalog of its collections, which numbered over twenty-two hundred items available for consultation. An author identified only as X sent a letter to the *Salem Gazette* praising the East India Society because they were vigorous and enterprising young men instead of "men advanced in years. . . . Most of your candidates are young, curious and full of enterprize, and will add much to your information and collection of curiosities." The writer went on to say that while many "men of lorded and contracted minds consider a Museum as they do fire works that give pleasure only while seen . . . it appears different to those who are enlightened by science." "Your researches," X added, "united to the researches of others, will assist the philosopher in discussing . . . the powers and faculties of the human mind."[82] The writer indicated that the society's active use of materials in its collections for research was tangible evidence of a new way to think about knowledge, one that emphasized practical application and experience over traditional study.[83]

The museum's collections were also part of public spectacles designed to promote the success of the community and locally owned specimens. The types of knowledge collected provide insights into what was valued by the community. The local newspaper, the *Salem Gazette,* announced in January 1801 that at the SEIMS annual meeting "one of the members was attired in a superb Mandarine dress presented to the Society by Capt. WILLIAM WARD."[84] The society's donation book verifies that a "Compleat Mandarine dress was the 71st item present to the society by Ward, who also donated a 'Chinese God.'"[85] These collections reflected a desire to demonstrate members' expertise and their intellectual superiority over these foreigners. The society also displayed its collections to the community in annual parades meant to project the superiority of white cultural identities. The mandarin dress was a controversial item at the society's second annual parade, in 1801, when a local reverend was appalled that one of the society's own members wore the foreign clothes instead of having a figure or a person of color don the exotic attire. A few years later, in 1804, the members of the SEIMS no longer dressed up as Asians and instead hired Black people dressed in authentic attire to carry the elegant palanquin that was a new prized addition to their collection. A white employee of the society was charged with making sure that the social distinction that separated the white man from all others was maintained in the display of these Asian collections.[86]

Overall, the collection amassed contained rare plants, animals, fossils, shells, artifacts, exotic clothing, weapons, and tools from across the globe. In 1799, members who were ship captains donated content from the lands of Sumatra, Surinam, Manila, the Cape of Good Hope, Mauritius, the western part of North America, and China. Occasionally the celebratory toasts of the society were also documented in detail. Thirteen toasts were published in the November 7, 1807, *Essex Register*. The tenth was to "*Our Museum*—May these emblems of the wants of the *savage*, teach us to value the blessings of the *civilized* state." This toast emphasized an evangelical zeal that underpinned the nature of the items explorers brought home. It also connected scientific learning to the mission of Americans to promote capitalism, republican values, and Christianity to the world. These items reminded visitors to the museum that their brethren in the SEIMS were acting out of more than just personal self-interest. An asterisk following the toast was linked to a note at the end of the article that read, "The Museum (in which this dinner was given,) is hung round with various implements of the *savage* nations on the N.W. Coast of America and other parts of the Globe."[87] The settler colonialism mind-set is clear in these toasts. The exotic items were meant both to capture the imagination of viewers and also to project an intellectual superiority so that viewers could imagine themselves as part of an expansive republic of knowledge that promoted progress to Indigenous peoples in far-off lands. The display of these objects offered Americans who were unable to visit distant lands a way to experience the thrill of settler colonialism.

The SEIMS collections were specifically designed to increase the knowledge of the members planning voyages and new business ventures. The society's by-laws and regulations stated that the society "shall purchase all approved Books of History, of Voyages and Travels, and of Navigation" that could be obtained. Furthermore, each member was obligated to "assist in collecting all valuable Publications, in every language" for the use of the society. Each member was given a blank journal in which to record their observations and "upon returning from Sea shall in all cases present the journals of their voyages to the President."[88] The society made copies of these journals for the collective use of its members. This collective action bound these members together for the promotion of new knowledge that was specific to their common interests.

Twenty-two years after the society's founding, it boasted that "sixty-seven journals of voyages made to various parts of the world (and in several instances to places rarely visited) have already been deposited" and were "open to the public inspection." This method of sharing information was an important public service for all seafarers who could access the volumes. Further, the members of the society were committed to sharing objects that represented the far-off environs they visited. In time the society employed someone to make a "catalogue" and arrange the collection "in a new and more scientific manner." The museum was open to visitors "at all times, free of charge" if they were accompanied by a member.[89] As the SEIMS example shows, across the early republic museums increasingly came to be seen as places for educational entertainment and as spaces for scientific learning, designed to reach ever broader audiences.

Budding scientists thrilled at the opportunity to form and join these new civic societies, which remained reliant on the resources provided by patronage. This patronage came in the form of well-known men of learning joining their convocation or through the financial wherewithal of affluent supporters. Once patronage was secured, a learned society could grow. The Academy of Natural Sciences (ANS), of Philadelphia, founded in 1812, seemed destined for a pedestrian existence until the social experimenter and scientist philanthropist William Maclure took an interest in the fledgling society. Maclure brought respectability and money to the institution, allowing the radical group to begin to develop a rich and diverse cabinet, publish a journal, and sponsor a scientific expedition into Florida designed to gather new specimens for original research.

Since most of the ANS's founding members did not have the reputation to be elected to the elite APS, they decided to found an institution of their own. This would help them share the costs for building a research cabinet. The ANS reached out via newspapers in 1812 to the "Cultivators and Owners of Land" in advertisements such as one in Philadelphia's *Star of Liberty* informing those who found interesting objects such as "Minerals, Ores, Stones, Marble, . . . Coal, Clays, Sands, Ochres etc. . . . that they may have them examined without cost . . . if directed to the Academy of Natural Sciences." The advertisement indicated that the goal of the academy was to develop the "resources of the country." Along with providing directions on packing specimens, the advertisement asked that the donor provide a "plain account of the soil in which they have been found, the name of the place, its distance and bearing from mountains from navigable waters, and from any great town."[90]

In 1815, the ANS advertised tickets for members of the public to their series of lectures on botany, mineralogy, and chemistry, which were very successful, especially with the "ladies of Philadelphia."[91] The success of the institution and its growing collections can be attributed, according to one scholar, to the "contributions from public-spirited savants" who favored the ANS instead of donating to Peale's museum, which was both privately owned and already supported by many of the elite.[92] Compared with the members of the APS, men who joined the ANS were not members of the elite, were not well known in the scientific community, and tended to be younger in age.

The ranks of the new society quickly swelled with members who longed to be taken seriously. These men sought support for their work and thus sought out a benefactor. William Maclure, a businessman recently settled from Scotland, was attracted to the mission of the ANS, which emphasized the importance of using science as a means of social reform with the goal of promoting a more equitable society.[93] In 1817 Maclure donated a significant sum to the society that enabled it to rise in popularity and significance, and the group elected Maclure president in return. Because of the society's focus on natural history and its encouragement of broader participation in knowledge collection and creation, it quickly supplanted the APS as a leader in promoting research in natural history.

Lastly, the ANS produced the *Circular to Captains and Voyagers*. At least two hundred copies of the eight-page circular were printed. The society's first publication, it informed the reader that their group had "directed their attention to the formation of a museum, illustrative of natural history," and since their work was "so important to the advancement of 'general science,'" they took the "liberty of requesting" that these sailors donate curiosities to help accomplish their work.[94] In the following pages the ANS provided "a few directions for the collection and preservation of specimens which may facilitate your labours, and render them more serviceable." Directions for the preservation of quadrupeds, birds, fish, insects, shells, plants, and minerals were given. "All other natural productions not particularized will be valuable acquisitions to the Academy. . . . Particularly specimens . . . from the Western coast of America, and other countries little explored." The final note of the publication told the reader that "the Academy have the pleasure of inviting your attendance at their Hall, No 35 Arch Street where their museum is deposited to which admittance can be at any time be gained through either of their members."[95] This invitation made clear that anyone could attend ANS meetings if they had relevant business; as with the SEIMS, at the heart of the ANS's mission was to be accessible to the public.

The ANS's new journal provided the organization's members with a means to publish their research findings. And importantly, on the final pages of every volume from 1817 to 1830 were listed the donations of specimens to their museum; the October issue in 1817 listed 157 distinct collections on six pages.[96] On January 17, 1817, Thomas Say submitted a one-page curator's report entitled "The Present Collection of the Academy of Natural Sciences of Philadelphia." The vastness of the collections may have overwhelmed him and the other curators since instead of a detailed listing of the collections, the report stated that the society had "four to five hundred volumes of Books" and "four to five thousand specimens of minerals native and foreign, numerous preparations of quadrupeds, birds, reptiles and dried plants, a large collection of native Insects and some foreign ones, a collection of several thousand shells native and foreign," and he insisted that the "articles are scientifically arranged."[97] As with Peale in his catalogs and newspaper announcements, this point was made to make sure that all who read this understood that the specimens were the real deal.

Shortly after his election to the presidency of the ANS in 1817, Maclure sponsored a privately funded effort to collect specimens in Florida. Maclure secured young scholars interested in natural history from the ranks of the APS to participate in the expedition and publish their findings in the ANS's journal. This made his organization a leading producer and distributor of the latest scientific information. The expedition included men who would become notable scientists, such as Thomas Say, George Ord, and one of Charles Willson Peale's sons, Titian Peale.[98] The expedition produced valuable additions and publicity about the ability of these members to conduct field research; however, it ended before its scheduled completion because of hostilities with Seminole and Creek Indians. This experience seemed to provide evidence for the need for military support and expertise for these types of expeditions. The ANS exemplifies how those who were not immediately accepted into the existing knowledge institutions found ways to establish their own institutions. Like the ANS, many of these new societies did not have connections to elite leaders as Peale did, and so they devised other means of building collections for their communities of scholars.

The movement to establish museums was not limited to urban locations within the Atlantic states. Residents in Cincinnati and Kentucky also worked to establish colleges, libraries, and learned societies. "On the subject of a museum" Dr. Daniel Drake reported that he confidently expected to see from "$5,000 to $6,000" to create a museum that would serve a "a complete school for natural history" with "the choicest natural and artificial curiosities in the Western Country."[99] In 1819 the *American Journal of Science* printed Drake's address, which took up more than four pages, and described him as someone who led a group of "citizens of Cincinnati [who] have recently instituted a society for the collection, preservation, exhibition, and illustration of natural and artificial curiosities, particularly of the *western country*."[100] The journal stated that the group "must of course solicit the aid of their fellow-citizens in all quarters of the extensive region."[101] Drake and his colleagues identified four broad classes of objects that the group sought. First, finding "metal and minerals" was considered "extremely interesting," and "every citizen of the western country must *feel* the necessity of a speedy development of its mineral resources."[102] They asked that detailed labels be affixed to each specimen so that viewers would learn how minerals could be profitable. Knowledge of animals, relics, and items created by "present savage tribes" were all viewed with an eye toward making profit. Drake's scheme embodied settler colonial ideals for expansion and control over knowledge based on the desire to exploit resources for white Americans. These leaders sought to reproduce the models designed by Peale and others in order to increase and diffuse knowledge for white settlers.

The plans for this western institution in Cincinnati were widely circulated across the country in newspapers, often under the headline "Science of the West." The stories reported the importance of expanding American naturalist studies, to correct erroneous studies by Europeans and to encourage mining for "useful minerals" and other natural resources.[103] Drake gave the speech celebrating the opening only a year later, in June 1820, illustrating that communities across the nation were embracing institutions of natural history.[104]

A transformation occurred in the country's first decades as the leaders of the United States struggled to decide how to create a vibrant and active citizenry dedicated to the work of scientific progress as then displayed in museums across the country. In contrast to the political turmoil and division between Federalists and Republicans over the work of natural history as encouraged by Jefferson and Peale around 1800, a new public-private partnership between the American military and learned societies emerged late in the second decade of the nineteenth century. In 1819 John C. Calhoun ordered Major Stephen H. Long to "explore the waters of the Missouri" on the "U.S. steamboat" called the "WESTERN ENGINEER," which launched from Pittsburgh to collect all manner of natural-history items, including "the inhabitants, soils, minerals, and curiosities."[105] Members of the APS were asked what to look for during the journey from Pittsburgh to "navigate the western waters as far as the Yellow Stone River," which was expected to take more than two years. The corps of scientists aboard the paddleboat included the ANS's Thomas Say, a botanist and geologist, and Titian Peale, a naturalist, landscape painter, and ornithologist. Other scientist members of the corps were a mineralogist, a zoologist, and a physician. Readers must have been thrilled when they read reports in periodicals about the Rocky Mountains, which had yet to be explored, and about "shining mountains 'from an infinite number of crystal stones of an amazing size,'" which might yield "more riches in their bowels that those of Indostan and Malabar . . . or in the mines of Peru."[106] The population eagerly awaited news of Long's expedition.

Increasingly, ventures such as SEIMS and the ANS provided American citizens outlets through which to promote their shared commitment to improving and expanding access to the collection and dissemination of useful knowledge. The patronage of wealthy elites proved helpful but was no longer an absolute requirement for these institutions to create a cabinet of useful content for their organizations. Specialized learned societies offered a means for the middling class and the emerging professional class to work together to disseminate the knowledge needed for their work and for their leisure interests. The members of these organizations were always careful to demonstrate their ties with their communities and frequently celebrated their collections and expansion of knowledge in their localities. They also opened their doors to nonmembers and promoted their collections as benefiting all Americans. Finally, these organizations linked the acquisition of knowledge with financial and moral advancements.

In the early republic, museums emerged as sites that helped Americans to engage with collections of artifacts and specimens from their own country and throughout the world. Leaders, especially on the Republican side of the political divide, hoped that engaging the populace with the wonders of nature would encourage learning, which would in turn ensure American prosperity. To accomplish this, museum collectors like Charles Willson Peale actively sought to make their enterprises seen as a public good.

These emerging museums were indeed public. Some museums, such as Peale's museum, required an admission fee to view the collection. Others charged no admission fee. The Salem East India Marine Society, which had no admission fee, demonstrated the importance of trade and highlighted the wealth of Asia. The Academy of Natural Sciences also opened its doors to nonmembers and developed a specialized collection to make use of the resources collected in the West and to promote the interests of like-minded citizen-scientists.

Collectors were especially successful in tying their mission to national aspirations of progress. Key to this success was their collective strategy of appealing to Americans via newspaper advertisements to participate in their museums by donating scientific curiosities. The shared experience of building scientific institutions by donating specimens that could be both viewed and utilized to produce new scholarship offered individual donors the opportunity to experience the wonders of nature. The dissemination of knowledge through lectures tied to museum holdings became a way to entice future citizen-scientists. In the end, while the collections were not open to everyone, they began to offer those in the middling classes a means to acquire a better understanding of the world in which they lived as well as some ties to bind diverse people together in the expanding republic.

The lack of established national knowledge institutions offered opportunities for new kinds of institutions that were better suited to emerging scientific disciplines such as natural history. Museums seemed perfectly suited to promoting access to diverse groups so that they could participate in the exciting scientific discoveries occurring every day. Men like Peale found a way to live in the world of traditional elite learned societies by making aspects of this new knowledge visible and useful through his preservation strategies and his commitment to life-long learning in a way that suggested that America offered opportunities for advancement through application and hard work. Nevertheless, although Peale and others like Scudder acquired diverse expertise, not everyone accepted them as equals. Also, most people never were accepted into the established learned societies. Instead, they devised new specialized societies to serve their own intellectual and local needs. In many cases their strategies were the same as Peale's, but their local institutions used museums to promote the intellectual needs of their communities amid the information revolution.

CHAPTER 4

NATIONAL AGRICULTURAL INSTITUTIONS

Democratizing Authority over Knowledge

An increasing number of Americans sought to engage with scientific discourse in the second and third decades of the nineteenth century. There was an explosion of new learned societies, libraries, schools, and lyceums, each of which promoted useful knowledge to an ever larger circle of information consumers. Alexis de Tocqueville famously was astonished at the scale on which "Americans of all ages, of all conditions, of all minds, constantly unite."[1] He was surprised that there were so many kinds of associations of which, "I confess, I had not even the idea," and he was greatly impressed by the fact that people in the "United States succeeded in setting a common goal for the efforts of a great number of men, and in making them march freely toward it."[2] He concluded that "in democratic countries, the science of association is the mother science; the progress of all the others depends on the progress of the former."[3]

Scholars have long explored the connections between the creation and the consumption of new knowledge. They have demonstrated a direct connection between popular participation in education and Americans' inventing their nation through scientific exploration and dissemination of knowledge.[4] An expanding democratic view of knowledge making allowed non-elite citizen-scientists to collect, codify, and even explain objects in the world in which they lived. The names of the institutions they established and joined signaled a growing trend toward specialization in scope and purpose. For example, the American Antiquarian Society, the Boston Athenaeum, the Association of American Geologists and Naturalists, the Medical Society of the District of Columbia, the Columbian Agricultural Society, the Washington Botanical Society, the Massachusetts Horticultural Society, and the South Carolina

Agricultural Society exemplify the specialization and geographic scope of these institutions. The goal of many of these institutions was to offer access to a growing community of people interested in participating in what we now call scholarship. Instead of emphasizing the social status of individuals, these groups focused on the intellectual worth of the ideas they offered. Nevertheless, different groups of Americans continued to disagree about what constituted "useful knowledge" and what kinds of institutions would best serve the diffuse and heterogenous society at large. Who could and should participate in the creation and dissemination of knowledge in the early republic became an important issue as a host of new people began to participate in what had once been the domain of the elites.

This chapter tracks increasing popular participation in the creation of scientific knowledge and how the federal government—at long last—became instrumental in enhancing that expertise.[5] The District of Columbia, as a neutral place designed to serve the collective interests of the country, was an important site for these discussions.[6] The federal city hosted several learned societies that demonstrate how specialized scientific interests evolved in the first three decades of the nineteenth century. Among the most significant examples of these were agricultural institutions, which served as a means for broad-based participation in scientific work. There was broad political support for expanding agricultural knowledge because of the importance of the agricultural industry across the country. This chapter also shows that the emerging bureaucratic institutions were critical for the development of scientific knowledge even if they supported scientific endeavors in unexpected ways, such as using international diplomatic and military expeditions to encourage the collection and deposit of seeds from across the world by specialized learned societies.

Agricultural Learned Societies

Agricultural sciences were critical to the explosion of scientific research in the eighteenth and early nineteenth centuries. From 1785 to 1800 many leaders urged local communities and states to establish agricultural societies to promote best practices in experimentation and seed exchanges. From the beginning, political leaders wanted to secure economic independence for their new republic by demonstrating American know-how in the form of agricultural knowledge. Independently generated agricultural knowledge was important to them since the United States' status as a former colonial space, which had been subject to Europe's system of bioprospecting, was seen as a source to be exploited instead of a site of intellectual equals. George Washington, in his eighth and final message to Congress, even devoted an entire paragraph to a broad-based plan of "public patronage" to establish agricultural societies "charged with collecting and diffusing information and enabled by premiums, and small pecuniary aids, to encourage and assist a spirit of discovery and improvement."[7] This call to the newly established nation, like his call for a national university, remained unfulfilled during his lifetime.[8]

Yet in the first decades of the nineteenth century, agricultural societies began to flourish in and around the new federal city, where a group of leading citizens established the Columbian Agricultural Society for the Promotion of Rural and Domestic Economy in 1809. Some of the same members formed the Agricultural Society of Prince George's County in the neighboring county in Maryland a few years later.[9] Leaders across Maryland formed a statewide organization in 1818. The new organization's constitution mandated that six of the elected "curators" be from "the Western and six from the Eastern Shore."[10] These curators were responsible for adding to and maintaining the collections of the society and amassing the "best samples of all the useful grains, roots, and seeds," as well as "all native fossils, marls, earth or substances proper for manure," needed for analysis by the members.[11] Virginia too boasted many agricultural societies, which reported their experiments in agricultural journals while also promoting the exchange of information via fairs and lobbying the state government for the establishment of a department of agriculture to conduct surveys and support a school of agriculture at the University of Virginia.[12]

Partnerships between government and agricultural societies became a vital part of the scientific infrastructure in the early nineteenth century and allowed a larger number of people to participate in knowledge making. These agricultural institutions not only produced journals, as other learned societies did, but also held annual fairs to promote the work of their members. This developed into a full-scale movement that went from the local level to the state and even the national level.[13] Even before the Columbian Agricultural Society (CAS) was founded, its future members participated in the early agricultural fairs on the national mall in 1804 and 1805. There individuals competed for awards provided by the city's government and private individuals for the best livestock.[14]

In 1810, the CAS established its journal, the *Agricultural Museum*, and also sponsored a number of exhibitions, beginning on May 16, 1810, at the Union Hotel in Georgetown. Among the visitors were President James Madison;

members of his cabinet, such as Albert Gallatin, William Eustis, and Robert Smith; and prominent citizens of the region, such as John Mason and William Marbury, all of whom donned clothing made from domestic fabrics. The *National Intelligencer* reported that the "exhibition" proved to "exceed any thing of the kind in the United States, and promises to be of great utility in the promotion of the Agricultural Arts." The newspaper also emphasized that the Society aimed to promote "domestic manufactures . . . by exciting a competition," and therefore handed out prizes ranging from $60 to $100 for outstanding examples of domestic livestock and fabrics.[15] A "Mr. Steinberger" from Shenandoah exhibited a twenty-seven-hundred-pound steer, believed to be the largest specimen ever raised in Virginia. Patriotic pride swelled across the country as newspapers reported and reprinted the dimensions of the livestock; the weights of beef, hide, organs, and tallow were recorded and announced after the animals were slaughtered and sold to consumers at the fair.[16] The evidence in hand was proof positive of the advancement of knowledge happening on the grounds of the federal city.

White men established and governed these societies, but their activities were sometimes more inclusive. In New York, James F. Brown, a former enslaved man who had secured his liberty by running away from Maryland, served as a gardener to the Verplank family in the Hudson Valley and participated in several agricultural and horticultural societies across the state.[17] In the District of Columbia, meanwhile, the Georgetown *Independent American* published advertisements that informed readers that "rooms of the ladies will be opened at half past twelve" and encouraged members of the society to bring their families and guests to the fair. Although it is unlikely that any society meetings were opened to women, it is evident that women were encouraged to participate in these celebrations of agricultural knowledge in the community.[18] The list of fair prizes as reported in newspapers such as the *Spirit of 'Seventy-Six* named female winners, including Martha P. Graham, of Dumfries, "for the best piece of cotton cloth for mens coats or womens dresses" and Sarah M. C. Mason, of Hollin Hall in Fairfax County, "for the best piece of Fancy Patterns for vests"; each woman received thirty dollars as a prize.[19] In fact, nine other prizes related to cloth were awarded to women. The popularity of the exhibition was so great that the CAS held a second fair in November 1810, which highlighted blankets and carpeting. Women again won many of the manufactured-cloth premiums.[20] In the end, the CAS dissolved because of the turmoil caused by the War of 1812, but it served as a catalyst for the development of a movement to establish a national botanical garden.

Spurred by the precedent set by the CAS, agricultural societies allowed more Americans to engage in the work of creating useful knowledge. These organizations relied on collective expertise, and they celebrated locally produced knowledge in many ways, including by presenting their findings and best works at public fairs, where prizes were given for the best examples of agricultural knowledge shared among their communities. Agricultural societies offered opportunities for the elite and regular farmers in an area to mingle and collaborate as equals.

This collaboration between elites and others in the society focused on how to improve the economic status of the members. Joel Poinsett, a leading diplomat, scientific expert in his time, and politician, began to donate minerals and antiquities to learned societies; he also donated seeds for use by institutions across the United States. His expeditions to South America and Mexico yielded several important collections, such as the famous poinsettia plant and his gift to the botanical garden in Philadelphia of "a valuable collection of plants of the south" including "fifty species of the *cactus*."[21] Poinsett also presented plants to other societies, including his own South Carolina Agricultural Society (SCAS). In 1823 members of the SCAS had argued that "the introduction of foreign seeds" would be critical to developing "some improvement in our present staple commodities."[22] This transformation would offer a diversification of resources and thus remove the temptation for everyone to grow the same commodity. The committee recommended that members of learned societies communicate with "the Consuls of the United States and such other persons as they may think proper" to secure appropriate seeds to use in the region.[23] The SCAS ordered that Poinsett's letter be printed with their report because he had specific information from his travels in Europe, South America, and Mexico about specific useful plants that might be imported into the region and outlined them in various levels of detail. The "*Agave Americana,* or the *American Aloes* would thrive in South Carolina," he wrote. The plant "when in maturity yields $150, the acre per annum," and "the juice of the Agave yields a great deal of spirit, much more than any other plant: an acre of the Agave will give more ardent spirits than an acre of Corn."[24] Poinsett introduced the reader to several pages of plants with an analysis of their viability in the climate of South Carolina. These examples are illustrative of his idea to collect agricultural specimens, and Poinsett became renowned for distributing seeds widely across the country and the world.[25]

Although men like Washington, Jefferson, Madison, and Poinsett actively participated in these organizations filled with diverse characters, some, such as the leading scientific figure Benjamin Silliman, worried about the amalgamation of elite savants with these new participants in organizations such as agricultural societies. By 1826 Silliman, eager to differentiate between those he viewed as amateurs from those that were true scientists, counted at least twenty-eight societies in the country spread across ten states and the District of Columbia. None of the enumerated scientific institutions were agricultural societies, although dozens of agricultural societies were formed in this period. The democratization of the creation and dissemination of knowledge exemplified in the early agricultural societies began to worry a new elite whose standing rested on their formal expertise.[26] Seed exchanges during the eighteenth century had relied on independent relationships and elite patronage.[27]

The Columbian Institute for the Promotion of Arts and Sciences and the National Botanical Garden

National leaders also focused on the cultivation of gardens, which they regarded as being akin to collecting specimens for museums and libraries, with an eye toward eventual medicinal, food, or trade purposes. Of course private gardens had existed since colonial times and continued to proliferate, offering spaces of escape and scientific materials for the wealthiest members of society; an example is the Woodlands, in Philadelphia, where "there was not a rare plant in Europe, Asia, Africa, from China and from the islands in the South Seas which William Hamilton had not procured."[28] Public gardens, however, which were thought to link together scientific, agricultural, and ornamental interests, were almost nonexistent. Washington and Jefferson first planned for a space in the federal city for a botanical garden in the 1790s; such a garden would, they believed, confer "social and moral benefits" and be a place "where one would be taught the principle of botany and landscape art."[29] Charles Willson Peale's museum, situated on public land, had a public garden, yet it was very limited in size. Then, a long-standing promise made many believe that the gardens founded by the famous colonial-era naturalist and botanist John Bartram in Philadelphia would be opened to visitors, but this promise did not immediately yield public gardens.[30]

Instead, the Columbian Institute for the Promotion of Arts and Sciences emerged in the federal city in 1816 as a "comprehensive learned society" with a federally approved charter to operate in the District of Columbia. The membership included some of the former members of the CAS, and they assumed the mantle for promoting scientific research in the region with a special mission to establish a national botanical garden.[31] The selection of the name Columbian Institute for the Promotion of the Arts and Sciences signified the importance of their purpose. The name Columbian became extremely common after the Revolution, as Americans began to emphasize their new identity, leading to naming the national capital the District of Columbia.[32] The first known use of the term *institute* to describe a society of learning was in 1795, when the French founded the Institut National des Sciences et des Arts, the name pointing to the comprehensive nature of this center of knowledge. The British later adopted the term to describe institutions of similar design, such as the Royal Institution of Great Britain, founded in 1799; the Royal Institute of British Architects, founded in 1834; and the Royal Archæological Institute, founded in 1843. The Royal Institution provided rooms for lectures and put out a publication to promote "useful discoveries; not only to those which might be made by the Institution and in this country, but in every part of the world."[33] Many leaders in the federal city saw this institution as a cornerstone to progress and tried to emulate these European models.[34]

The members of the Columbian Institute instituted a broadly defined agenda of scientific knowledge, as articulated in a letter to the editors of the *Daily National Intelligencer* in 1816. The new association would not "be local" and it would "extend to all classes of citizens," promoting the "discoveries of the learned . . . for public utility."[35] Many viewed this as an organization for the nation. The *Otsego Herald*, of Cooperstown, New York, reported that the institute was "a national society on the plan of the Institute of France and the Royal Society of Great Britain."[36] These reports spurred a call for all citizens and their representatives to cooperate and support this institution in order to fulfill Washington's desire for a national university.[37] The *Intelligencer* article expressed the hope that Americans "at some future day will resort to finish their education in different branches of science at the NATIONAL SEMINARY, to which, a Botanical Garden and Mineralogical Cabinet will be an important appendage."[38] The expectations were for the Columbian Institute to focus on national scientific aims to improve the conditions for all Americans.[39]

Shortly after founding the society, the membership of the Columbian Institute elected Edward Cutbush, a leading naval surgeon, as president. Cutbush, a graduate of the University of Pennsylvania in 1794, had served in the navy until 1820. After resigning from the navy, he had served as a professor of chemistry at the Columbian College, in the District of Columbia, and then as a professor of chemistry and medicine at Geneva College, in New York, where he had also served as the institution's first dean, a position he held until his death in 1843. Cutbush's scientific interests included practices to promote the health of soldiers and sailors. His book *Observations on the Means of Preserving the Health of Soldiers and Sailors and on the Duties of the Medical Department of the Army and Navy, with Remarks on Hospitals and Their Internal Arrangement* was the standard text for American military doctors for years. In it, he lamented doctors' lack of knowledge of natural history, especially in botany and mineralogy. Physicians typically relied on botanical gardens in treating their patients, and Cutbush energetically sought to develop a public botanical garden in America's federal city.[40]

In his initial address to the institute, Cutbush outlined the objectives of the group, and he encouraged members to build the scientific infrastructure needed to educate increasing numbers of men. His twenty-six-page address asserted that the expansion of knowledge of the natural history of the United States was crucial to finding medicinal cures for ailments and that "every individual in our Republic should be animated with a patriotic zeal."[41] Thus, Cutbush viewed part of the institute's mission to be to help prepare industrious citizens, whose interest in "the examination of the natural productions of his country . . . offer rich mines of knowledge yet unexplored; the woods, the waters, and the bowels of the earth court an examination by aid of the Institute." He also hoped to demonstrate the importance of a botanical garden and the goals of scientific improvement to the nation's representatives, as well as "the artist, agriculturalist, and manufacturer [and] to the nation at large." On every page Cutbush reiterated the importance of securing access to the materials within a garden, museum, and a library to the expansion and dissemination of knowledge. He made eight separate references to the establishment of a garden, four to the establishment of a mineralogical cabinet, three to a museum, and he mentioned the need for a well selected library twice.[42]

Given that Cutbush pushed for the establishment of a botanical garden, it is not surprising that the Columbian Institute had significant success with this project. After lobbying Congress and the president for several years, members of the institute secured five acres of land for a botanical garden in 1820. The group quickly went to work, erecting a wooden fence and planting honey locust trees that would eventually serve as a natural fence to protect the specimens in the garden. Surviving records only sparsely document when and what was planted in the garden; however, a significant list of plants arranged in Linnaean order was published in William Elliot's *Washington Guide* and included, among other items, *Antirrhinum canadense* (toadflax), which had many medicinal uses, including treating digestive-tract problems and as a diuretic, as well as *Aristolochia serpentaria* (Virginia snakeroot), commonly used in small doses by Indigenous peoples to cure rattlesnake bites and treat fevers and stomach disorders. The Columbian Institute was critical in bringing together different types of scientific expertise to achieve common goals, including the establishment of a national garden in the federal city. The garden was not just a place where the elite could take leisurely strolls in the capital city. It was a site that served scientific purposes, promoting the discovery of new knowledge to be utilized by the federal government and the local citizenry. After the Columbian Institute's charter expired in 1841, the garden reverted to the federal government and became the model for present-day botanical gardens.[43]

Central to the work of a botanical garden was the exchange and cultivation of seeds and plants from both within the United States and across the globe. Merchants who collected and sold seeds and plants organized them according to the scientifically prescribed Linnean system and created catalogs for consumers to peruse. Seed merchants and dealers operated on the East Coast in the late eighteenth and early nineteenth centuries.[44] Newspaper databases contain significant relevant lists of people selling seeds via advertisements. Some began to publish catalogs to allow customers to peruse their seed storehouses. The earliest example of a broadsheet catalog listed in America's Historical Imprints was published in New York in 1798 by Jon Langdon.[45] Similar catalog sheets published by Bernard M'Mahon in Philadelphia in 1803 and Samuel Gundy in New York later in 1815 were inexpensive to print and posted in public places throughout the cities.[46] The broadsides listed a variety of vegetables, flowers, and other plants, along with a note stating that the seeds were guaranteed to be from the previous year's cultivation and could be transported easily. Finally, the notices informed the consumer that catalogs would be available in the stores, which suggests the availability of a much greater variety. Langdon's broadsheet listed at least 204 varieties of plants for sale. A thirty-six-page catalog of seeds published in 1813 for M'Mahon shows not only the variety of plants available but also that his "repository of seeds of Garden Vegetables, of the Grasses, Grains, and Roots, used in Rural Economy; of plants used in dying and other arts" offered access to sustenance as well as medicinal home remedies and beauty for the home. He claimed to have more than thirty-seven hundred items in his collection and he added their "true *Linnean* or *Botanical* as well as their English names" as well as a promise to provide articles on common uses of the plants.[47]

These plants for sale in merchants' catalogs offered wider access to the world of the learned elites, as illustrated by the 1819 do-it-yourself kit created by William Cobbett. Cobbett was a newspaper editor who supported reforms for the poor, promoted democratic ideals, and advocate agricultural knowledge for all. He moved between England and the United States, leaving England when he feared being incarcerated for his radical views on universal manhood suffrage.[48] Cobbett imported "no less than one hundred and fifty-four barrels of field and garden seeds" from England and arranged them in "boxes" that included "a large assortment of seeds for the field and for the Garden."[49] In some cases, a purchaser would receive up to a pound of particular seeds, which was advertised as containing "fifty sorts of seeds."[50]

Each box included a list of seeds and an accompanying pamphlet explaining how to raise a host of vegetables for a "large garden." Cobbett hoped his pamphlet and seeds would be of practical use "to many persons and may tend to promote improvement in Gardening and Farming" across the "United States."[51] The sale of seeds to a growing number of consumers in the first decades of the nineteenth century, along with the encouragement for experimentation, resulted in the proliferation of agricultural societies made up of diverse groups of people, including the elite, professionals, and a growing number of yeoman farmers. Participation in botanical work offered a space in which people could meet and express their expertise on a more level ground.

The work of collecting and disseminating agricultural knowledge was a global enterprise, and Americans deployed several methods to ensure that they did not lag behind their global competitors. Starting in the 1790s, a nascent diplomatic corps of American consuls abroad assisted with trade and helped American seamen and merchants resolve diplomatic issues. The work of a consul was diverse, and most scholars focus on their political and diplomatic work as the eyes and ears of the early republic in foreign cities.[52] Yet, significantly, consuls also secured commercial and scientific knowledge, helping American science advance back home.

Joel Roberts Poinsett exemplified the expanding number of people who actively collected all kinds of materials while serving on diplomatic missions. Poinsett, a wealthy son of a South Carolina physician, was educated at the University of Edinburgh and at the age of twenty-two traveled extensively in Europe, as far east as Russia and the contested lands of the Nogais along the Caspian Sea.[53] Along the way, Poinsett mastered several languages, and his journeys during the first decade of the nineteenth century stimulated his desire to acquire profitable specimens of seeds and other useful knowledge for the United States. His experience abroad also secured him an appointment as US "agent for seamen and commerce" for South America.[54] Albert Gallatin, treasury secretary in the administration of President James Madison, wrote to Madison on August 15, 1810, that he had "found a gentleman who appears to me peculiarly fitted in every respect" to serve the needs of the country.[55] Elite members of organizations such as the New York Historical Society and the American Philosophical Society had collected publications about Latin America throughout the late eighteenth century, but there were few examples of scientific specimens of natural history from South America. Now, Poinsett's keen curiosity and observation skills provided a window on the commercial and scientific opportunities in the Southern Hemisphere.[56]

After serving for four years, Poinsett returned to his native South Carolina, where in October 1818 he received a request from Secretary of State John Quincy Adams on behalf of President James Monroe for "sources of intelligence . . . which you may think it useful to the public to communicate to the Executive Government of this Union."[57] Poinsett provided a detailed report describing the governing details and figures related to overall exports and imports of several South American states. He also provided examples of commodities as well as methods of production and cultivation for each of the countries of the southern continent.[58]

Latin America was a seen as critical to the diplomatic, economic, and scientific promotion of liberty in the Western Hemisphere. In the words of the historian Caitlin Fitz, "A new order for the New World was emerging" during the age of revolutions, and US elites believed they were destined to lead the emerging republics.[59] James Monroe appointed a diplomatic mission, the South American Commission, in 1817 and hoped that Poinsett would agree to return to South America. The president was unable to persuade him, however. Instead, he found Ceaser Augustus Rodney, John Graham, and Theodorick Bland. Also, part of the group were their appointed secretary, Henry

Brackenridge, and William Baldwin, who served as the ship's surgeon. The expedition's primary focus was on diplomacy, and there was no mention of collecting or exploring for botanical specimens. Nevertheless, despite its limited diplomatic impact, this expedition was significant as the first by the United States to collect plants in South America.

William Baldwin exemplified the American naturalists who were at the center of a diffused network of scientists with links to urban sites and traditional scientific leaders. Baldwin was appointed to serve because of his connection with the Columbian Institute and Edward Cutbush. Baldwin led the initiative to secure botanicals because of his work as a doctor and his independent medical research.[60] After completing part of his medical studies at the University of Pennsylvania, he served as a ship's surgeon for several years in order to secure the funds needed to finish his medical education. His experiences became a source for his 1807 dissertation, published as *A Short Practical Narrative of the Diseases Which Prevailed Among American Seamen, at Wampoa in China, in the Year 1805*. In his work, Baldwin regularly "drew 10 to 16 ounces of blood" from patients, but he also liberally used a variety of medicines made from plants such as jalap, calomel, opium, Peruvian bark, and rhubarb.[61]

Baldwin exchanged correspondence and specimens with Henry Muhlenberg, a Pennsylvania botanist, and he conducted botanical explorations into eastern Florida while stationed at St. Mary's and Savannah, Georgia.[62] While at naval headquarters in Washington, DC, Baldwin found "some lovers of science" who were interested in assigning him to the journey on the US frigate *Congress* to South America because of his knowledge of natural history. The Columbian Institute's "president, Dr. Cutbush, (the oldest Surgeon in the Navy,) enabled me to promote its interests," wrote Baldwin, and he joined the institute.[63] The members of the institute showed him their impressive collections of specimens and their library, with "the best modern works," but his letters identify the weakness of the armchair scholars who published works but did not participate in active fieldwork.[64]

Baldwin conducted excursions and collected plants at every stop the frigate made along the way, including Rio de Janeiro and locations throughout the Rio de la Plata region, such as Buenos Aires, Montevideo, and Maldonado. While there, he consulted with local experts, including Aimé Bonpland, who had served as Alexander von Humboldt's collaborator on his famous botanical expedition to South and Central America from 1799 to 1804. Baldwin's infectious enthusiasm for botanical and agricultural knowledge ensured successful interactions. He promised to share specimens such as Georgia's sea island cotton and 137 other specimens from North America, while Bonpland sent a large collection of plants to Baldwin. The news of this exploration was shared in the *American Farmer*, which reported that Baldwin had been directly responsible for introducing the "*Arabian Date bearing Palm* into South Carolina, Georgia, Alabama, and Louisiana." Baldwin's expedition was deemed a "benefit to the country, or utility to science."[65]

Baldwin's exceptional work was the talk of the country and was communicated in the *Journal of Foreign Medical Science and Literature* in the form of a reprint from the *Quarterly Journal of Science and Arts*. It helped him secure a spot with Major Long's overland expedition to the West in 1820, during which he died of consumption.[66] Yet his legacy lived on. Baldwin's collections and journals remained significant and were deposited in the academy's archives; they also spurred more calls for scientific expeditions to promote agricultural pursuits. As gathering specimens through fieldwork became more important to the burgeoning agricultural societies, emerging professional men like Baldwin were not just purveyors of items but advanced knowledge in their own right.[67] Baldwin's indirect relationship with the federal government in this role as both surgeon and a collector of botanical knowledge on behalf of scientific organizations offers an important insight into the development of early American scientific knowledge.

Botanical gardens and seed exchanges were critical to the development of knowledge institutions in the first decades of the nineteenth century. As a form of knowledge production they offered tools for many budding scientists, doctors, and those who experimented with plants as a means for providing medicinal relief and new commodities to develop wealth in the new republic. Seed exchanges not only promoted access to the materials but also offered means to develop trade and diplomatic networks with people across the land and seas. In the end, the botanical gardens and the seeds that made their growth possible offered opportunities for more people to participate in a plant-growing economy that required increasingly specialized knowledge. Participation in this environment helped to bring together different people to promote the creation and spread of valuable knowledge that would improve the conditions for the people in their country.

Funding Expeditions and Fueling the Imaginations of an Active Scientific Citizenry

Direct federal support for scientific endeavors remained controversial, especially when the expenditures focused on improvements that were not directly beneficial to the whole country. Amid the partisan divide emerging between the Jacksonian Democrats and John Quincy Adams and the National Republicans, who eventually would become known as the Whigs, expenses on scientific ventures became a target for political factions.[68] Although it is true that there were distinct divisions between the emerging groups that formed the second party system regarding what the federal government could and should be utilized for, especially when it came to internal improvements, these divisions often masked the serious intellectual distinctions between the political parties.[69] Among the most important distinctions between Jackson's populist movement and those who they believed were corrupt elites seeking to form an intellectual aristocracy was that the Jacksonians believed in those with natural talents more than those who acquired talent through formal learning. For Jackson and his followers, this corruption was exemplified by those who espoused knowledge that was not useful to the common man, and they imagined themselves as the voice of the people, who eschewed formal book learning and served as the intellectual foil to bookish men who had learned in colleges instead of from practical experiences.[70]

John Quincy Adams hoped to promote an active scientific agenda for the United States and kick-start perpetual improvement. He hoped to rise above partisanship by keeping many of James Monroe's cabinet members, but this was wishful thinking and did not acknowledge the bitter partisan divides occasioned by the election of 1824. Still, in his first annual message to Congress he called for that body and the country to build Washington's national university on "the spot of earth which he had destined and bequeathed to the use and benefit of his country," which remained "still bare and barren."[71] The importance of this reminder to the country that there was an unfinished mission that had been bequeathed to Americans from their founding father cannot be overestimated. Washington's name held immense authority and evoked a patriotic duty in people across the country. Adams reminded the country that in order to maintain "her station among the civilized nations of the earth" the United States had to be like the "governments of France, Great Britain, and Russia," who invested the "genius, the intelligence, the treasures of their respective nations to the common improvement of the species" in the advanced study of science and exploration. Adams's goals for the country also included a host of other institutional endeavors, such as a national observatory and a trip to the polar regions, yet all of these projects fell victim to partisan divisions led by Jacksonian Democrats in the Congress.[72]

Adams, like Washington and Jefferson found ways to promote his agenda for national knowledge institutions despite the partisan opposition. Adams was particularly adept at using public-private partnerships in the federal city to advance his agenda. Tobias Watkins, a friend to John Quincy Adams and a leading member of the Columbian Institute, founded the *Baltimore Medical and Physical Recorder* and *The Portico: A Repository of Science & Literature,* in which he published many pieces of medical scholarship. In 1826 he addressed the Colombian Institute and argued that "if it be true, that 'Liberty is Power,' how infinitely must that power be augmented when to Liberty is added *Knowledge!*"[73] His twenty-seven-page speech was published and distributed to advance the institute's goal to increase knowledge. The learned society focused on bringing the diverse interests and groups across the country to "unite with the members of the Institute" in a common cause. They hoped that their group would eliminate "the animosities which are so apt to be engendered by political debate" and in the end make the United States "preeminent in the arts and sciences, as she already is in Liberty and the power that Liberty gives."[74] Watkins encouraged Americans to emulate the models of the National Institute in France and the Royal Academy of Britain but in addition to develop expertise "among the poorer classes of society" to promote their rise from poverty to "usefulness."[75] These powerful words inspired his compatriots, but Watkins's work came under attack once he was convicted of embezzling money in his role as fourth auditor of the United States. Jacksonians used the scandal to diminish his scientific authority and as proof of the problems with putting too much power in the hands of centralized institutions not enumerated by the Constitution.[76] Ultimately these public-private partnerships had limited success because the Jacksonian Democrats continually found ways to impede their political opponents.

Surprisingly, major sources of advocacy for scientific exploration were the emerging lecture circuit and lyceums, which stimulated public participation in expanding new knowledge. Lyceums offered a vibrant platform for nineteenth-century Americans to hear new voices speak about exciting new ideas and scientific discoveries.[77] Much like museums, lyceums were a new type of institution that energized and connected diverse communities of Americans, who believed they were taking part in a common national improvement effort as they heard a variety of new schemes to promote scientific knowledge for the public good.[78] Some of these lectures sought to introduce new plants to serve as a basis for new commodities for cultivation, such as a lecture proposing to introduce the "Tea-Plant in the United States" given to the Lyceum of Natural History in New York.[79] That same organization published "a Catalogue of Plants" growing "within thirty miles of the City of NEW-YORK," which was picked up by newspapers across the country, inspiring others to act.[80] No fewer than thirteen newspapers published the advertisement, and one wrote that "more than thirteen hundred species" were identified in the volume and that "it is an invaluable document for the man of science everywhere."[81] Increasingly, Americans across the country embraced the idea of self-improvement by going to lectures and then putting new ideas into action in their communities. By 1850 approximately four hundred thousand Americans were attending lectures in lyceums each week.[82] Lyceums, like museums, served a broader community than just the elite and they offered not only educational opportunities but also entertainment, including shows with racist tropes embedded in them. Lyceums also offered opportunities for nineteenth-century stars such as Ralph Waldo Emerson to travel on the lecture circuit and spread their knowledge to new listeners across the country.[83]

Some of these new voices presented exciting propositions to encourage a new round of expeditions across and even into the globe itself. The most famous and outrageous endeavor was proposed by Captain John Cleves Symmes Jr. Symmes, born in New Jersey, was a veteran of the War of 1812 and the nephew of his namesake, who had served as a delegate to the Continental Congress and become a significant land developer in the Northwest Territories. Following the war, the younger Symmes became dedicated to the idea that became known as the Theory of Concentric Spheres. In a circular broadsheet he announced "TO ALL THE WORLD! I declare the earth is hollow and habitable within; containing a number of solid concentric spheres . . . open at the poles," and he assured readers that he stood "ready to explore the hollow" if he received support.[84] Symmes asked for "one hundred brave companions, well equipped" and proposed "to start from Siberia in the fall season with reign deer and sleighs, on the ice of the frozen sea." Inevitably, the explorers would find a "warm and rich land stocked with thrifty vegetables and animals, if not men, on reaching one degree north-ward of lat. 82."[85] This information was published widely across the country, and Symmes promised that his soon-to-be-published treatise would provided evidence for his claims. He also promoted his ideas by joining the lecture circuit and writing letters to secure supporters.[86]

It is easy to dismiss Symmes as a crackpot, yet many Americans embraced his ideas as fresh and important for the future of the country. President John Quincy Adams supported a modified version of Symmes's idea; although he did not subscribe to the hollow-earth theory, he did want Americans to explore the world, including the polar regions, to secure natural resources.[87] James McBride, a merchant and future president of the Miami University (Ohio) board of trustees, championed Symmes and his work. McBride created a scrapbook that contained related content that he personally had gathered from 1820 to 1855, including newspaper clippings and personal manuscript notations of the Symmes lectures he had attended, as well as "A List of Books tending to elucidate and support Symme's Theory of the Earth."[88] McBride was instrumental in collecting Symmes's disjointed, separately published circulars and ideas in a volume published in 1826 under the title *Symmes's Theory of Concentric Circles*. The foreword promised that the "nett profits were . . . to be paid to Captain Symmes toward enabling him to promote and establish his principles" by conducting an expedition to explore the polar regions.[89] Finally, McBride made a mounted wooden model of the earth for Symmes, which he used during his lectures.

In addition, Symmes and his supporters from Kentucky, Ohio, and South Carolina sent petitions to their representatives in Congress, who dutifully presented them to the Senate and House of Representatives of the 17th Congress, where the proposals died. Other followers included Thomas Spottswood Hinde and Jeremiah N. Reynolds. Hinde even wrote to Thomas Jefferson in 1824 hoping to secure his support, but to no avail.[90] After becoming a convert to Symmes's theory Reynolds joined him on the lecture circuit, where they "charged fifty cents admission" and made many converts to their shared work.[91] Although their attempts to obtain support from the federal government fell apart due to Jacksonian Democrats' disdain for these kind of projects, Reynolds continued to lecture and find supporters. In 1829 he secured assistance for an expedition to the South Pole. This expedition ended with a mutiny, and he was set on shore in Chile. After he traveled on foot to Valparaiso, he gained passage aboard an American ship in 1832. Reynolds wrote several works of fiction, such as *Mocha Dick: Or the White Whale of the Pacific*, which influenced Herman Melville's *Moby Dick*, in 1839.[92]

Jackson and his supporters saw explorations championed by Symmes and Reynolds and the Adams administration's scientific agenda overall as both a folly and a dangerous task for the central government to undertake. Jackson wrote to John Branch, a senator from North Carolina and later Jackson's choice as secretary of the navy, on March 3, 1826, that "Instead of building lighthouses of the skies, establishing national universities, and making explorations round the globe; their language will be, pay the national debt" and promote "national independence, & defence."[93] Any "surpluss revenue amonghst the several states [should be used] for the education of the poor—leaving the superintendence of education to the states respectively. This will be the safe course to perpetuate our happy goverment." This response to Adams's message delivered three months earlier, in which he had called for the federal government to become the "instrument for the improvement of the condition of men" through a robust set of "seminaries of learning" to assure that the United States would "assum[e] her station among the civilized nations of the earth," became a keystone to the Democratic campaign against the Adams administration, twisting Adams's call for lighthouses of the skies to "lighthouses in the skies."[94] The Jacksonians expertly utilized their press machine to ridicule the scientific agenda as both fanciful and out of touch with the concerns of regular people. Jacksonian editors became effective, aggressive, and opportunistic advocates for Jacksonian candidates.[95] One person's improvement was another's boondoggle. Although Jacksonians deemed scientific expeditions to explore the territories of the United States acceptable, there were a growing number of calls for reform amid the discontent emerging in the "era of good feelings," as the 1820s came to be called. A chief reason for the discontent was a great belief in the supposed corruption of many in the federal government, and American voters came to believe that Andrew Jackson was the person to stop the unnecessary and unconstitutional measures promoted by the National Republicans.

Adams's loss of the presidency in 1828 seemed to doom the use of scientific expansion to help local societies gather and disseminate new knowledge. Before he left office, however, Adams enacted a few initiatives to promote his agenda, using the existing bureaucratic structure of consuls spread across the globe. In 1827 the Treasury Department issued a circular to the consuls of the United States. The president asked that "trees and plants not heretofore known in the United States" that can be cultivated in the country be collected and sent via the navy and other "Commanders of such public vessels," as well as the "Masters of the merchant vessels of the United States," who they believed would be moved by "their well-known public sprit—to lend their gratuitous co-operation" to see these specimens returned to the country for the promotion of the commercial and scientific advancement of Americans.[96] The circular also included a six-page set of instructions for the care and packing of the specimens while in the custody of the seamen, which was one page longer than the order justifying the action.[97] This scientific initiative was justified by invoking the needs of national security and the improvement of commercial opportunities through American expertise in natural history. Several specimens sent to the Department of Treasury ended up in the collections of the Columbian Institute.

After Jackson assumed power, local, specialized learned societies, including local agricultural societies, flourished in a new political environment that emphasized decentralization, moving activities for scientific improvement firmly to the local or state level. Agricultural societies were widespread by the late 1820s, and their popularity was growing. By 1841, 912 agricultural societies existed in various localities in the United States.[98] Additionally, the number of specialized publications increased dramatically; this, however, was only a first step toward disseminating new agricultural know-how to the American public. When these societies met, their members typically shared the bounty of their harvests, and they gathered to hear the addresses of their leaders and to share tributes via toasts to their convictions and their brethren.

For example, Henry Alexander Scammell Dearborn, son of former secretary of war and major general Henry Dearborn, served in several political offices, including the House of Representatives and several state and local elected offices. He also served as the longtime president of the Massachusetts Horticultural Society. In this capacity he delivered an address every year, several of which were printed and distributed as a means to diffuse the society's knowledge. In his first anniversary address, on September 19, 1829, Dearborn connected the advance of civilization with advances in horticulture. He also stated that "the co-operation of individuals, by means of variously organized societies . . . has been one of the most efficient means of accelerating the progress and the bounds of knowledge."[99] He extoled the advances made in literature, history, natural science, and other fields of knowledge.[100] Dearborn concluded his speech by pointing out that all human knowledge was interconnected, with horticulture being central to all. These addresses moved many listeners toward the realization that as a next step the country needed to establish agricultural experimental stations and to seek federal support for the needed expertise in agricultural chemistry and agricultural botany.[101]

Yet at the heart of the agricultural-society movement were successes at the state level. DeWitt Clinton's program of internal development in New York provided state support to the Albany Lyceum, which promoted and published knowledge as a means to encourage best practices among its community.[102] The program in New York created more than fifty new agricultural societies and led to the establishment of the New York Board, which published three volumes of *Memoirs of the Board of Agriculture of the State of New York* from 1821 to 1826. Citizens across the state submitted their findings to the editor, George William Featherstonhaugh. Lamenting the publication of the final volume, he hoped that "an enlightened legislature will appreciate the benefits" of the publication. He also expressed the wish that his journal would "serve as an example to sister states" and, like the late law to improve agriculture, "call into active employment the genius skill and industry of thousands of our fellow citizens."[103] No further state support was forthcoming, however. Nonetheless, the publication encouraged the rise of a popular agricultural press. The Rochester *Genesee Farmer* and the *Cultivator* of Albany both advocated for the establishment of a state agricultural society. In 1833 they successfully established a statewide agricultural society with the *Cultivator* as its primary publication. State funding provided support for both publications and for the county societies and their fairs in 1841.[104]

Yet some scientists resented the claims that these contemporary publications made about advancing scientific knowledge. Joseph Henry, a professor of natural science at the College of New Jersey, wrote a letter in 1838 to an unnamed journal condemning it for providing suspect information about the powers of electricity.[105] Henry repeated the claim that "a salad of mustard or water cresses may be produced in a few moments by the assistance of electricity and that rain water apparently free from any noxious animalcule in an hour may be rendered full of insects." He immediately assured the editor that this was a falsehood and that both were "without foundation." Henry proceeded to reveal the first example was a story originally published as a piece of fiction by an American traveling in "Europe who saw a Parisian juggler perform the 'sleight of hand' as the important discovery of a new electrical action." The second was the result of "wonderful accounts of the experiments by Mr. Cross . . . which . . . have been proved to be incorrect."[106] Henry disdained the growing popular participation in science because it offered imposters an avenue to spread misinformation. Abhorring ignorance and unprofessional behaviors by fellow scientists as well, Henry called for the development of a scientific code of conduct.[107]

Henry did not suffer fools. He confided in a letter of August 9, 1838, to his friend and fellow scientist Alexander Dallas Bache his disappointment with the nation's premier scientist, Benjamin Silliman, the founder of the *American Journal of Science*. Henry reminded Bache of their goal: "We must put down quackery or quackery will put down science." He listed several examples of science that he viewed as evidence of swindlers and imposters but reserved his greatest criticism for those who had positions of authority over knowledge. First, he pointed to the ill-advised practice of allowing questionable scientists to testify before congressional committees, which then produced reports using "flattering terms" and stated that "in the opinion of several scientific gentleman and in their own estimation" the discoveries presented to them were sound and "worthy of the confidence of the public and the patronage of Congress." This incensed Henry, leading him to publish a correction and protest "on behalf of the scientific character of the United States against the custom of publishing scientific articles among the documents of Congress before their true character is ascertained."[108]

Henry also indicated that he had confronted Silliman on the inadequacy of the reviewers for the *American Journal of Science* and suggested that a new group of collaborators from different departments of science was needed to participate in the publication of his journal. Nonetheless, "the hint was not however taken and shortly after the name of the Professors son was attached to the Journal."[109] In the end, Silliman did acquire some new collaborators. Henry, however, maintained vigilance to ferret out pretenders who sought to dupe the masses, and he longed for the day when American scientists would have what one scholar has called an "*Esprite de Corps.*"[110] In other words, Henry wanted scientists to professionalize the field of scientific endeavor.

Despite his imperiousness, it is easy to understand Henry's frustration with the increasingly popular and numerous scientific publications. The New York Agriculture Society's journal the *Cultivator* alone printed at least twenty-six articles about the impact of electricity upon agricultural pursuits in the years 1834–40. Interestingly enough, Henry's letter to the editor may actually have increased the interest of the editors in stories about electricity, since even more articles were published after Henry's corrective letter, including an article written in 1840 titled "The Science of Agriculture." Further, the journal began

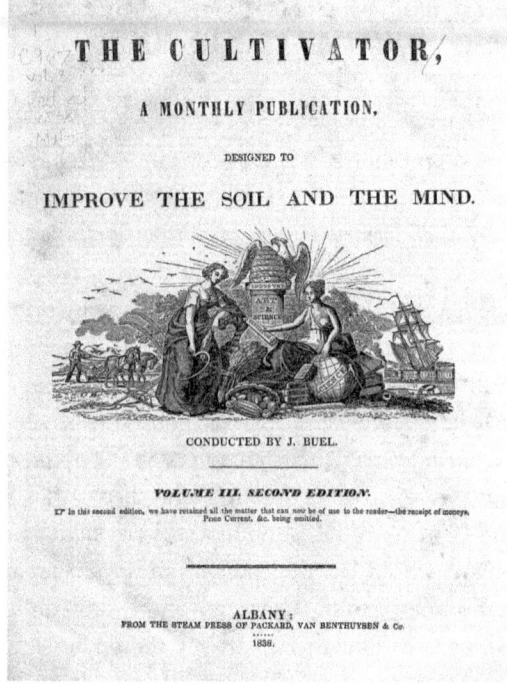

FIG. 8. Title page of the New York State Agricultural Society's journal, *The Cultivator*. The illustration shows the interconnectedness of agricultural knowledge and scientific activity. (Courtesy Smithsonian Institution)

publication of a series of twenty-five articles titled "A Dictionary of Terms Used in Agriculture and Its Kindred Sciences." These essays focused on the power of electricity to accelerate growth of plants and to assist the movement of farm machinery. Nevertheless, one entry lamented that "the effect of electricity on vegetation has not received the attention it deserves. That plants push forward much faster where the electric currents are active is well known."[111] As shown by this example, these journals, which were popular, democratic, and accessible to a general population, did not necessarily present accurate information. In fact, they often seemed to present misinformation.

There was a tension, then, between a commitment to democratizing knowledge and a commitment to promoting accurate scientific information, validated by researchers in the field. These trends accelerated in the 1830s and 1840s. The image emblazoned on the *Cultivator*'s title page demonstrates the Agricultural Society's vision of the totality of knowledge (Fig. 8). Several crucial elements are obvious in the image, including the embrace of art and science, the promotion of both the advances of technologies, evidenced by the train and ship in the background, and also respect for classical knowledge in the form of books and scrolls. Surrounding the muses, likely Polyhymnia and Urania, are the tools of knowledge. Crucially the New York Agriculture Society connected these symbols within the context of the American nation, including familiar American emblems such as the beehive of industry and the eagle of the republic. The growth of knowledge is symbolized through cultivation, and knowledge is available to the common people who plow the fields in order to reap the treasures of the earth. Progress, made possible by mankind's utilization of knowledge, is the clear message of this image. Thus, agricultural societies represented the best qualities of the republic because they embraced all knowledge and all men.[112]

A call for national support came eleven years later from Dearborn himself. His speech to the Berkshire Agricultural Society suggested that the majority of citizens in the United States pursued agricultural cultivation and that the entire national industry relied on the success of those pursuing agriculture. After evoking George Washington's call for agricultural improvements, Dearborn made his own, stating that agriculture served as "not only the emblems but the trophies and conclusive evidence of an antecedent and exalted state of civilization . . . and of the progress and moral improvement and intellectual cultivation." Dearborn concluded that a "wise national administration" would focus less on theoretical sciences and more on promoting advances in agricultural knowledge as a means to unite the science and the arts.[113] In 1841, after reading Joel Poinsett's address espousing the value of a single national institution to coordinate the work of "every branch of knowledge,"[114] Dearborn suggested that the national institution also create a botanical and a zoological garden. He believed that adding agricultural knowledge would offer Americans the ability to experiment and "diffuse intelligence on all the numerous branches of rural economy." He suggested that the national institution use the land on the mall for this purpose. Further, the creation of an "extensive experimental farm . . . would prove to be indispensible at the national capital." He even suggested that agricultural societies should associate with the National Institute and colleges, much as the European role models he cited did. Finally, the goods created at the experimental site would yield money for reinvestment.[115]

Charles Lewis Fleischmann, a naturalized citizen from Germany who worked in the US Patent Office, had submitted a similar suggestion for an agricultural institution to Congress in 1838. Fleischmann appealed both to the duty of humanity and to the notion of improving civilization, as well as to the congressional committee's sense of practicality since the government needed to contend with a growing population and many demanded access to federal land.[116] Even more importantly, he argued that the institution he suggested for teaching and performing agricultural experiments and research was built upon a successful German model and offered the added benefit of acculturating and training the mass of citizens to acquire the goal of all humanity: wealth. Fleischmann wrote that "when wealth is produced by agriculture, it banishes idleness and the vices connected with it; it renders . . . the population strong, healthy, and industrious; it is the source of domestic happiness and contentment."[117] Some scholars see Fleischman's plan as an important part of a progressive advance toward federal legislation in 1862 and 1887 as well as complementary state actions.[118] His plan was certainly an important building block for improved resources for agricultural research.

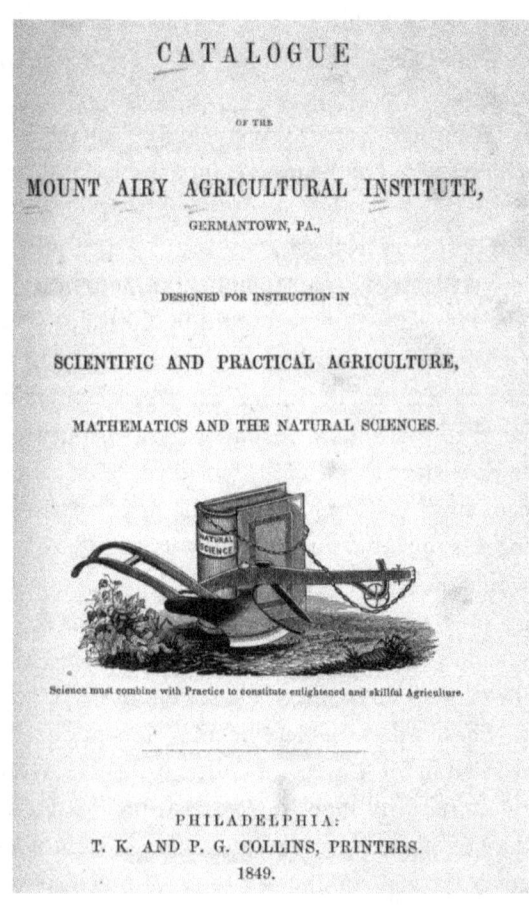

FIG. 9. Title page of the *Catalogue of the Mount Airy Agricultural Institute*, of Germantown, Pennsylvania, 1849, showing the institute's emblem and motto, a good illustration of the linkage between knowledge and agriculture. (Courtesy Pennsylvania State University, HathiTrust CC0)

In fact, many Americans believed that agriculture was the only scientific field that utilized all aspects of knowledge. The Mount Airy Agricultural Society adopted a symbol to demonstrate how farmers and science had become interconnected (Fig. 9). Just as significantly, the image conveys that science should be useful. The society's motto stated this message and also communicated the point through the image of the plow that is tethered to the book on natural science.

Amid political democratization, a democratization of the authority over knowledge also emerged in the first part of the nineteenth century, and the two processes mirrored each other. Americans were told that they were important contributors to the success of their country. This success was rooted in the expansion of liberty of the mind, which would promote security, enlightenment, and economic success for all participants. Still, some believed that these advancements needed to be managed by national authorities and organizations that could guide popular participation in scientific endeavors. The proliferation of associations, agricultural and otherwise, reflected a broad consensus about the status and importance of scientific discourse to a diverse population that was directly connected to the advancement of political expansion and internal improvements. Still, some leaders, especially Jacksonians, worried about these activities being centralized, while others, such as Professor Henry and scientists like him, saw a need to control popular scientific activities and publications. America's democratic society filled with joiners seemed to be at odds with the need to establish a system of authoritative knowledge.

CHAPTER 5

A NATIONAL RESEARCH INSTITUTION

Citizen Science and Controlling the Information Revolution

Into the antebellum era, Americans continued to debate the purpose of a national institution to organize knowledge, who it should benefit, and who ought to be able to create and disseminate new knowledge. These debates took on new importance in 1826, when the wealthy Englishman James Smithson directed in his last will and testament that if his inheritors died with no heirs, his estate was to be given in trust to the United States "to found at Washington, under the name of the Smithsonian Institution, an Establishment for the increase & diffusion of knowledge among men."[1] Those unlikely events came to pass, and the United States received the money from Smithson's estate in 1836. The money from this gift removed the strongest objection by those who claimed that there was no constitutional mandate to utilize federal money to establish a national institution of knowledge.[2] Nevertheless, a decade passed before what became the Smithsonian Institution was created in 1846, and its early years were fraught with internal debates.

The establishment of the Smithsonian Institution reflected a fractious American society during the antebellum period. The divergent interests of the citizens involved in deciding on how to spend the Smithson money resulted in ongoing power struggles over what type of institution to establish. Factions formed in Congress that mirrored those in society. In the House of Representatives, John Quincy Adams remained the lone advocate for a national observatory, while other politicians believed the country needed a national university, a teacher's college, an agricultural research center, a national library, a national learned society, or an institution dedicated to expanding scientific knowledge through research. Each faction believed the type of institution it championed to be the proper one for the nation.

Previously, scholars have analyzed the founding of the Smithsonian as a tale of petty squabbles between politicians and as a missed opportunity to promote a national institution following the French model or as a story of heroic visionaries who made sure that Smithson's resources did not go to waste.[3] This chapter tells the broader story at the heart of the Smithsonian's founding, the story of the politicized nature of knowledge in this period and the ways in which politicians, the US citizenry, and an emerging transatlantic professional class of scientists tried to manage the sprawling impact of the information revolution.

Most importantly, scientific leaders in the United States in this period were greatly influenced by a German epistemological framework that emphasized careful methodological study by experts who developed and communicated their methodological process for all to see. Therefore, they focused on constructing a system designed to limit citizen-scientist participation. They envisioned regular Americans participating in the work of science only as procurers of specimens and as nameless hidden laborers assisting a new class of experts whose training assured authoritative analysis. In the end, the Smithsonian Institution was established as an institution designed to provide something for everyone, professionally trained scientists and citizen-scientists alike, but it turned into an elitist institution that sought to establish control over Americans engaged in scientific work in the antebellum period.

What began with debates over a national university in the 1790s ended with the Smithsonian in the 1830s. Whereas political leaders such as Washington had envisioned a national university to establish a new generation of leaders for the American republic, the Smithsonian championed a different way for Americans to engage with scientific knowledge. After nearly half a century, what was believed to be appropriate training in scientific knowledge changed from a training based on classical texts to one based on deep disciplinary knowledge. This change resulted in a new kind of credentialed expertise that looks very much like what we have today.

The Smithson Bequest

We know surprisingly little about why James Smithson bequeathed his wealth to the United States. We do know that the gift was contingent upon his only nephew, Henry James Hungerford, dying without children. There are some good reasons to believe that he wanted to specifically help the United States develop the needed scientific infrastructure while snubbing the intellectuals in England. It seems likely that Smithson was impressed with the United States, and English newspapers and magazines reported frequently about US plans to celebrate the fiftieth anniversary of the Declaration of Independence during the time he was writing his will. Also, even though he was renowned for his own scientific work in chemistry and geology, the British Royal Academy offended him when they questioned his work, and he held a grudge even after he was vindicated. Further, Smithson was greatly impressed by William Maclure, an immigrant to the United States who was instrumental in the formation of the Academy of Natural Sciences in Philadelphia, as discussed in chapter 3. Finally, it is possible that he was impressed by the ambitious scientific agenda proposed by John Quincy Adams in his first annual address on December 6, 1825. All these circumstances may have converged and influenced Smithson's decision.[4]

The first two weeks following President Jackson's December 17, 1835, report notifying Congress about the Smithson inheritance entrusted to the United States saw at least forty-two articles published by newspapers across the country outlining the news of the bequest. Of these at least ten reported that the institution would be some form of "national university," "National College," or "institution of learning." The remaining articles focused on reprinting excerpts of Smithson's will, emphasizing the part about "diffusion of useful knowledge among men," and offering related excerpts of the correspondence between government officials over the will.[5] Americans were fascinated by the variety of possibilities this generous donation offered.

Politicians immediately began to debate how to take advantage of this new opportunity. Some saw the impact that national institutions such as the US Military Academy and the US Coast Survey had had on scientific advancements and hoped the Smithson money would ensure that the United States could participate in cutting-edge scientific research. John Quincy Adams ushered efforts successfully through the House of Representatives and presented a report to Congress on January 19, 1836, recommending that Congress accept the gift and "carry into effective execution the noble purpose of an endowment for the increase and diffusion of knowledge among men."[6]

The Senate's debates were more complex. The South Carolinian senators, John C. Calhoun and William C. Preston, worried that the federal government would overreached its authority. Such an overreach might lead to an active federal agenda that would eventually promote an abolitionist program designed to limit or eliminate slavery. They used delay tactics and arguments denying that Congress had the authority to accept the gift. Preston argued that the gift was not appropriate since the Constitution did not bestow any power on Congress to act for "national objects" and "establish an university." When these arguments failed, they claimed that accepting benefits from a foreigner would be beneath the dignity of the country.[7] Preston saw no reason to receive the proceeds as a beneficiary for "this District . . . to raise foreigners to immortality by getting Congress as the *parens patriae* of the District of Columbia to accept donations from them."[8] In the end, these attempts failed, and the Senate joined the House of Representatives in passing legislation in July 1836 approving the authorization of the president to secure the claim through the agent Richard Rush.[9]

The debates only intensified once Rush secured the Smithson legacy after brilliantly navigating the complex Chancery Court case in England.[10] After securing the money, President Martin Van Buren directed Secretary of State John Forsyth to issue a circular letter to "persons versed in science and in matters relating to public education, as to the mode of applying the proceeds of the bequest."[11] Although Forsyth addressed the letter to seven intellectual leaders, it quickly became a national discussion amplified by the periodical press. Diverse constituents in antebellum America petitioned Congress regarding the appropriate means for diffusing knowledge.[12]

At least eleven proposals focused on using the Smithson money to establish educational institutions.[13] For example, Steven Chapin, president of the Columbian College in Washington, DC, advocated for an institute of higher learning that would complement his struggling college. Thomas Cooper, former president of South Carolina College and a noted chemist who held racist views of enslaved African Americans, believed the institution should only admit "graduates of other colleges" and insisted on a strict curriculum of sciences and mathematics. "No Latin or Greek; no mere literature" should be taught, he wrote; instead the focus ought to be on "things, not words." Cooper firmly objected "to all *belles-lettres,* and philosophical literature, as calculated only to make men pleasant talkers."[14] In this, his views aligned with those of Jeffersonians, who thought that education promoting republican values was needed. Cooper's ideas also provided an intellectual bridge to the Jacksonian Democrats, who eschewed anything that appeared to elevate classical learning and older ideas of aristocratic education. Cooper's proposal reflects a new understanding of what served as useful knowledge in the antebellum period.

Francis Wayland, president of Brown University, disagreed with Cooper. Wayland argued that the nation needed an institution devoted to the classics and that the Smithsonian could meet that need. He believed that the Smithsonian would enable students who had finished their collegiate studies to continue their "classical and philosophical education" before engaging in their professional training. This, he wrote, would "add to the intellectual power of the nation."[15] The Indiana Democratic congressman Robert Dale Owen (son of Robert Owen, founder of the utopian community at New Harmony, Indiana) promoted the idea of free public education for all and thus called for the bequest to provide a facility designed to train teachers—although now he is mostly remembered for his role in championing the Romanesque Revival architectural style of the Smithsonian's "Castle."

Some imagined specialized institutions to promote and spread scientific knowledge and were committed to engaging more fully with the transatlantic community of scholars.[16] Walter R. Johnson, a renowned expert in education, sent a memorial to the House of Representatives in 1838. Johnson asked that Congress use the Smithson money for the establishment of a "National Institution for the prosecution of experiments and reseaerches in those physical sciences which are required by the public service, and for the general welfare of the country."[17] Johnson's experience in preparing reports for federal agencies made him acutely aware of the government's need for scientific expertise.[18] Johnson pointed to England, Scotland, France, and Prussia as examples of countries with active centrally sponsored scientific institutions and argued that the establishment of an "institution for practical science" was "no novel project for the enlightened government of a civilized nation to entertain."[19] Johnson carefully outlined nine major objectives emphasizing agricultural, security, and a wide range of commercial interests that needed to be centrally funded to promote the "public interests" through "prosecuting researches in physical science."[20] The whole country would benefit from any advances in scientific knowledge. As noted in chapter 4, Charles Lewis Fleischmann likewise submitted a proposal for a national agricultural educational institution focused on applied research in 1838. Fleischmann hoped to unite the efforts made by the agricultural societies in the states.[21] The vision offered by these men emphasized the state as tool for organizing knowledge, thereby acting to promote a form of national progress through expansive scientific work.

The bequest finally removed the long-standing obstacle to a national institution dating back to the nation's first half century, when Roger Sherman objected to funding such an institution from the US Treasury unless it provided direct benefits to citizens. Van Buren's direction to receive proposals from experts demonstrated the desire to secure the best feedback from leading thinkers, yet the fact that so many citizens had their own ideas about how the money should be used was evidence that this institution needed to serve the people. The only question remaining was the one that was present from the very beginning: What kind of institution would best serve the diverse needs and interests of a republican society?

Developing a Republic for Scientists

In essence, Johnson and Fleischmann proposed a system modeled on German precedents because they hoped the Smithsonian Institution would unite the work of scientific and governmental authorities in the young republic. The diffuse nature of the German state and the expansive number of learned societies that connected the German populace to developing state-sponsored infrastructure seemed vaguely familiar to Americans.[22] American students had begun to attend renowned universities in Berlin, Leipzig, Halle, Heidelberg, and Göttingen as early as 1769. After reading advertisements in American newspapers, an influx of American students enrolled at these universities from 1830 to 1870. In an 1820 issue of *Spooner's Vermont Journal*, the University of Göttingen boasted that "our University is at present frequented by about fifteen hundred students of all civilized nations," including America, and that it had "the best of Professors in every department of Science."[23] In an 1827 issue of the Philadelphia *Album and Ladies' Weekly Gazette*, an article described the epistemological framework of German universities.[24] This framework rebuked traditional models and instead rested on a public commitment to science via participation in local learned societies, which emphasized mutual scientific interest and learning from professors who were active members within the organizations.[25] Thus, Americans viewed German universities as promoting opportunities for wider participation in the creation and dissemination of knowledge than existed in the United States. Students who studied at German universities could learn to be specialists in a domain of knowledge and then return to the United States as leaders in a new epistemological method that could be used to train new scientists instead of philosophers.

For many Americans, scientific knowledge became the key to unity and progress, and many believed that a learned society promoting the national interests of the United States was critical to the success of the nation. In May 1840, a group of elites in Washington, DC, led by Joel Poinsett—Martin Van Buren's secretary of war, renowned diplomat, and collector of natural-science specimens—formed a learned society that they hoped would serve as the "National Institute for the Promotion of Science," which would "promote Science and the Useful Arts, and ... establish a National Museum of Natural History."[26] The breadth of this proposed national institution was reminiscent of Joel Barlow's *Prospectus of a National Institution,* published in 1806. Poinsett's group envisioned a strong institution with experts in medicine, chemistry, geology and mining, and other areas that would centralize national research in Washington.

Peter Stephen Du Ponceau, the then president of the American Philosophical Society and an honorary member of the National Institute, wrote a letter to the National Institute for the Promotion of Science congratulating it on its founding and pledging his support. Du Ponceau emphasized the importance of the institution for the future of the United States since "no free nation" can exist without advancements in science, and he doubted that the organization could succeed as a national institution without the support of the government. Du Ponceau saw science as a means to promote national unity and pride; "above all, it will soften the rage of party spirit, which threatens to involve us in the fate of the Roman Republic."[27] As a centralized national organization, this institution could direct a scientific agenda and act as a conduit between the learned societies across the nation and those around the world. He hoped that this institution could help the United States overcome its deficiencies in scientific infrastructure.

Joel Poinsett was the perfect person to lead the new organization since he had spent a lifetime collecting all forms of knowledge and had learned how to secure maps, books, natural-history specimens, and even ancient artifacts.[28] Poinsett had a keen eye for useful commodities, and periodicals widely published his findings, including rich natural resources available for commercial exchange.[29] Once he had secured items, Poinsett liberally donated collections of interest to a variety of institutions, including his hometown museum, the Charleston Literary and Philosophical Society.[30] In 1827 Poinsett sent to the Charleston society "three cases of minerals" containing "a miscellaneous collection of beautiful specimens ... and a geological suite of the minerals composing the mountains and mines of Tlalpujahua."[31] The College of Columbia in New York and the American Philosophical Society also received various minerals and antiquities as donations. The APS published a list of thousands

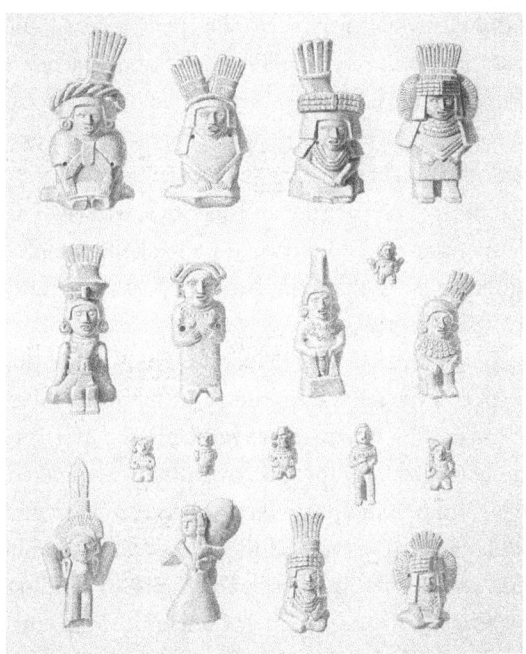

FIG. 10. Mexican artifacts given to the American Philosophical Society. Drawing by Maximillian Franck for publication in 1829. (Courtesy The Trustees of the British Museum)

of "Mexican Antiquities" donated by Poinsett, which he had collected during the five years he spent there as the US minister to Mexico.

These donations included an original manuscript later known as Montezuma's Tribute Roll, precious metals and minerals, pottery, vases, shells, musical instruments, and "Copies of the Ancient Sacrificial Stone, Calendar Stone, and Goddess of war, modeled in Wax from the originals in the National Museum of Mexico," which was extremely rare.[32] Having a replica in the United States made scholarship on Mexico possible. These tools became critical to building the scientific and scholarly apparatus for American experts such as William Prescott, who relied on such collections for his classic work on Mexico, which established a new historiographical framework for understanding early contact between Indigenous peoples and Europeans.[33]

Three decades of service had made Poinsett a master of using relationships to accomplish broader goals. He targeted government officials and decreed that "Governors of States, and Diplomatic, Consular, and Commercial Agents" who were not already members "shall *ex officio* be considered as corresponding members" of the National Institute. Poinsett also asked the secretaries of the army and the navy to circulate a request to aid the National Institute and "establish cabinets to receive and preserve all contributions" gathered at their duty stations.[34] This action was similar to the call made by the South Carolina Agricultural Society mentioned in chapter 4, but Poinsett was now able to use his authority as secretary of war to make sure it happened. This order also encouraged officers to build their own cabinets on ships and posts and incentivized them to add to national collections. The soldiers and sailors were asked to make sure that "the various specimens as collected should be packed carefully in suitable boxes, and be consigned to the Quartermaster's Department" and sent to the National Institute in Washington.[35]

Collections soon flooded the society from across the globe. The scale of the donations was overwhelming, especially after the secretary of the navy, Abel Upshur, declared that the collections of the newly approved United States Exploration Expedition were officially property of the US government and called for a new process to manage these important specimens gathered by persons funded by the government on behalf of the people of the United States. This declaration broke with a tradition established by Lewis and Clark of sending items from exploring expeditions to Peale's Museum in Philadelphia. Poinsett's political acumen seemed to ensure that the National Institute would become the custodian of the scientific treasures of the United States.[36]

The leaders of the National Institute believed their organization was unique among learned societies across the world. In the minutes of their regular meeting in March 1841, members stated that they were the "first experiment . . . made of a popular Institution of Science . . . intended for the benefit of the people," and "it is right that they should take part in its administration." This institution was meant to benefit all Americans, and anyone could become a member. This created a mutually beneficial relationship between scientific leaders and ordinary Americans: the former performed work on behalf of the latter, while the latter actively engaged in the governance of the institution and the production of new knowledge. Poinsett trusted that ordinary Americans would benefit from the leadership of chosen "officers and scientific branches of the Institution, and will I am sure cheerfully submit to their management of them." The duty of leaders, therefore, was to remain well versed in the latest scientific discoveries and to present them to the people in a way that was economical and "applicable to the arts, and useful to our manufacturers and mechanics," thus encouraging them to share their own experiments and findings with the institution.[37]

Support in Congress accelerated when the National Institute surprisingly secured an ally in Senator William C. Preston of South Carolina. Preston believed the plan for a national learned society was more appropriate than the establishment of a national university, which he still deemed unconstitutional. Together with Missouri Senator Lewis Linn, Preston introduced bills to Congress in 1841 that would incorporate the National Institute and make it responsible for administering the new Smithsonian Institution. The bill called for the interest generated from the Smithson fund to be used to erect buildings and "procure the necessary books and philosophical instruments, to arrange collections to prescribe the duties of the professors and others belonging to the said Smithsonian Institution" in exchange for free visitor admission; and delegated works of art and natural history owned by the United States were to be deposited, preserved, and arranged in the buildings of the future Smithsonian Institution but managed in the meantime by the members of the National Institute.[38] While the country seemed ready for the Smithsonian to be led by the National Institute, no action was taken on the bills presented to Congress. Poinsett became increasingly frustrated with the delay, stepped away from the society, and returned to private life. He believed that active members of the organization could shepherd the process forward by calling a great national scientific convention, and he remained active in the National Institute from his home in South Carolina while focusing on the newly created United States Agricultural Society and his own hometown South Carolina Agricultural Society.[39]

In 1844, National Institute members sponsored a convention in Washington that was designed as a national effort to match conferences in Germany and other European countries. Americans read about several annual conferences in Europe and wondered why the United States did not participate. National conferences such as the annual Congress of Philosophers, first held in 1822 at Leipzig, and the 1828 event at Berlin saw scientists share "communications of observations from all quarters of Germany" in all aspects of natural sciences.[40] A letter to the editor of the *New York Evening Post* enviously asked, "Why cannot we have an American Institute?" The author wrote about the Society of German Naturalists and Philosophers, who gathered yearly to promote the common cause of science.[41] The leaders of the National Institute hoped that an annual meeting in Washington would help to unify the disparate learned societies in the country and enable the society to emerge as the true national leader in science.

The result seemed to be a success: the Literary and Scientific Convention was attended by hundreds, including President John Tyler and other government dignitaries, "strangers and citizens," and "a large number of Ladies." The "several fine specimens of natural and artificial productions, sent by the members of the Institute ... excited great admiration." This was the "first convention of scientific men" ever assembled in the capital, and newspapers hoped that "the public" would "understand and appreciate the noble and laudable objects" of the learned society, which would "diffuse light and knowledge throughout the world."[42] Newspapers continued to celebrate the large number of attendees and the broad scope of topics discussed at the convention.[43] However, some elites, including emerging scientific specialists, questioned the seriousness of the event because of the broad-based participation and viewed it as more political than scientific in nature.

Not everyone was in favor of all learned societies throughout the country being led by a single national institution that was so closely tied to the nation's political leaders. Some viewed the National Institute's conference as a power grab by self-aggrandizing, politically motivated pretenders. The small Association of American Geologists, founded in 1840 by men of the state geological surveys across the country, was particularly suspicious of the National Institution's designs. The AAG had planned to hold their fourth annual meeting in Washington, but now they worried that the massive National Institute meant to subsume their smaller body since they had called for a meeting at the same time. The ambitions of the National Institute were well known. In 1841, Henry L. Ellsworth, of the Patent Office, spearheaded an effort to establish a national agricultural society; a meeting held in Washington, DC, was well documented in periodicals. The group was addressed by a committee from the National Institute whose instructions were to "explain to them that a Department of Agriculture already exists in the Institution and to suggest that all of their objects might probably be sooner and better accomplished by uniting with the National Institution."[44] This goal of unifying the scientific aims of the diverse institutions across the country remained elusive, however, as smaller organizations and scientists worried that the National Institute's open call to membership had filled its ranks with D-list scientists and ambitious politicians rather than real scientists.[45]

This mistrust intensified following a disagreement between the members of the National Institute, the scientific corps of the Exploration Expedition, and the commander of the expedition, Lieutenant Charles Wilkes, over who should own, care for, and interpret the collections gathered by the expedition. Traditionally, a sponsor, in this case the federal government, received two specimens of everything collected during an expedition. Naturalists could use any other items they collected for their own private use. This norm was challenged with regard to the Exploration Expedition. Congress named the National Institute the caretaker of the collections and appropriated five thousand dollars to make them available on the second floor of the Patent Office in Washington, DC, which is why members of the National Institute believed the collections were their responsibility and under their control. In May 1841, Colonel John James Abert, commander of the Corps of Topographical Engineers, naturalist, and a founder of the National Institute, reported to Poinsett that "20 tons more of the collections" had arrived, noting that a quarter of the boxes that contained "the most choice articles" were surprisingly labeled as private. When members of the institute unpacked the crates, they discovered that there were no instructions indicating cataloging procedures, likely because the naturalists had believed they would be handling the items themselves. The naturalists might also have kept the cataloging procedures to themselves to ensure their employment once they returned. Indeed, when the ship returned to port many were fired, including the experienced naturalist Titian Peale, son of Charles Willson Peale.[46]

Questions over who owned the specimens and who had access to them to disseminate the expedition's findings resulted in a debate over what constituted an expert. Lieutenant Wilkes described the mishandling of the collections to Senator Tappan and told him that Congress should withdraw the powers granted to the National Institute and instead entrust them to experts employed by the federal government.[47] Tappan agreed, saying that "the National Institute was not intended to be a branch of the Government of the nation, to be sustained and supported," and that the sooner they "disabuse themselves, of this delusion and turn to their own resources, the sooner the society may commence a career of usefulness and honor."[48] Tappan and Wilkes wanted to emphasize that science was performed by those with specific expertise, which gave them authority in their field.[49]

The challenges surrounding authority and authentic scientific knowledge became more problematic with the surge of showmen and business-oriented characters such as P. T. Barnum, who made a living commodifying and constructing stories about natural-history curiosities. Their exhibits allowed a growing middling class to view exceptional natural and scientific wonders for the admission price of twenty-five cents. Barnum was notoriously opportunistic in constructing stories about his exhibits. One of the most well known at the time, the Feejee Mermaid, and has been explored by scholars at length.[50]

Barnum's advertising of the Feejee Mermaid in 1841 coincided with the widespread interest about the collections returned from the Pacific expedition. Importantly, Barnum offered a compelling challenge designed to get people to determine the authenticity of the specimen that was on display. The result was a series of many hysterical stories printed in newspapers of people arguing for or against its authenticity.

When the exhibit made it to Charleston, South Carolina, in 1843, these debates nearly resulted in a duel between a gentleman of note who believed that it was indeed an authentic creature of nature and others who suggested that it was an obvious forgery. In the meantime, people continued to flock to see what the fuss was about. Barnum's invitation to allow individuals to decide for themselves about the authenticity of his collections provide a form of democratization over knowledge. Interest was stoked by Barnum's clever use of advertisements in newspapers invoking unspecified "scientific gentlemen."[51]

In fact, Barnum reveled in the controversy that arose when expert naturalists such as John Bachman challenged both the authenticity of the mermaid and the qualifications of untrained men, such as a lawyer and one of the editors of the *Charleston Courier*, to determine its authenticity. The war of words between the two men in the newspaper had less to do with the actual nature of the mermaid and more to do with a man's ability to discern and to publicly participate in conversations about scientific knowledge.[52] Barnum's exhibits offered a glimpse into how authority in science could impact a democratic society. Individual learning and experiences were critical in a society in which many citizens, at least among white men of all classes, increasingly saw themselves as social and political equals. Many Americans believed they had access to a wide range of knowledge, including scientific manuals and literature, and were perfectly capable of determining whether specimens like the mermaid were humbugs.[53]

As more people participated in scientific exploration, fights over what constituted authentic information seemed to resemble political fights. The emerging professional scientists, armed with degrees from colleges, worried about casual dabblers in science who lectured at local lyceums or published their ideas in pamphlets or periodicals. For example, Dr. Alfred Post, in an address delivered to the New York Academy of Medicine, reported that "some members were apt to give way to desponding thoughts on account of the prevalence of charlatanism and the hold which it had gained among the community," but he assured his audience that their "system of scientific medicine" had a solid foundation and would prevail over time.[54] Joseph Henry corresponded with several scientists who worried about the "charlatanism" that was widespread in their country. John Torrey wrote to Henry in 1838 asking that he speak directly to Congress since several frauds were being perpetrated upon the US Navy in order to promote their procurement of items. Henry's friend and colleague scientist Alexander Bache and he corresponded regularly about the need to expose unqualified people whom they referred to as charlatans.[55] Further, they worried about the impact of politicians upon the veracity of scientific work and thus hoped to establish a community free from the impact of the whims of a democratic polity and guided only by the truth discerned by employing rigorous scientific methods. In a letter to Samuel B. Morse on February 24, 1842, Henry made it clear that he expected that the members of Congress would yet again fail to recognize the value of his invention because in their minds "the electro-magnetic telegraph is associated with many chimerical projects constantly brought before the public."[56] Over and over, scientists like Post, Torrey, Bache, and Henry showed their disdain for quacks; in their view, most politicians simply did not have the qualifications to interfere with the authentic work of scientists. In other words, the neutrality that they believed was provided by science offered a freedom from the messiness of politics, and many hoped the Smithsonian would become a model for truth.

Building an Institution to Promote Research in the United States

The founding of the Smithsonian represented a host of interests—including those who wanted a national university, a national observatory, a national library, a national learned society, a series of applied scientific institutions, or literary foundations—and necessitated political compromise. The debates over what kind of knowledge should be privileged continue to this day. The modern Smithsonian Institution is best known by the American public as a collection of museums meant for the people of the nation and the world. Despite Henry's efforts, the idea of democratic access ultimately prevailed, though it took decades to fully realize this dream.

Adams dropped demands for a national observatory, as did Robert Dale Owen and the other advocates for a college. They still hoped for their programs to succeed; however, they chose a compromise program that developed a system for the administration of the funds. The final vote in the House was

85–76, and that in the Senate was 26–13. The bill establishing the Smithsonian Institution that President James K. Polk signed into law on August 10, 1846, represented ten years of negotiation and compromise.[57]

This compromise, orchestrated by Poinsett and his associates at the National Institute, provided an administrative structure to the governance of the Smithsonian.[58] The legislation described the Smithsonian's new building as having display space for "objects of natural history," as well as a "chemical laboratory, a library, a gallery of art, and the necessary lecture rooms."[59] Reflecting the federal government's strong commitment to the institution, the board of regents included the president, the vice president, the chief justice, three members of the House, and three senators. The legislation also specified that the board include the mayor of the city of Washington and "six other persons . . . two of whom shall be members of the National Institute in the city of Washington . . . and the other four thereof shall be inhabitants of States, and no two of them of the same State."[60] The group's role was to oversee the business of the institution, including selecting a site for a facility on public grounds and hiring officials to supervise the institution's day-to-day operations.[61] Because of the contentiousness surrounding decisions about the mission of the institution, the composition of this group was carefully balanced to represent the competing interests involved.

The legislation directed that all "objects of art, natural history, plants &c., belonging to the United States," including those in the hands of departments of the executive branch, must be delivered to the institution so that they could be properly classified and arranged to "facilitate the examination and study of them."[62] The design of the institution's administration reflected the multivalent goals of the National Institute for the Promotion of Science and clearly demonstrated a balance of several political interests. However, some on the board, notably the professor and scientist Alexander Dallas Bache, wanted to stack the deck to promote a scientific-research agenda by selecting a particular kind of scientist to lead the organization. He and his fellow compatriot scientists called themselves the *Lazzaroni* or "scientific beggars," and they were committed to professionalizing American science and uprooting charlatans who used their political influence and elite status to secure scientific positions.[63]

Bache solicited letters from sources around the country and in Europe to promote his preferred candidate, Joseph Henry, a scientist and professor at Princeton. At the same time he also undermined the interests of the supporters of the leaders of the National Institute, now led by Francis Markoe, an expert on museums, and Rufus Choate, a senator from Massachusetts and a leading member of the Whig Party, who supported a large national library. Bache made it clear to his colleagues that he was "anxious" to see the Smithson money used to fund "scientific research" performed in their underfunded colleges and universities. He wanted to make sure that the Smithsonian became the "true national institute."[64] His behind-the-scenes work laid a solid foundation for Henry's election by winning seven votes.[65]

The scientists knew they had won the day. As Bache told Henry, "Science triumphs in you today my friend and come you must. Save this great National Institution from the hands of charlatans."[66] But they also recognized that they needed to carefully implement a program to realize their goals, which is why Bache had written to Henry on December 4, 1846, that his nomination came with a price: he needed to "appoint an assistant Secretary who shall act as Librarian and Professor Charles C. Jewett of Brown University" to mollify the "library part of the Board."[67] Jewett's addition as an administrative member of the Smithsonian leadership served as an institutional reminder that there were important interests in Congress that wanted to create a more broadly based institution.

Once in place in Washington, Joseph Henry detested how politicians interfered with the work of scientists. In Henry's mind, they were imposters who had no business taking part in the organization of his institution. In a letter to his wife, Harriet, on December 22, he wrote that he was "hampered with the law of congress that directs that a building be erected" to hold collections of natural-history specimens and the collections of the Exploration Expedition.[68] Henry was further exasperated when he saw the requirements for establishing a large library and even wondered about the utility of establishing a wide-scale lecture series. Henry and several of his colleagues thought that "politics" had no place in the work of a scientist. To his friend Eliphalet Nott, long-serving president of Union College and a champion of scientific education, Henry reported his intent to promote scientific research rather than to create a "pile of brick and morter filled with objects of mere curiosity intended for the embellishment of Washington and the amusement of those that visit that city."[69] He declared that there were too many commitments for the money available, and he worried that the entirety would be spent on objects of useless knowledge. He wished instead to expand the knowledge of humanity through new research to be published in a journal printed by the Smithsonian. Only scholars who held authentic credentials, that is, experts in specialized, field-specific knowledge, were to conduct that research and be published by the Smithsonian.[70]

Henry subsequently moved to wrest control over the Smithsonian from politicians and place it fully in the hands of scientific experts. On December 8, 1847, Henry submitted a "Programme of Organization of the Smithsonian Institution," written in consultation with experts, which the regents approved. Two broad themes emerged as priorities: "To Increase Knowledge" and "To Diffuse Knowledge."[71] Each of these two broad areas had two subsections that defined the mission of the Smithsonian as being to "stimulate men of talent to make original researches" by conferring monetary and other awards on the leading scientific scholarly projects of the day and to "appropriate annually... income for particular researches, under the direction of suitable persons."[72] In order to widely distribute knowledge, Henry proposed a regular serial publication titled *Smithsonian Contributions to Knowledge* to share the Smithsonian's scientific advances throughout the world. This publication, which continued from 1848 to 1916, was well received in Europe.[73] Carefully vetted scientific projects stood at the core of his agenda. In turn, Henry and his collaborators limited the scope of popular participation in the work of the institution and also established boundaries for those who supported the parts of the Smithsonian's mission dealing with popular education and a library.

Originally, the plan to implement Smithson's will had made clear that "regard must be had to certain requirements of the act of Congress establishing the institution. These are a library, a museum, and a gallery of art, with a building on a liberal scale to contain them."[74] In other words, a museum, a gallery of art, and a library were part of the agenda of the institution as passed by Congress. However, Henry deemed these forms of knowledge less valuable and only honored them because they were included in Congresses' mandate. Henry thought that collections of books and museum artifacts were items of dead knowledge, which were only valuable if serious researchers could engage with them. His preferences and ideas were no secret. In his diary, John Quincy Adams made note of Henry's plan to circumvent the "Act of Congress" since "he has a different plan of organization which is evidently sliding into a job."[75] Henry simply believed that he knew better than any politician how best to increase and diffuse knowledge, and he had no qualms about using his position as the director of the organization to implement his agenda.

During the Smithsonian's early years, various factions emerged over what type of institution ought to be formed and whom it should serve. Joseph Henry emphasized a research agenda, while the assistant secretary and librarian of the Smithsonian, Charles C. Jewett, stressed the importance of bibliographic knowledge, and Spencer F. Baird, the curator of the Smithsonian, emphasized natural-history collections. Yet despite their differing visions, these men were all cast from the same mold. Each focused on his particular area of expertise and relied on that to frame his understanding of the world and to generate authority for his community of knowledge. In essence, despite their differences over the focus of the Smithsonian's mission, they all sought to increase and diffuse knowledge, each in his own way.

Henry's "Programme of Organization" comprised thirty-five typescript pages and included three appendixes, which included Jewett's plan to establish a national library and two reports supporting the Smithsonian's first major scientific project, known as the Meteorological Project.[76] Henry demonstrated a clear preference for the first part of the plan, which focused on increasing knowledge "by stimulating researches."[77] The second component, titled "Details of the Plan for Diffusing Knowledge," offers even more insights into Henry's goal for the institution. He aimed to create a series of publications produced by the Smithsonian to publish its newly produced research, and he made clear that only selected experts would produce scholarship. He also wanted to provide subventions to help scholars get their books published.[78] Importantly, the idea of building a library and a museum as part of the plan to widely diffuse knowledge was secondary to publication. The library was to be limited to collecting a small and focused collection to promote the immediate research needs of the institution. Overall, Henry prioritized scholarly publications and authorized funds to collect the books or specimens needed to conduct new research, but he did not envision the Smithsonian as a site of public education. His priorities were exemplified by the projects he supported.

Henry's enthusiasm and support for the meteorological project rested on his belief that in order to answer definitively what caused weather phenomena, there needed to be a large-scale effort to gather data for scientists to analyze.[79] The Smithsonian acted as a central hub for this ambitious endeavor; it established collecting standards and coordinated a nationwide network of volunteer weather observers. At its zenith the program included more than six hundred correspondents across the United States and in Canada, Mexico, Latin America, and the Caribbean. These volunteers were told that they were part of an "extended system" designed to better understand the cause of "American Storms."[80] Its leaders saw this program as a "grand meteorological crusade" to finally answer age-old questions about why there were particularly severe hurricanes and tornadoes in America.[81]

The plan offered institutional support to observers in the form of tools. The backbone of the program was the blank log sheets distributed to volunteers to fill out and submit to the Smithsonian. Observers recorded a wide range of phenomena, such as "thunderstorms, tornadoes, lightning, hailstorms, aurora borealis, meteors, solar and lunar halos, frosts, depth of frozen ground and opening and closing of waterways and their extreme rise and fall, the temperature of wells and springs, and the occurrences of earthquakes."[82] The Smithsonian leaders organized volunteers into three classes to determine who would receive the limited number of free scientific instruments to help record the data. First-class observers received a barometer, a thermometer, wind vanes, a rain gauge, and some even hygrometers. Second-class observers typically did not receive a barometer, while third-class observers received no instruments from the Smithsonian. Newspapers had widely reported that observers would be provided instruments, but the costs of the requested instruments exceeded the two thousand dollars allotted by the Smithsonian for their purchase.[83] Some states, such as New York, also agreed to purchase barometers and other instruments.[84] By 1852 the Smithsonian was telling the populace that instruments were available for loan from the organization or for purchase at a reasonable price.[85] With limited resources available, Henry and his colleagues saw this program as a perfect example of citizen science designed to promote new knowledge. Henry even recorded in his pocket notebook that "every man is a valuable member of society."[86]

Despite suggesting that all citizens were valuable contributors, Henry and his scientific compatriots did not assign equal value to all their fieldworkers. The distinctions between those who labored and gathered data, on the one hand, and those who would scientifically interpret the data had long been a problem. In recent years we have become more aware of Americans scientists' exploitation of women. This practice became institutionalized in the Smithsonian's massive meteorological study. Many women who were consistently faithful observers and returned their logs regularly never received instruments despite repeated requests. Further, women often struggled to receive new recording logs despite being better observers than their male counterparts. Some had to rely on help from their husbands to get new blank forms for recording their volunteer labor.[87]

Women also worked as low-paid clerical assistants and processed data received from observers. They prepared data for scientists, who utilized it in publications. These scientists hired men and women students and paid them "as cheaply as possible" over seven years to process the massive datasets.[88] Male clerks felt threatened by their female counterparts, so the women's offices were moved to the basement of the Patent Office Building; later, women were forced to work from their homes. Some of these women received credit for their work, but the overwhelming majority did not. Similarly, the volunteer citizen-scientists were not named in Lorin Blodget's 1857 publication *Climatology of the United States*. The professional scientists never recognized the labor of the women clerks and volunteer citizen-scientists.[89] By the mid-nineteenth century, then, knowledge making in the United States had become the domain of formally educated experts. The impulses of earlier decades to be more inclusive had been shut down. Instead a new system of gatekeepers was established that erased the contributions of those who had not been formally trained. Knowledge making and dissemination were restricted to a Brahmin class of intellectuals.

Despite Henry's ambivalence toward the Smithsonian's libraries and museums, both he and Jewett agreed that an important way to diffuse knowledge was through a national catalog of the collections of academic libraries throughout the country. This would assist researchers in locating resources. Both Henry and Jewett wanted to make the Smithsonian "a centre of bibliographic reference" by securing "catalogues and statistics of all the Public Libraries in the United States."[90] They hoped to establish a national network of libraries and librarians coordinated by the Smithsonian. Jewett's work resulted in a series of critically important products that helped professionalize librarianship.[91] Jewett's success had a profound impact on building a movement of library cooperation and promoting a sense of shared professionalism, both of which helped to communicate the value of books to a wide base of users. In 1850, Jewett presented his "Plan for Stereotyping Catalogues by Separate Titles; and Forming a General Stereotyped Catalogue of Public Libraries in the United States" to the fourth annual meeting of the American Association for the Advancement of Science, Henry's home professional organization, which he had helped found.[92] Jewett's paper was an anomaly; the other scholarship dealt with scientific topics.

Subsequently, Jewett and other librarians decided to hold their own meeting in New York in 1853. The conference was well covered in the periodical literature, with press coverage noting the presence of librarians serving large libraries in cities and academic settings but also librarians at "various Young Men's Institutes, Mechanics' Libraries, and Students Libraries at College," and all were interested in hearing about the Smithsonian's plans.[93] In contrast to

Henry, the librarians acknowledged the profound impact libraries had "upon the people of this country, who are taught in our extended system of common schools to enjoy and demand the highest and freest intellectual advantages; the number of institutions which are already commenced and projected, and the liberal endowments they have occasionally received, alike demand that information be generally diffused" in an efficient manner for widespread access.[94] Jewett, who was unanimously elected chairman of the conference, remarked that he was inspired by the commitment of his colleagues across the country to "better diffusion of a knowledge of good books, and for enlarging the means of public access to them."[95] Thus despite their differences, Jewett and Henry shared the view that knowledge came from expertise in specific fields of study, which could then be communicated to the masses.[96] Not everyone agreed with their claims to be the builders of knowledge institutions.

Some Americans questioned Joseph Henry's agenda and saw his vision as esoteric and designed for elites, thus not fulfilling the high aims of James Smithson or the needs of the American people. A blistering critique published in the *Baltimore American* and reprinted in newspapers across the country questioned the value of the work of the Smithsonian. Titled "The Smithsonian Institute.—A Mystery," the piece described a stranger's visit to the institution in "our National Metropolis" as a bizarre experience. The visitor first encountered the building "in the centre of a small prairie," which was reminiscent of "Basaltic delusions . . . amongst the canons [canyons?] and buttes of New Mexico."[97] The building was described as a "mausoleum," in which the visitor encountered "imitation sphynxes" and "brazen instruments" and objects only to be seen "on State occasions" and their value "only comprehended . . . by the scientific few." The author indicted Henry's haughty demeanor, which showed "general contempt for uneducated opinion," and concluded by asking, "What results worthy of the people who accepted this trust, have sprung from these investments?" The answer was "NOTHING."[98]

The article condemned all aspects of the organization and its administration, deeming the scientific work performed by the Smithsonian insignificant and a "lamentable waste" of the resources devoted to the endeavor. The author also added that Henry had warned against accepting excessive donations of books and that "the Professor . . . does not seem to consider an extensive library indispensable to the success" of his system. Instead of Henry's dense scheme, "at the base of the monument to Washington there should be founded a Free College for the instruction of American youth," since this institution would provide education for the "improvement of our people in the departments of civil progress as West Point has provided . . . in Military science [and thus] will give a practical application" of the Smithson bequest.⁹⁹ The *Alexandria (VA) Gazette* reported on the *Baltimore American*'s "able article" and suggested that "it is probable that the views of the American may meet with much more favor from the people of this country, than Professor Henry imagines," indicating that there were many who wanted to see the bequest used to benefit the people more broadly. These people remembered the debates over the national university, and many more invoked Washington's vision for a national university. Gone was the historical idea of a university for an elite few; now there was a reimagined national university suggested by their founding father, who they believed sought broader access.¹⁰⁰

In the end, for whom was the Smithsonian designed? An image published in 1858 in a Canadian magazine depicts a lecture room filled to capacity in which Joseph Henry is surrounded by instruments and is conducting experiments on "acoustics applied to public buildings" (Fig. 11).¹⁰¹ The accompanying article demonstrates that people outside the United States were interested in the scientific work done by the Smithsonian. The *London Illustrated News* reported on figures associated with the Smithsonian and American scientific work, and

FIG. 11. Lecture Room, Smithsonian Institution. *Canadian Journal of Industry, Science & Art* 3, no. 14 (1858): 114. (Courtesy American Antiquarian Society)

the Royal Society of London began promoting the Smithsonian's work as early as 1851.[102] Other countries were starting to take the United States more seriously as a producer of innovative scientific work.

The Smithsonian Institution can be seen as one version of a national university. Its design included both a research arm and a library and museum. When established, it appeared to be an institution built from political compromise. The institution was supposed to be an open collection for citizens to view and use. In several annual reports, the Smithsonian announced that its collections were "freely open to any persons engaged in original research."[103] The *Tenth Annual Report*, in 1855, after the completion of its building, now known as the Castle, detailed that several associations had utilized the spaces in the building to conduct their meetings. Importantly, the building had been planned to "accommodate the meetings of literary, scientific, and other associations which might assemble at the seat of government" as long as the groups had no "party or sectarian character."[104]

While those who established the institution claimed that it was accessible to a broad community of users, it is hard to track whether it really was open to all. The same annual reports that touted the open nature of the Smithsonian also emphasized the increasing burden that physical collections and excessive users placed on the institution. Joseph Henry never hesitated to remind all who would listen that the main purpose of the institution was to support scientific research, not to gather collections for the general use of the population. After dismissing Jewett in 1853 and shortly thereafter jettisoning the bulk of the institution's library, as well as the responsibilities of serving as a national library, Henry hoped to remove the museum as well.

By the mid-nineteenth century, many scientists were emphasizing the need to separate the world of science from the domain of politics. They sought to establish the Smithsonian Institution as a research facility devoted to promoting specialized scientific knowledge. Ironically, it barred the participation of the citizen-scientist. Instead, it promoted a new class of elite scientists. These learned men sought to be free from those whom they viewed as amateurs and charlatans and to create a new professional class to study specialized disciplines. They also believed that their notion of scientific knowledge trumped others.

The Smithsonian's leadership believed it benefited all by allowing the few to organize and spread knowledge throughout the republic in an efficient manner. In the end, the decades-long debates over the purpose and nature of knowledge institutions within the United States changed how people thought about and participated in the creation and dissemination of knowledge. By 1850 scientific research had become an all-powerful way to understand the world. Science became a universal truth distinctive from humanistic understanding of texts, the arts of practical application, or the science of social organization and politics. Ironically, this new way of categorizing knowledge created more divisions through specialization. Many saw the battle between Jewett and Henry over the mission of the Smithsonian as a battle between advocates for literature and advocates for the sciences.

CONCLUSION

Americans continued to debate the best ways to generate, validate, and diffuse new knowledge after the establishment of the Smithsonian, and these debates continue today. The Smithsonian's independence from the impulses of politicians was critical to its early scientists, such as Joseph Henry and others, during the debates over how Americans would become informed citizens. Many naively believed they could create a knowledge institution free from biases so long as it focused on scientific knowledge. The Smithsonian eventually did acknowledge some failings of these foundational ideas, for example, when it issued the "Human Remains Task Force Report to the Secretary" in January 2024. That report concedes that the Smithsonian, like other institutions, strayed from "objective" science when it "amassed collections of human skeletons and organs to help document racial and other differences among human beings." The report acknowledges the pervasive influence, in the institution's early years, of the "ideology of white supremacy, manifest in systems of slavery, segregation, immigration restrictions, and expansionism, [which] was deeply embedded in American society and government policy," and that "the Smithsonian's practices reflected what has come to be referred to as 'scientific racism.'"[1] In other words, these flawed ideas of how human knowledge was framed were baked into the foundation of the institution itself.

These acknowledgments are important because the Smithsonian transformed the way the national government directed the effort to expand and diffuse knowledge toward creating an informed citizenry. Ironically, it is this very effort to recognize nonscientific political and cultural influences that has drawn the wrath of recent critics, who claim to want to erase the signs of a supposedly "divisive, race-centered ideology" from what had once been "a symbol of American excellence and a global icon of cultural achievement."[2] Thus the question whose knowledge is authoritative in a republic has come up yet again.

The modern Smithsonian Institution is best known to the American public as a collection of museums meant not only to educate the people of the nation but to benefit the wider world. Despite founding director Joseph Henry's efforts, the idea of democratic access ultimately prevailed to a degree, though it took decades to fully realize this dream. In fact, Henry's goal for an institution devoted solely to scientific research proved impossible for many reasons. Most importantly, the natural-history specimens collected by the federal government, including the massive collections of the United States Exploration Expedition, were transferred to the care of the associate secretary and curator Spencer F. Baird. Then, once Baird assumed leadership of the Smithsonian after Henry's death, he emphasized the importance of the collections and worked to expand them. In 1876, he led the installation of the Smithsonian's exhibit at the Centennial celebration in Philadelphia. An archivist at the Smithsonian Archives wrote that "Baird's most important triumph . . . came as he was able to convince most of the Centennial exhibitors to avoid the hassle and expense of shipping their displays home by donating them to the Smithsonian."[3] Baird filled sixty boxcars with donations, which provided the impetus for congressional appropriations for a national museum building that opened in 1881.

In the end, Henry's research emphasis and Baird's museum emphasis both came to fruition and continue to coexist as the two main pillars of the Smithsonian. Today, visitors flood into the capital city to visit the Smithsonian's impressive collections. They are educated by professional curatorial staff members, who work diligently to convey diverse stories in their exhibits. Yet many operations receive little or no attention and remain out of the sights of casual visitors to the Smithsonian. Several research centers, including the Smithsonian's Libraries and Archives, its Museum Conservation Institute, the Astrophysical Observatory, the Conservation Biology Institute, the Environmental Research Center, the Marine Station, and the Tropical Research Institute, are staffed by credentialed experts and generate new, specialized knowledge. This Smithsonian is an amazing success story because it was not limited to one specialized type of knowledge; it is a diverse institution with diverse interests, yet all fit within the same epistemological paradigm that emerged between the

American Revolution and the eve of the American Civil War through the necessary public and political engagement over what constituted useful knowledge in a republic.

As this book shows, a radical transformation—an information revolution—occurred between the era of the American Revolution and the Civil War. The expansion of the federal government's role in promoting the spread of knowledge came shortly after the creation of the Smithsonian Institution with the creation of an independent Department of Agriculture through the passage of the Morrill Act in 1862. This law promoted an expansion of agricultural knowledge and the establishment of land-grant colleges to serve the needs of the people. Further, the Morrill Act provided for the federal government to use federal lands for the territories to promote practical and useful knowledge to the people across the country, including the southern states once they had rejoined the Union.[4] This information revolution was profound, and it was evident in the people's acceptance of the host of emerging institutions.

This change can be seen in the success of the various land-grant colleges that were focused on engineering and technical knowledge. Daniel Coit Gilman wrote a piece in 1867 for the popular magazine *North American Review* that was published widely as a pamphlet and in other magazines across the country under the title "Our National Schools of Science." Gilman was instrumental in founding the innovative Sheffield Scientific School at Yale and eventually became the first president of Johns Hopkins University. In this piece he made the point that the Morrill Act had donated public lands for the establishment of institutions for the "Benefit of Agriculture and the Mechanic Arts" as part of a clear mandate from the people to establish national institutions for the "common welfare of all the inhabitants" of the United States. Gilman reminded his readers that "national banks" and "national securities" were preferred by "workingmen, farmers, mechanics, teachers, ministers, and other men of little income and less savings" than rich capitalists. He also wrote that the nation had established a national railroad and a "National Academy of Sciences," as well as a "national Department of Education." Gilman wanted everyone to understand that a new age of national institutions had dawned for the United States and that key among these institutions were the "national schools of science." These schools were not for the elite but were designed to "secure the liberal and practical education of the industrial classes."[5] In the end the change profoundly altered the way early Americans participated in the creation and dissemination of knowledge, culminating in the proliferation of new sources and institutions of information. This process in turn shaped the way American citizens participated in the democratic polity.

From the earliest days of the republic, George Washington and many elite leaders had envisioned the need for a national university to educate the future leaders of the nation. One of the few founders who had not received a college education, Washington greatly esteemed learning and hoped that such an institution would serve as a centralized location where the youth of the nation could learn about the privileges and duties of citizenship in their nascent republic. He embraced the Enlightenment's understanding of the universal nature of knowledge and believed that the quest for knowledge would serve to improve humanity. In order to eliminate discord, promote mutual goals, and progress, Washington and many Federalists wished to establish an institution designed to initiate and nurture bonds of affection among the nation's youth through the acquisition of common knowledge and shared experiences. They worried that without constant vigilance their new nation was destined to devolve into factions filled with unscrupulous men who held designs that promoted their own self-interests. The republic needed to bring together the best young men in the nation and provide them with a safe place, free from the corruption of the older institutions of Europe, to mature as the rightful inheritors of the goals of the American Revolution.

Yet almost a half century later, when the Smithsonian was established, the notion of what constituted a national university had changed. Instead of a universal institution designed to promote a common vision for a homogenous citizenry, a plethora of special-interest institutions has risen across the United States. Different types of organizations and institutions tailored their research and lecture agendas to the information needs of their communities, empowering citizen-scientists in the process. As more people participated in the democratizing of knowledge in the United States, challenges arose. With the influx of new practitioners of science in the early republic, many elites worried that it was becoming exceedingly difficult to trust the quality and veracity of information generated and disseminated.

With diversified participants came an expansion in the creation of new information and projects in the new nation. Some scientists who became military engineers after receiving specialized scientific training at West Point and other military academies participated in the expansion of civil-engineering projects, mapped the West, and located the vast mineral resources in the region. Others collected and studied natural oddities and sent their findings to traditional institutions. When ignored, they formed their own institutions and organizations. Some of these groups and individuals became very successful. Others formed museums or presented their findings at newly established lyceums. Some of these new citizen-scientists believed that the earth was hollow and called for expeditions to travel to its center. This slew of activities in the realm of knowledge making and dissemination offered interested Americans many new opportunities to learn about or participate in scientific projects. However, many leaders believed that expanding access to the public sphere also provided an opportunity for charlatans to defraud the citizenry, and so they sought different means to create access to knowledge by shoring up or reinstituting hierarchies.

On a related note, the development and enhancement of several communication networks converged with the expanding transportation network to produce a political, market, transportation, and communication revolution. Taken together, all of these factors produced an information revolution in the early American republic. As newspapers, magazines, almanacs, catalogs, and documentary histories proliferated in the young republic, this expansion in the number and range of sources led to a need for organizing information in the United States. These burgeoning sources of information were critical for expanding businesses and other kinds of needed knowledge institutions, and in a republic it was crucial for the citizenry to be educated participants in the spread of knowledge. Leaders and citizens alike therefore regarded knowledge as something to be produced in the United States and a core part of self-governance. Access to new information markets offered more opportunities for a diverse and engaged citizenry to participate in the public sphere. The citizen-scientist who took part in what had been solely the domain of elites best exemplifies this change.

In turn, the emergence of a variety of knowledge institutions in the United States helped promote a new type of specialized scholar and scholarship. Government remained an important gatekeeper in establishing official sanction for institutions, while more proto-professional groups established a basic level of self-regulation over their nascent disciplines. Some hoped that the National Institute for the Promotion of Science would govern the flood of new scientists and new information sources in the nation. Yet by the time that the Smithsonian was established, few trusted a universal society to perform this work. Instead, many relied on national institutions focused on individual branches of knowledge to establish their own means of control to make sure their members only conducted and published good, reliable science. For example, the American Academy for the Advancement of Science grew out of the Association of American Geologists and Naturalists. The academy's membership requirements were stringent and moved away from the democratic approach of the National Institute and other groups that allowed anyone interested and able to pay to become a member. Instead, the AAAS demanded that those admitted already be members of specialized learned societies, college professors, or civil engineers employed in public works. The AAAS established the journal *Science,* the model publication for academic and scientific research to this day.

This dynamic also informed the founding of the Smithsonian. Although legislators intended the Smithsonian to fulfill the many information needs of the nation, the way the leadership of the new institution implemented its mission assured that a new type of science arose, spurring a radical change toward further specialization of scientific knowledge. Joseph Henry and other leading scientists demanded an institution that promoted original research. Convinced that only expert scientific research would improve the human condition, Henry wanted the Smithsonian to serve as a catalyst for science rather than emphasizing the collection and display of knowledge. This required a rejection of citizen science in favor of credentialed experts focusing solely on their own specialized subject fields, who were thought to operate above the fray of politics. The ideal scientist, in this understanding, was a neutral actor, free from the influence of politicians and the populace.

Joseph Henry's design for the Smithsonian thus intended it to operate above politics and to efficiently apply its limited resources toward scientific research to promote the expansion of knowledge. Further, Henry hoped that the Smithsonian would serve as a nexus to tie together colleges and eventually the research universities in the United States. He insisted that rather than being a single national institution serving the different needs of the nation, the Smithsonian should concern itself with a few specialized tasks, including that of acting as a clearinghouse for natural history. At the same time, the Smithsonian would also become a museum, whose collections would communicate knowledge to a larger public and create a more democratic arena for sharing information with the American people, who would benefit from the work produced by these credentialed scientists. Thus the Smithsonian became the depository for the vast number of specimens collected by various agencies of the US government over the years. The Smithsonian also showcased the technical and scientific knowledge of the United States to both its citizens and the world. It coordinated the US exhibits at world's fairs as well as various industrial exhibitions, most importantly at the 1876 Centennial Exposition. Publications highlighting the significance of the collections on display at these fairs communicated to foreign visitors and observers that the United States belonged among the elite scientific nations of the world.

It was no accident that specialized institutions connected to specific disciplinary studies developed independently after the Smithsonian was established to promote natural-history research. Agricultural and technical colleges proliferated as a means to test and impart practical knowledge, and they developed experimental stations to promote their needs. In addition, diverse types of libraries developed to support a wide range of scholarship. The push for public libraries to promote the educational needs of the poor resurfaced in the 1880s, and the specialized needs of scholars led them to advocate for a true national library led by Ainsworth Rand Spofford at the same time. Supporters of educational agendas remained committed to the establishment of a national university, yet the call for this institution went unfulfilled. Instead, schools and teaching colleges were founded throughout the nation as the US population continued to increase. Toward the end of the nineteenth century, knowledge came to be measured in terms of its practical application and its contribution to material progress in the country.

Although far distant in time, the debates over a national university in the early republic speak to present-day questions concerning information creation and dissemination in our digital age. We are living at a time when the shift from the printed word and physical libraries to digital technology and virtual-learning environments is rapidly changing what it means to be an informed citizen. Although most commentators see the digital revolution as democratizing knowledge, the debates over the national university suggest that it will be a more complex process. While information will be more widely available, some forms of knowledge may become more highly specialized and inaccessible. The ease of dissemination may make every person believe that he or she is an expert, in which case the authority of knowledge may be open to question. Information revolutions change not only what is known but also how citizens participate in the democratic process. Figuring out the implications of these changes for the present system of American government is the task at hand. Learning from the fate of Washington's national university may provide some clues as to where we as a nation are headed.

NOTES

INTRODUCTION

1. "Laying the Corner-Stone of the Smithsonian Institute: A Glorious Jubilee," *Baltimore Sun*, 3 May 1847.
2. Dallas, *Address Delivered on Occasion of Laying the Corner Stone of the Smithsonian Institution*, 4.
3. Rhees, *Smithsonian Institution*, 1:6.
4. James Green, "Rise of Book Publishing," esp. 93–94.
5. "Table of American Publications in the Year 1835," *Booksellers' Advertiser & Monthly Register of New Publications, American & Foreign* 2, no. 1 (1 Mar. 1836): 2; James Green, "Rise of Book Publishing," esp. 124–27.
6. Groves, "Periodicals and Serial Publication: Introduction," 225–27.
7. Tucher, "Periodical Press," 391.
8. Grasso, *Speaking Aristocracy*, 1–16.
9. Pasley, *"Tyranny of Printers,"* 1–23.
10. Waldstreicher, *In the Midst of Perpetual Fetes*, 1–14; Neem, *Creating a Nation of Joiners*.
11. Brown, *Strength of a People*, xxiii.
12. Brown, *Knowledge Is Power*. The essays in Gross and Kelley, *Extensive Republic*, are indispensable for understanding print culture in this period.
13. John, *Spreading the News*.
14. See Castel, "Founding Fathers and the Vision of a National University"; Thomas, *Founders and the Idea of a National University;* Boonshoft, *Aristocratic Education and the Making of the American Republic;* Justice, *Founding Fathers, Education, and "The Great Contest";* Pangle and Pangle, *Learning of Liberty;* Kelley, *Learning to Stand and Speak;* Cremin, *American Education: The National Experience;* and Rudolph, *American College and University.*
15. Gochberg, *Useful Objects*, 1–12; McMullen, *American Libraries Before 1876;* Ostrowski, *Books, Maps, and Politics;* Shera, *Foundations of the Public Library;* Augst and Carpenter, *Institutions of Reading;* Davidson, *Reading in America;* Henkin, *City Reading;* Library of Congress, *Librarians of Congress;* Shera, "Jewett and Spofford"; Carpenter, "Libraries"; Kaplan, *Men of Letters in the*

Early Republic; Wolff, *Culture Club;* Cole, "Library of Congress Becomes a World Library"; Ray, *Lyceum and Public Culture in the Nineteenth-Century United States;* Wright, *Cosmopolitan Lyceum;* Porter, *Eagle's Nest;* Orosz, *Curators and Culture;* Charles C. Sellers, *Mr. Peale's Museum;* Brigham, *Public Culture in the Early Republic;* Fernandez-Sacco, "Spectacular Masculinities"; Schwartz, *Collecting the Globe;* Alexander, *Museum Masters;* Sifton, "Disordered Life"; Schofield, "Science Education of an Enlightened Entrepreneur"; Hart and Ward, "Waning of an Enlightenment Ideal"; Hendrickson, "Western Museum Society of Cincinnati"; O'Malley, "'Your Garden Must Be a Museum to You.'"

16. Hindle, *Pursuit of Science in Revolutionary America;* Dupree, *Science in the Federal Government;* Greene, *American Science in the Age of Jefferson;* Daniels, *American Science in the Age of Jackson;* Kohlstedt, *Formation of the American Scientific Community;* Oleson and Brown, *Pursuit of Knowledge in the Early American Republic.*

17. Nichols, *Stephen Long and American Frontier Exploration;* Richard G. Wood, *Stephen Harriman Long;* Benson, *From Pittsburgh to the Rocky Mountains;* Sioli, "Breaking into the Trans-Mississippian Frontiers"; Wooster, *American Military Frontiers.*

18. Schiebinger and Swan, *Colonial Botany;* Parrish, *American Curiosity;* Schiebinger, *Plants and Empire;* Strang, *Frontiers of Science.*

19. Of critical importance to my understanding of this topic are the collected essays in McDonald, *Thomas Jefferson's Military Academy,* specifically Wagoner and Coalwell McDonald, "Mr. Jefferson's Academy," and Crackel, "Military Academy in the Context of Jeffersonian Reform"; Coalwell McDonald and McDonald, "West from West Point"; Scott, *Capital Engineers;* Mark Smith, *Engineering Security;* and Alder, *Engineering the Revolution.*

20. Jennifer Green, *Military Education and the Emerging Middle Class in the Old South;* Wells and Green, *Southern Middle Class in the Long Nineteenth Century;* Jonathan Wells, *Origins of the Southern Middle Class.*

21. Neem, "From 'Ancients and Axioms' to 'Every Branch of Science'"; Kimball, *Orators and Philosophers.*

22. Yokota, *Unbecoming British,* 8–12; Branson, *Scientific Americans,* 1–4; Winterer, *American Enlightenments,* 1–4.

23. Headrick, *When Information Came of Age,* 3–14; Sloan and Burnett, *Enlightenment.*

24. Branson, *Scientific Americans,* 2–4.

25. May, *Enlightenment in America;* Cotlar, *Tom Paine's America;* Kerber, *Federalists in Dissent;* Allgor, *Parlor Politics.*

1. A NATIONAL UNIVERSITY

1. "George Washington's Last Will and Testament, 9 July 1799," *Founders Online*, National Archives, https://founders.archives.gov/documents/Washington/06-04-02-0404-0001.
2. Kayser, *Washington's Bequest to a National University*; see also Kayser, *Bricks Without Straw*, 12–14. The shares remained unused because the federal government never established a national university. In 1825 all rights and interest of the Potomac Canal Company were transferred to the Chesapeake and Ohio Canal Company, but the stocks were deemed worthless, so that upon their transfer to Washington's nephew Lawrence Lewis in 1832 he refused to turn them in for cash.
3. See Hoyt, *National University*; Hoyt, *Memorial in Regard to a National University*; Madsen, *National University*; Castel, "Founding Fathers and the Vision of a National University"; Quattlebaum, *National University Movement in the United States*; Leibiger, *Founding Friendship*; Longmore, *Invention of George Washington*; Richard Norton Smith, *Patriarch*; Wagoner, *Jefferson and Education*; I. Bernard Cohen, *Science and the Founding Fathers*; Hayes, *Road to Monticello*; and Gilreath, *Thomas Jefferson and the Education of a Citizen*.
4. American Philosophical Society Minutes, 1787–1798, 71.
5. Justice, *Founding Fathers, Education, and "The Great Contest,"* 1.
6. See Brown, *Strength of a People*, xiii–xvii; Winterer, *American Enlightenments*, 3; and Kaestle, *Pillars of the Republic*, 183–85. The literature on the history of education is extensive. Core studies are Neem, *Democracy's Schools*; Beadie, *Education and the Creation of Capital in the Early American Republic*; Rudolph, *American College and University*; Thelin, *History of American Higher Education*; Cremin, *American Education: The National Experience*; Pangle and Pangle, *Learning of Liberty*; and Tyack, *Law and the Shaping of Public Education*. For the aristocratic impulse to control a democratic push via education, see Boonshoft, *Aristocratic Education and the Making of the American Republic*.
7. Wilder, *Ebony and Ivy*; Rudolph, *American College and University*, 23; Gordon S. Wood, *Empire of Liberty*, 472–73; O'Shaughnessy, *Illimitable Freedom of the Human Mind*, 2–3.
8. Hindle, *Pursuit of Science in Revolutionary America*, 3. Critical to understanding the underlying philosophical differences between the Federalists and Jeffersonian Republicans is Neem, "From 'Ancients and Axioms' to 'Every Branch of Science.'" See also Winterer, *American Enlightenments*, 1–9; Headrick, *When Information Came of Age*, 4–12; and Brown, *Knowledge Is Power*, 5, 268–86.

9. Nestor, "From the (Philadelphia) Independent Gazetteer, June 3," *Massachusetts Gazette*, 19 June 1786, 2. My thanks to James Ambuske for this observation on the name Nestor.
10. Ibid. I am grateful for the insights from Winterer, *American Enlightenments*, 2–4.
11. The author claimed to be "a Foreign Spectator" but was later identified as Nicholas Collin. Although Oswald later would become associated with the anti-federalists, this series encouraged readers to seek ways to promote "federal sentiments" and to recognize the necessity of "a general Federal spirit," which required the inculcation of virtue through moral improvement and, importantly, developing new institutions. "An Essay on the Means of Promoting Federal Sentiments in the United States, by a Foreign Spectator," *Independent Gazetteer*, 13 September 1787; "An Essay on the Means of Promoting Federal Sentiments in the United States, by a Foreign Spectator (Continued from 548)," ibid., 15 September 1787. For an exceptional analysis of Collin's essays, see Boonshoft, *Aristocratic Education and the Making of the American Republic*, 107–9, 170–81.
12. Rush, *Plan for the Establishment of Public Schools and the Diffusion of Knowledge in Pennsylvania*, 27.
13. Price, *Observations on the Importance of the American Revolution*, 51.
14. Benjamin Rush to Richard Price, 25 May 1786, in Rush, *Letters of Benjamin Rush*, 1:388–89.
15. Price, *Evidence for a Future Period of Improvement in the State of Mankind*, 12, 20–24.
16. Rush, *Thoughts upon Female Education*, 5.
17. Pangle and Pangle, *Learning of Liberty*, 101–5; Kerber, *Women of the Republic*, 210–11; Zagarri, *Revolutionary Backlash*, 168–69; Bilder, *Female Genius*, 123–24, 132–50.
18. Opal, *Beyond the Farm*; Opal, "Exciting Emulation"; Adam R. Nelson, "Perceived Dangers of Study Abroad, 1780–1800"; Georgia Legislature, *Colonial Records of the State of Georgia*, 378; Boonshoft, *Aristocratic Education and the Making of the American Republic*, 167–71. Additionally, Johann Forster developed a plan to establish a "new National extensive & useful Institution for the Education of Youth in America." https://diglib.amphilsoc.org/islandora/object/text%3A191030. See Robson, "Pennsylvania's 'Lost' National University." Forster's plan, though developed in 1783, was lost before being disseminated.
19. Rush, *Plan for the Establishment of Public Schools and the Diffusion of Knowledge in Pennsylvania*, 14.

20. Rush's role in early calls for education is well documented. See Messerli, "Columbian Complex"; Terrell, "'Republican Machines'"; Kuritz, "Benjamin Rush"; Binger, *Revolutionary Doctor*; and Justice, "'Great Contest.'" Rush also helped found and govern Dickinson College (1783), in Carlisle, Pennsylvania, and Franklin and Marshall College (1787), in Lancaster. For the role of education in republican polity, see Brown, *Strength of a People*, 85. For how many saw the state's role in education, see Gordon S. Wood, *Empire of Liberty*, 16–34. See also Brown, *Strength of a People*, 49–118.
21. Benjamin Rush, "Address to the people of the united states," *American Museum; or, Repository of Ancient and Modern Fugitive Pieces &c. Prose and Poetical* 1, no. 1 (Jan. 1787): 8.
22. "To Friends of the Federal Government: A Plan for a Federal University," in Rush, *Letters of Benjamin Rush*, 1:491–95. In an editorial note, Butterfield writes that the ascription is almost unnecessary since the paper is in the tone and style of Rush. Rush, *Letters of Benjamin Rush*, 1:495n1.
23. Benjamin Rush to Jeremey Belknap, 5 November 1788, in Rush, *Letters of Benjamin Rush*, 1:496.
24. This appears to be the first public mention of an institution that would be like what the Smithsonian would become.
25. Benjamin Rush, "Plan of a Federal University," *American Museum; or, Repository of Ancient and Modern Fugitive Pieces &c. Prose and Poetical* 4, no. 5 (Nov. 1788): 443.
26. According to George Washington's Mount Vernon, Washington owned copies of the *American Museum*; see https://www.librarything.com/profile/GeorgeWashington.
27. *Records of the Federal Convention of 1787*, 2:325. My thanks to Zachary Schrag for his important questions about copyright and these helpful sources: Patterson, *Copyright in Historical Perspective*; Goldstein, *Copyright's Highway*; and Rose, *Authors and Owners*.
28. *Records of the Federal Convention of 1787*, 2:325.
29. 1 Annals of Cong.1551 (1790).
30. Hoyt, *Memorial in Regard to a National University*, 27–28; Castel, "Founding Fathers and the Vision of a National University," 282; Madsen, *National University*, 21–24.
31. "Henry Knox's Notes on the State of the Frontier, January 1790," *Founders Online*, National Archives, https://founders.archives.gov/documents/Washington/05-05-02-0042.
32. Richardson, *Compilation of the Messages and Papers of the Presidents*, 1:66.
33. Ibid., 1:68.

34. US Constitution, article 1, section 8, "Copyrights and Patents."
35. 2 Annals of Cong. 1550–51 (1791). Stone was speaking of the recently enacted bill to promote the progress of science and the useful arts, also known as the Copyright Act of 1790. See also Donner, "Copyright Clause of the U.S. Constitution"; and Charlene Bangs Bickford, Kenneth R. Bowling, William C. diGiacomantonio, and Helen E. Veit, eds., *Documentary History of the First Federal Congress of the United States of America, March 4, 1789–March 3, 1791, Digital Edition* (Charlottesville: University of Virginia Press, 2020).
36. John Fenno, "Importance of a Proper System of Education—Establishment of Federal University Recommended," *Massachusetts Centinel* (Boston), 16 January 1790, 148.
37. Hayes, *George Washington*, 43, 112, 125; see also chap. 2.
38. McDonald, *Sons of the Father*, xii–xiv; Leibiger, *Founding Friendship*, 140–52. For their collaborations on a national university, see 57, 150, 152, 215–16.
39. "To John Adams from John Trumbull, 19 October 1805," Founders Online, National Archives, https://founders.archives.gov/documents/Adams/99-02-02-5106; John Adams to Benjamin Rush, 19 March 1812 and 22 April 1812, in Rush, Jefferson, Adams, and Biddle, *Old Family Letters*, 1:372–73 and 377; Harrison, *Powerful Mind*, 1.
40. "From George Washington to George Chapman, 15 December 1784," Founders Online, National Archives, https://founders.archives.gov/documents/Washington/04-02-02-0149.
41. George Chapman, *Treatise on Education*, 81–82. This work remained part of Washington's collection and is identified in his inventory; see https://www.librarything.com/catalog/GeorgeWashington.
42. "From George Washington to George Steptoe Washington, 5 December 1790," Founders Online, National Archives, https://founders.archives.gov/documents/Washington/05-07-02-0017.
43. Glover, *Founders as Fathers*, 111–21.
44. Isaac, *Take Note!*, 29–35.
45. "To George Washington from William Rawle, 6 July 1787," Founders Online, National Archives, https://founders.archives.gov/documents/Washington/04-05-02-0230.
46. For the New York Society Library circulation records for Washington, see https://cityreaders.nysoclib.org/Detail/entities/1288. See also the interesting story of the book that was 221 years overdue in Belinda Goldsmith, "George Washington's library book returned 221 years late," *Reuters*, 20 May 2010, https://www.reuters.com/article/us-library-washington/george-washingtons-library-book-returned-221-yrs-late-idUSTRE64J4EG20100520.

47. "To George Washington from William Rawle, 18 January 1791," *Founders Online*, National Archives, https://founders.archives.gov/documents/Washington/05-07-02-0136.
48. Hayes, *George Washington*; Harrison, *Powerful Mind*, introduction and conclusion.
49. "From George Washington to the Officials of Washington College, 11 July 1789," *Founders Online*, National Archives, https://founders.archives.gov/documents/Washington/05-03-02-0089.
50. Hayes, *George Washington*, 23.
51. Bowling, *Creation of Washington, D.C.*, 219–20, 226–31.
52. "To George Washington from David Stuart, 18 April 1792," *Founders Online*, National Archives, https://founders.archives.gov/documents/Washington/05-10-02-0173; Bowling, *Creation of Washington, D.C.*, 230–31.
53. "To George Washington from the Commissioners for the District of Columbia, 24 June 1793," *Founders Online*, National Archives, https://founders.archives.gov/documents/Washington/05-13-02-0099; Arnebeck, *Through a Fiery Trial*, 163, 202–3.
54. "To George Washington from the Commissioners for the District of Columbia, 23 December 1793," *Founders Online*, National Archives, https://founders.archives.gov/documents/Washington/05-14-02-0365.
55. "To George Washington from Thomas Johnson, 23 December 1793," *Founders Online*, National Archives, https://founders.archives.gov/documents/Washington/05-14-02-0373.
56. "From George Washington to Thomas Johnson, 23 January 1794," *Founders Online*, National Archives, https://founders.archives.gov/documents/Washington/05-15-02-0088.
57. Costanzo, *George Washington's Washington*, 31–32. See note 7 in "To George Washington from the Commissioners for the District of Columbia, 23 December 1793." In what is considered to be the first economics book about the United States, Blodget outlined the need for a national university. See Blodget, *Economica*. Blodget later claimed to have met Washington during the Revolutionary War and pitched the idea of a national university to him. Although this is possible, it seems unlikely since Washington reached out to David Stuart to learn more about Blodget's qualifications, saying that he had only "a very slight acquaintance with him personally, and less knowledge of his abilities." "To George Washington from David Stuart, 18 April 1792," *Founders Online*, National Archives, https://founders.archives.gov/documents/Washington/05-10-02-0173; Bowling, *Creation of Washington, D.C.*, 230–34.

58. Steele, "'The Yeomanry of the United States Are Not the Canaille of Paris,'" 27–29.
59. Addis, *Jefferson's Vision for Education*, 4, 11–12; Boonshoft, *Aristocratic Education and the Making of the American Republic*, 60–69, 136–38, and for ornamental education, chap. 5.
60. "To George Washington from Thomas Jefferson, 23 February 1795," *Founders Online*, National Archives, https://founders.archives.gov/documents/Washington/05-17-02-0380.
61. In a letter to a friend, Jefferson described the Geneva faculty as the best in Europe. See "From Thomas Jefferson to John Banister, Jr., 15 October 1785," *Founders Online*, National Archives, http://founders.archives.gov/documents/Jefferson/01-08-02-0499 (last modified 30 Dec. 2015).
62. Boonshoft, *Aristocratic Education and the Making of the American Republic*, 138–43.
63. "From Thomas Jefferson to George Washington, 23 February 1795," *Founders Online*, National Archives, https://founders.archives.gov/documents/Jefferson/01-28-02-0209.
64. Shawen, "Thomas Jefferson and a 'National' University," 309, 320–21; Virginia and Virginia (Colony), *United States Statutes at Large*, 11:525–26. This gift greatly embarrassed Washington, who did not want to gain personally from his service, so he divested himself of these shares as well as the one hundred shares in the James River Company bestowed upon him by the Virginia legislature in 1785. See notes 6 and 7 to "George Washington's Last Will and Testament, 9 July 1799," *Founders Online*, National Archives, https://founders.archives.gov/documents/Washington/06-04-02-0404-0001.
65. Shawen, "Thomas Jefferson and a 'National' University," 319.
66. "From George Washington to John Adams, 15 November 1794," *Founders Online*, National Archives, http://founders.archives.gov/documents/Washington/05-17-02-0112 (last modified 13 June 2018).
67. "To John Adams from Edmund Randolph, 16 November 1794," *Founders Online*, National Archives, https://founders.archives.gov/documents/Adams/99-02-02-1586.
68. Randolph wrote to John Adams that if he were asked for his opinion by "Mr. D'Ivernois [an opponent of the French Revolution who sought refuge for himself and his faculty colleagues], it would be, to adopt a settlement in Pennsylvania or the Federal city, on the best terms, which can be obtained." Ibid.
69. "From George Washington to Thomas Jefferson, 15 March 1795," *Founders Online*, National Archives, https://founders.archives.gov/documents/Washington/05-17-02-0441.

70. Kerber, *Federalists in Dissent*; Greene, *American Science in the Age of Jefferson*. Here I also rely on the understanding of the conflict over access to the public sphere by scholars like Christopher Grasso in *A Speaking Aristocracy*.
71. Here I am grateful for many conversations with Johann Neem and for his exceptional essay that unpacks this very complex idea, "From 'Ancients and Axioms' to 'Every Branch of Science.'"
72. Kimball, *Orators and Philosophers*.
73. Neem, "From 'Ancients and Axioms' to 'Every Branch of Science,'" 321.
74. I have greatly benefited from the excellent essays in Ragosta, Onuf, and O'Shaughnessy, *Founding of Thomas Jefferson's University*, of which see esp. Eastman, "'The Powers of Debate Should Be Sedulously Cultivated'"; Neem, "From 'Ancients and Axioms' to 'Every Branch of Science'"; and Gibson, "Medical Education in the Nineteenth Century."
75. Onuf, *Mind of Thomas Jefferson*,167–77; Hayes, *Road to Monticello*, 213–19.
76. The University of Edinburg was the second eye of scientific learning in Europe that Jefferson mentioned when discussing the University of Geneva.
77. "To Thomas Jefferson from William Thornton, 22 May 1796," *Founders Online*, National Archives, https://founders.archives.gov/documents/Jefferson/01-29-02-0075; Mauviel, "Volney, Constantin-François de Chasseboeuf."
78. Quotations are from William Thornton, "On National Education," n.d. [1795–97], in *Papers of William Thornton*, 347.
79. Washington and Hamilton exchanged five letters from 1 September to the end of November. Washington initially wanted to include a statement about the university in his Farewell Address to the American people. Instead, Hamilton persuaded him that it was an inappropriate forum and that he should address the issue directly to Congress. "From George Washington to Alexander Hamilton, 1 September 1796," *Founders Online*, National Archives, https://founders.archives.gov/documents/Washington/05-20-02-0394; "To George Washington from Alexander Hamilton, 4 September 1796," *Founders Online*, National Archives, https://founders.archives.gov/documents/Washington/05-20-02-0402.
80. "From George Washington to George Steptoe Washington, 23 March 1789," *Founders Online*, National Archives, https://founders.archives.gov/documents/Washington/05-01-02-0334; "From George Washington to George Steptoe Washington, 5 December 1790."
81. I have learned much from Glover, *Founders as Fathers* (see esp. 103–31); and Boonshoft, *Aristocratic Education and the Making of the American Republic*, 98–117.

82. "To George Washington from Robert Coram, 5 March 1791," *Founders Online,* National Archives, https://founders.archives.gov/documents/Washington/05-07-02-0287.
83. Cotlar, *Tom Paine's America,* 115–60; Cotlar, "'Every Man Should Have Property.'"
84. Coram, *Political Inquiries,* 57.
85. Ibid., 94.
86. Ibid., 101; Boonshoft, *Aristocratic Education and the Making of the American Republic,* 231.
87. "To Thomas Jefferson from Robert Coram, 5 March 1791," *Founders Online,* National Archives, https://founders.archives.gov/documents/Jefferson/01-19-02-0105.
88. See Cotlar, *Tom Paine's America,* esp. chap. 4.
89. "From George Washington to the U.S. Senate and House of Representatives, 7 December 1796," *Founders Online,* National Archives, https://founders.archives.gov/documents/Washington/05-21-02-0142.
90. 6 Annals of Cong. 1694–95 (1797).
91. William Thornton to George Washington, 13 September 1796, in *Papers of William Thornton,* 395–97.
92. "To George Washington from the Commissioners for the District of Columbia, 21 November 1796," *Founders Online,* National Archives, https://founders.archives.gov/documents/Washington/05-21-02-0105.
93. Commissioners of the District of Columbia, *Memorial of the Commissioners Appointed Under the Act "For Establishing the Temporary and Permanent Seat of the Government of the United States," and on So Much of the President's Speech as Relates to the Establishment of a National University,*12 December 1796, 153, in American State Papers, ProQuest Congressional, https://congressional-proquest-com.mutex.gmu.edu/congressional/docview/t47.d48.asp037_misc.91?accountid=14541.
94. Ibid.
95. Martin, *Government by Dissent,* 83–114.
96. Estes, *Jay Treaty Debate;* Leibiger, *Founding Friendship,* 192–222.
97. Commissioners of the District of Columbia. *Memorial of the commissioners;* 6 Annals of Cong. 1600–1601 (1797).
98. For an explanation of the debate, see Oberle, "Institutionalizing the Information Revolution," 44–47; scholars can also view the debates in 6 Annals of Cong. 1697–1711 (1797).
99. 6 Annals of Cong. 1706–7 (1797).
100. 6 Annals of Cong. 1701 (1797).

101. Arnebeck, *Through a Fiery Trial*, 393.
102. Ibid., 393–94; National Capital Planning Commission, "Foggy Bottom / Northwest Rectangle Heritage Trail Assessment Report," 23; S. S. Moore, *Traveller's Directory*, 23. I am grateful to Kenneth Bowling for his assistance over the years in trying to locate this site.
103. 8 Annals of Cong. 345 (1799).
104. George Washington University, Office of the University Historian, *Fate of Washington's Bequest to a National University*.
105. "To Thomas Jefferson from Joel Barlow, 15 September 1800," Founders Online, National Archives, https://founders.archives.gov/documents/Jefferson/01-32-02-0093.

2. A NATIONAL ACADEMY

1. "From Thomas Jefferson to the American Philosophical Society, 28 January 1797," *Founders Online*, National Archives, https://founders.archives.gov/documents/Jefferson/01-29-02-0218. See also Spero, "Other Presidency," 321–60. The two philosophers referred to were Benjamin Franklin and David Rittenhouse.
2. "To Thomas Jefferson from Benjamin Rush, 4 January 1797," *Founders Online*, National Archives, https://founders.archives.gov/documents/Jefferson/01-29-02-0197.
3. "From Thomas Jefferson to the American Philosophical Society, 28 January 1797," *Founders Online*, National Archives, https://founders.archives.gov/documents/Jefferson/01-29-02-0218.
4. American Academy of Arts and Sciences, *American Academy of Arts and Sciences, 1780–1940*, 1–2.
5. State of Massachusetts, *Act to Incorporate and Establish a Society for the Cultivation and Promotion of Arts and Sciences*, 1.
6. See Greene, "Science, Learning and Utility"; Greene, *American Science in the Age of Jefferson*, 3–36, 60–90.
7. Crackel, *Mr. Jefferson's Army*; Crackel, "Military Academy in the Context of Jeffersonian Reform."
8. For the learned society as information system, see Dupree, "National Pattern of American Learned Societies,." On how the army, especially its engineering corps, was critical to building a national infrastructure by providing expertise to the private sector, see William D. Adler, *Engineering Expansion*.
9. See, e.g., Hindle, *Pursuit of Science in Revolutionary America*, 248–79, 382–85; and Greene, *American Science in the Age of Jefferson*, 1–36.

10. Dupree, "National Pattern of American Learned Societies," 21.
11. Headrick, *When Information Came of Age*.
12. Kerber, *Federalists in Dissent*, 174.
13. Jefferson used the phrase *empire of liberty* frequently. To best understand Jefferson's vision for the republic it is critical to note the importance of renewal and growth of from the fertile lands of the west: "From Thomas Jefferson to Benjamin Chambers, 28 December 1805," Founders Online, National Archives, https://founders.archives.gov/documents/Jefferson/99-01-02-2910. See also Gordon S. Wood, *Empire of Liberty*, 357; Neem, *Creating a Nation of Joiners*, 2–9; Opal, "Exciting Emulation"; and Boonshoft, *Aristocratic Education and the Making of the American Republic*.
14. On the importance that Jefferson placed on widespread access to education, see Neem, "'To Diffuse Knowledge More Generally through the Mass of the People.'"
15. Higginbotham, "Military Education Before West Point"; Kohn, *Eagle and Sword*; United States Army Corps of Engineers, *U.S. Army Corps of Engineers*.
16. Higginbotham, "Military Education Before West Point," 25.
17. Alder, *Engineering the Revolution*, 69.
18. Headrick, *When Information Came of Age*, 96–123.
19. Heine Barnett, "Mathematics Goes Ballistic"; Bamford, "Public Schools and Social Class, 1801–1850"; Hearl, "Military Education and the School Curriculum, 1800–1870."
20. Gillispie, "Scientific Aspects of the French Egyptian Expedition, 1798–1801," 447–49.
21. "National Institute in Egypt," *Aurora General Advertiser* (Philadelphia), 19 April 1799, 3; "Intelligence: National Institute in Egypt from the Western Printed at New York," *Weekly Magazine of Original Essays, Fugitive Pieces, and Interesting Intelligence*, 4 May 1799, 128.
22. Among newspapers reprinting this news were several New York papers, such as the *Commercial Advertiser*, 8 December 1801, 2; the *Evening Post*, 9 December 1801, 2; and the *Spectator*, 9 December 1801, 2.
23. See, e.g., Sonnini, *Travels in Upper and Lower Egypt*; and "Advertisement," *Mercantile Advertiser* (New York), 16 June 1801. Also, the work of members of the Institute of Egypt was frequently mentioned in newspapers.
24. "To Thomas Jefferson from Volney, [25 June 1801]," Founders Online, National Archives, https://founders.archives.gov/documents/Jefferson/01-34-02-0354.
25. Oberle, "Institutionalizing the Information Revolution," 95–109.
26. "Horatio Gates to Robert Livingston Discussing the Haitian Revolution, the Louisiana Purchase and Key French Figures," 12 February 1803,

American History, 1493–1945, https://www.americanhistory.amdigital.co.uk/Documents/Details/GLC06611.
27. "From George Washington to Antoine-Jean-Louis Le Bègue de Presle Duportail, 23 April 1783," *Founders Online*, National Archives, https://founders.archives.gov/documents/Washington/99-01-02-11144.
28. On the need for scientifically trained men, see Webb, "Origin of Military Schools in the United States Founded in the Nineteenth Century," 1–26; and Crackel, *West Point*, 5–51.
29. "National Institute in Egypt," *American Mercury* (Hartford, CT), 25 April 1799, 4, America's Historical Newspapers (Readex); "National Institute in Egypt," *Connecticut Gazette* (New London), 1 May 1799, 3, America's Historical Newspapers (Readex).
30. Bonaparte, *Copies of Original Letters from the Army of General Bonaparte in Egypt*, vii–xx; see also "Letter X," on p. 67, which outlines the planned reorganization of Egypt.
31. Commission des sciences et arts d'Egypte and Emperor of the French Napoleon I, *Description of Egypt. First Edition. Antiquities, Descriptions, Volume One*; Commission des sciences et arts d'Egypte and Emperor of the French Napoleon I, *Description of Egypt. First Edition. Antiquities, Descriptions, Volume Two*. Subsequent editions had as many as five volumes of content.
32. See Norry, *Account of the French Expedition to Egypt*; Institut d'Égypte, *Memoirs Relative to Egypt*; and Ripault, *Report of the Commission of Arts to the First Consul Bonaparte*.
33. Crackel, "Military Academy in the Context of Jeffersonian Reform." See also Crackel, *West Point*; and Crackel, *Mr. Jefferson's Army*. On curriculum reform, see Wagoner and Coalwell McDonald, "Mr. Jefferson's Academy."
34. Dupree, "National Pattern of American Learned Societies."
35. Grasso, *Speaking Aristocracy*, 13.
36. Here I rely on Grasso, *Speaking Aristocracy*; and Brown, *Knowledge Is Power*.
37. Kerber, *Federalists in Dissent*, 75.
38. Quoted in ibid., 77.
39. Kerber, *Federalists in Dissent*; Greene, *American Science in the Age of Jefferson*; Grasso, *Speaking Aristocracy*.
40. Strang, *Frontiers of Science*. Strang's work is particularly illustrative of this process on the frontier, and examples abound in his excellent work. See esp. 1–21 and 162–207.
41. United States, ed., *Account of Louisiana*.
42. Spero, *Scientist Turned Spy*, esp. 110–21.
43. Ibid.

44. "American Philosophical Society's Instructions to André Michaux, [ca. 30 April 1793]," *Founders Online*, National Archives, https://founders.archives.gov/documents/Jefferson/01-25-02-0569.
45. Ibid.
46. "Expedition Behind Enemy Lines," American Academy of Arts & Sciences Archives, https://www.amacad.org/news/expedition-behind-enemy-lines.
47. American Academy of Arts and Sciences, *American Academy of Arts and Sciences, 1780–1940*, 3.
48. Gordon S. Wood, *Empire of Liberty*, 357.
49. Adam Rothman, in *Slave Country*, also makes it clear that westward expansion required military efforts. See also American Philosophical Society, "Concerning inquiries to be made by Major Long of the Indians," 30 March 1819, American Philosophical Society Archives, box 1; and Long, *Account of an Expedition from Pittsburgh to the Rocky Mountains*.
50. Dzurec, "Of Salt Mountains, Prairie Dogs, and Horned Frogs"; Neem, "From 'Ancients and Axioms' to 'Every Branch of Science.'"
51. I delivered parts of these findings in my paper "Science, Skepticism, and Societies: The Politics of Knowledge Creation in the Early Republic" at the American Philosophical Society conference Networks: The Creation and Circulation of Knowledge from Franklin to Facebook, Philadelphia, 7 June 2019. I am grateful to the American Philosophical Society for sponsoring the research panel.
52. "To Thomas Jefferson from William Short, 9 October 1791," *Founders Online*, National Archives, https://founders.archives.gov/documents/Jefferson/01-22-02-0192.
53. Mauviel, "Volney, Constantin-François De Chasseboeuf."
54. "To Thomas Jefferson from William Thornton, 22 May 1796," *Founders Online*, National Archives, https://founders.archives.gov/documents/Jefferson/01-29-02-0075.
55. "To Thomas Jefferson from Alexandre Lerebours, 17 May 1796," *Founders Online*, National Archives, https://founders.archives.gov/documents/Jefferson/01-29-02-0069; "Early Proceedings of the American Philosophical Society for the Promotion of Useful Knowledge, Compiled by One of the Secretaries, from the Manuscript Minutes of Its Meetings from 1744–1838," *Proceedings of the American Philosophical Society* 22, no. 3 (1884): 227, 238.
56. Hahn, *Anatomy of a Scientific Institution*, 203.
57. Ibid., 159–251.
58. Gordon S. Wood, *Empire of Liberty*, 369–74; Kerber, *Federalists in Dissent*, 67–94; Dzurec, "Of Salt Mountains, Prairie Dogs, and Horned Frogs," 82–83.

59. "Climenole: A Review Political and Literary. No. 12," *Port-Folio* (Philadelphia), 17 November 1804, 361.
60. Carter, *"One Grand Pursuit."*
61. Coalwell McDonald and McDonald, "West from West Point"; Stanton, *American Scientific Exploration, 1803–1860*.
62. Edling, *Revolution in Favor of Government*, 121.
63. Puls, *Henry Knox*; Alder, *Engineering the Revolution*; United States Army Corps of Engineers, *U.S. Army Corps of Engineers*; Crackel, *West Point*.
64. Fredriksen, "Williams, Jonathan"; "Jonathan Williams," Biographical Directory of the United States Congress, https://bioguide.congress.gov/search/bio/W000523; "14th Congress: Pennsylvania 1814," Mapping Early American Elections, https://earlyamericanelections.org/maps/meae.congressional.congress14.pa.county.html.
65. "To Thomas Jefferson from Jonathan Williams, 24 January 1796," Founders Online, National Archives https://founders.archives.gov/documents/Jefferson/01-28-02-0459.
66. Meeting minutes, 6 April 1798, in "Early Proceedings of the American Philosophical Society for the Promotion of Useful Knowledge," 269–70.
67. Mucher, *Before American History*; Snead, *Relic Hunters*; DeLucia, "Fugitive Collections in New England Indian Country"; Delucia, *Memory Lands*; DeLucia, "Antiquarian Collecting and the Transits of Indigenous Material Culture."
68. Meeting minutes, 19 January 1798, in "Early Proceedings of the American Philosophical Society for the Promotion of Useful Knowledge," 266–67; Meeting minutes, 16 February 1798, ibid., 267–68.
69. Meeting minutes, 1 June 1798, ibid., 269–71.
70. American Philosophical Society, "Philosophical Society Meeting," 7 December 1798, American Philosophical Society Minutes, 1787–1798, 236–38; Curator's Record of Donations to the Cabinet, 1769–1818, 1:44, https://diglib.amphilsoc.org/islandora/object/text%3A290237; Jonathan Williams to Samuel Hodgdon, "Barrels Belong to the Philosophical Society," 13 October 1798, in United States Department of War, Papers of the War Department, https://wardepartmentpapers.org/s/home/item/65061.
71. "To Thomas Jefferson from Jonathan Williams, 12 December 1802," *Founders Online*, National Archives, https://founders.archives.gov/documents/Jefferson/01-39-02-0134.
72. Crackel, "Military Academy in the Context of Jeffersonian Reform"; American Philosophical Society, "Members, American Philosophical Society," *American Philosophical Society Members Database*, 2012, https://www.amphilsoc.org/members.

73. Wagoner and Coalwell McDonald, "Mr. Jefferson's Academy," 118–19.
74. Wade, "Military Offspring of the American Philosophical Society." The best data gathered for the groups comes from their membership lists. In 1809 the USMPS had 212 members, most of whom were young men from the Corps of Engineers. In 1809, 34 of those members, or 16 percent, also belonged to the APS. Many of these cadets would later be elected to the APS.
75. Jonathan Williams, "Military Philosophical Society," 12 November 1802, The Thomas Jefferson Papers, Library of Congress, 2, http://hdl.loc.gov/loc.mss/mtj.mtjbib011976.
76. See Jonathan Williams to Charles Cotesworth Pinckney, 18 March 1807, and Pinckney to Williams, 11 December 1807, in The Papers of the Revolutionary Era Pinckney Statesmen Digital Edition, https://rotunda.upress.virginia.edu/founders/PNKY-01-03-02-0009-0050.
77. Wade, "Military Offspring of the American Philosophical Society," 105.
78. "Establishment of the United States Military Philosophical Society," 1 December 1805, Henry Knox Papers; Dzurec, "Of Salt Mountains, Prairie Dogs, and Horned Frogs," 82; Parrington, *Colonial Mind, 1620–1800*, 357–95; Nash, "American Clergy and the French Revolution," 3.
79. Jonathan Williams, *United States Military Philosophical Society: The Address* (Washington, DC, 1808), 5–9, American Periodicals Series II (Proquest), http://mutex.gmu.edu/login?url=https://www.proquest.com/reports/united-states-military-philosophical-society/docview/127552298/se-2?accountid=14541.
80. Ibid., 2.
81. Metchie J. E. Budka, "Minerva Versus Archimedes," *Smithsonian Journal of History* 1, no. 1 (January 1966): 62.
82. Ibid.
83. See "science, n.3b," *OED Online*, http://www.oed.com/view/Entry/172672?redirectedFrom=science, and "art, n.1.3a," ibid., http://www.oed.com/view/Entry/11125, both accessed 29 September 2012.
84. Benjamin Henry Latrobe to John Reich, 16 January 1807, in Latrobe, *Correspondence and Miscellaneous Papers*, 2:365–67.
85. Forman, "United States Military Philosophical Society, 1802–1813."
86. Ibid., 278.
87. Zuersher, "Benjamin Franklin, Jonathan Williams, and the United States Military Academy," 99.
88. Numerous newspapers and magazines covered the story. See, e.g., "United States Military Philosophical Society," *Medical Repository of Original Essays and Intelligence* 3 (Feb.–Apr. 1806): 421–22; "United States Military Philosophical

Society," *Poulson's American Daily Advertiser* (Philadelphia), 30 July 1806, 3; and "Under the auspices of that scientific officer, Colonel Jonathan Williams, commanding the United States corps of Engineers at West Point, in the State of New York, a Military Philosophical Society has been instituted," *Raleigh (NC) Register*, 11 August 1806.

89. Jonathan Williams, *Extracts from the Minutes of the United States Military Philosophical Society* . . . , 6 October 1806, 4, American Periodicals Series.
90. Partial lists of the collections from the extracts of society minutes. See Wade, "Military Offspring of the American Philosophical Society."
91. "Letters from Dr. Mitchill to Judge Spencer, on the Fortifications Erecting at New York," *American Register; or, General Repository of History, Politics and Science* 4 (2 Jan. 1808): 312.
92. National Park Service, "Castle Williams," https://www.nps.gov/gois/learn/historyculture/castle-williams.htm.
93. Williams, *Extracts from the Minutes of the United States Military Philosophical Society* . . . , 3.
94. Wade, "Military Offspring of the American Philosophical Society," 106.
95. "Extracts: From the Minutes of the United States Military Philosophical Society at a Stated Meeting Held October 6, 1806 in the Fundamental School in the School of Engineers and Artillerists in the School of Cavalny [sic] in the School of the Navy," *United States Military Philosophical Society. Extracts from the Minutes of the United States Military Philosophical Society at a Meeting[s] Held October 6, 1806, January 30, 1808 [and] December 28, 1809 (1806–1809)* (Washington, DC, 6 Oct. 1806), American Periodicals Series II (Proquest), quotation from pp. 4–5.
96. Zuersher, "Benjamin Franklin, Jonathan Williams, and the United States Military Academy," 101.
97. "Extracts: From the Minutes of the United States Military Philosophical Society at a Stated Meeting Held October 6, 1806."
98. Pike, *Account of Expeditions to the Sources of the Mississippi, and Through the Western Parts of Louisiana.*
99. "To Thomas Jefferson from Jonathan Williams, 5 March 1808," *Founders Online,* National Archives, https://founders.archives.gov/documents/Jefferson/99-01-02-7553; "Thomas Jefferson to Congress, 18 March 1808," American State Papers: Military Affairs, no.79, 1:229, https://congressional-proquest-com.mutex.gmu.edu/congressional/docview/t47.d48.asp016_mil.aff.79?accountid=14541.
100. "Thomas Jefferson to Congress, 18 March 1808," American State Papers: Military Affairs, no.79, 1:228–30.

101. "To Thomas Jefferson from Jonathan Williams, 5 March 1808," *Founders Online*, National Archives, https://founders.archives.gov/documents/Jefferson/99-01-02-7553. It is unclear whether Jefferson made changes or approved of what Williams called his "rough draft"; however, Williams's letter clearly asks for input from Jefferson.
102. "Thomas Jefferson to Congress, 18 March 1808," American State Papers: Military Affairs, no. 79, 1:228.
103. 19 Annals of Cong. 1559 (1809).
104. Ibid.; 20 Annals of Cong. 234 (1810).
105. Crackel, *West Point*, 72–73.
106. Forman, "United States Military Philosophical Society, 1802–1813," 283–85; Fairchild, *History of the New York Academy of Sciences*, 12–13.
107. Wade, "Military Offspring of the American Philosophical Society."
108. Colin Wells, *Devil and Doctor Dwight*, 139–41, 149.
109. "Miscellany, Communicated for the Palladium," *New-England Palladium* 21, no. 25 (1 Apr. 1803), 1.
110. Hofstadter, *Idea of a Party System*.
111. Adams is quoted in Wagoner and Coalwell McDonald, "Mr. Jefferson's Academy," 118.
112. "From John Adams to Thomas Jefferson, 20 August 1821," *Founders Online*, National Archives.
113. Sylvanus Thayer to George Graham, 29 August 1817, in Thayer, *West Point Thayer Papers*.
114. Naughton, "Professional Military Education," 85–86.

3. A NATIONAL MUSEUM?

1. Yokota, *Unbecoming British*, 8–12; Branson, *Scientific Americans*, 1–4; Winterer, *American Enlightenments*, 1–4; Neem, "From 'Ancients and Axioms' to 'Every Branch of Science'"; Brown, *Strength of a People*; Headrick, *When Information Came of Age*, 3–14; Sloan and Burnett, *Enlightenment*.
2. Francis Hopkinson, "An Address to the American Philosophical Society, Held at Philadelphia, for Promoting Useful Knowledge: Delivered January 16, 1784," in Hopkinson, *Miscellaneous Essays and Occasional Writings*, 1:363–64.
3. Ibid., 1:365.
4. The scholarship on non-elite participation in the scientific enterprise is vast. My understanding of this topic comes from Branson, *Scientific Americans*; Lewis, "Gathering for the Republic"; Winterer, *American Enlightenments*, esp. 1–17; Lewis, *Democracy of Facts*; Parrish, *American Curiosity*; and Brown, *Strength of a People*.

5. See Parish, *American Curiosity*; Schiebinger, "Prospecting for Drugs"; Carney, "Out of Africa"; and the exceptional essays in Bleichmar and Mancall, *Collecting Across Cultures*, which offer critical insights. See also Snead, *Relic Hunters*; Gochberg, *Useful Objects*, 1–12; Christopher Iannini, *Fatal Revolutions*; and Bennett, *Florida Explored*.
6. For an understanding of the educational nature of the museum in the early republic, Brigham, *Public Culture in the Early Republic*, is exceptional. See also the excellent recent book by Reed Gochberg, *Useful Objects*.
7. The scholarship on exploration is vast and offers important insights into the importance of westward expansion. Some of the most useful sources for me include Ronda, *Beyond Lewis & Clark*; Sioli, "Breaking into the Trans-Mississippian Frontiers"; Mizelle, "Displaying the Expanding Nation to Itself"; Schwartz, *Collecting the Globe*; Guidone, "Empire's City"; Goetzmann, *Exploration and Empire*; Nichols, *Stephen Long and American Frontier Exploration*; Stanton, *American Scientific Exploration, 1803–1860*; Orsi, *Citizen Explorer*; and Bennett, "1817 Florida Expedition of the Academy of Natural Sciences."
8. "A Representation of the Figures Exhibited and Paraded Through the Streets of Philadelphia, on Saturday, the 30th of September, 1780," Printed Ephemera Collection, Library of Congress, https://search.worldcat.org/title/1226918671.
9. The historian Gary B. Nash even wrote that Peale sold out; see Nash, *First City*, 140. In general, the literature on Charles Willson Peale is extensive, and I found the following sources especially useful: Brigham, *Public Culture in the Early Republic*; Ward, *Charles Willson Peale*; Hart and Ward, "Waning of an Enlightenment Ideal"; Hindle, Miller, and Richardson, *Charles Willson Peale and His World*; Charles C. Sellers, *Mr. Peale's Museum*; Laura Rigal, *The American Manufactory*; Fernandez-Sacco, "Framing 'The Indian'"; Antony Adler, "From the Pacific to the Patent Office"; Appel, "Science, Popular Culture and Profit"; Porter, "American West Described in Natural History Journals, 1819–1836"; Ellis, "Founding History, and Significance of Peale's Museum in Philadelphia, 1785–1841"; and Peale, *Collected Papers of Charles Willson Peale and His Family*. A major project to collect the family papers, *The Collected Papers of Charles Willson Peale and His Family, 1735–1885*, was completed by the Smithsonian and produced on 449 microfiche. From this a five-volume set of selected papers was produced that is indispensable for researchers: *The Selected Papers of Charles Willson Peale and His Family* (hereafter cited as Peale, *Selected CWP*).
10. Charles C. Sellers, *Mr. Peale's Museum*, 215–335; Ward, *Charles Willson Peale*. To understand the notion of ambition among the founders' children, I relied on Opal, *Beyond the Farm*, esp. vii–xiv, 186–87.

11. Charles C. Sellers, *Mr. Peale's Museum*, 12.
12. Charles Willson Peale to John Beale Bordley, 5 December 1786, in Peale, *Selected CWP*, 1:195–96. Wilson and Ord's *American Ornithology*, with colored plates published in America, seems to have been the first of American bird books.
13. Wonders, *Habitat Dioramas*, 23–45; Wilson and Ord, *American Ornithology*. The best example is a diorama for the white-headed eagle. On museum preferences for displays, see Peale, *Selected CWP*, 1:148n3; Lucas, *Story of Museum Groups*; and Rader and Cain, *Life on Display*.
14. "Extract of a Letter from Halifax, Nova-Scotia," *Pennsylvania Packet* (Philadelphia), 31 October 1786. Peale became obsessed with developing the best techniques and utilizing the latest technology to preserve animal skins. He and his son Titian spent hours poring over manuals and handbooks and experimenting to perfect preservation methods.
15. Charles Wilson Peale to George Washington, 31 December 1786, in Peale, *Selected CWP*, 1:464.
16. See, e.g., *Independent Gazetteer* (Philadelphia), 17 November 1786, 2; *Middlesex Gazette* (Middletown, CT), 27 November 1786, 2; and *Massachusetts Spy* (Worcester), 30 November 1786, 427.
17. "To George Washington from Charles Willson Peale, 31 March 1787," *Founders Online*, National Archives, https://founders.archives.gov/documents/Washington/04-05-02-0112. In the end, Peale struggled for three more years to find the proper method for preserving animals skins.
18. *Pennsylvania Packet*, 1 March 1787, 3.
19. Charles C. Sellers, *Mr Peale's Museum*, 9.
20. Advertisement in *Pennsylvania Packet*, 7 July 1786, in Peale, *Selected CWP*, 1:448. The editors of the *Selected CWP* note that this advertisement ran in the *Pennsylvania Packet* thirty-nine times from 7 July to 12 November 1786; Peale also used the same advertisement in the *Freeman's Journal; or the North American Intelligencer* and in the *Independent Gazetteer*, both also Philadelphia publications.
21. Charles Willson Peale to David Ramsay, 15 October 1786, in Peale, *Selected CWP*, 1:456.
22. Charles Willson Peale to Christopher Richmond, 22 October 1780, in ibid., 1:457–58.
23. "Mr. Peale ever desirous to please," *Maryland Gazette* (Annapolis), 2 November 1786.
24. See Peale, *Selected CWP*, 1:458n4.
25. "Philadelphia, August 26," *Pennsylvania Mercury, and Universal Advertiser* (Philadelphia), 26 August 1788, 4.

26. Elias Hasket Derby Jr. to Charles Willson Peale, 3 September 1796, Derby Family Papers.
27. "American Intelligence," *State Gazette of South-Carolina* (Charleston), 22 September 1788; "The Following Curiosities Have Lately Been Presented to Mr. Peale's American Museum, in Philadelphia," *Massachusetts Centinel* (Boston), 31 December 1788, 1.
28. Fisher, *Recollections of Joshua Francis Fisher*, 183; Charles C. Sellers, *Mr. Peale's Museum*, 38–40. Regarding the title supercargo, I am grateful to Anthony Guidone for pointing me to James Fichter's book *So Great a Proffit: How the East Indies Trade Transformed Anglo-American Capitalism* above definition. Fichter argues that the East Indian trade created and elevated this new position.
29. Charles C. Sellers, *Mr. Peale's Museum*, 38–40.
30. "Sundry Late Communications to Mr. Peale's MUSEUM Philadelphia, Viz," *Massachusetts Centinel* (Boston), 2 September 1789, 191.
31. "Advertisement," *Freeman's Journal; or, The North-American Intelligencer* (Philadelphia), 27 August 1788, 4.
32. Brigham, *Public Culture in the Early Republic*, 34.
33. "Late Additions to Peale's Museum," *General Advertiser* (Philadelphia), 28 August 1792, 2.
34. Charles C. Sellers, *Mr. Peale's Museum*, 12; Sifton, "Pierre Eugene Du Simitiere (1737–1784)"; Hans Huth, "Pierre Eugène Du Simitière and the Beginnings of the American Historical Museum"; Sifton, "Disordered Life"; Orosz, *Eagle That Is Forgotten*; Iannini, *Fatal Revolutions*.
35. Hart, "'To Encrease the Comforts of Life'"; Gordon S. Wood, *Empire of Liberty*, 541–57.
36. Charles C. Sellers, *Mr. Peale's Museum*, 8–20; Peale, *Selected CWP*, 1:449–50.
37. Peale, *Guide to the Philadelphia Museum*, 2.
38. Wonders, *Habitat Dioramas*.
39. "To the Citizens of the United States of America, Mr. Peale Beg Leave to Present the Following Address," *Mail; or, Claypoole's Daily Advertiser* (Philadelphia), 16 January 1792, 3.
40. Peale, *Selected CWP*, 2, pt.1: 265.
41. Ibid., 2, pt.1: 267.
42. Charles C. Sellers, *Mr. Peale's Museum*, 101–3.
43. Peale, *Selected CWP*, 2, pt. 1: 269.
44. At least 219 pieces of correspondence between Jefferson and Peale were gathered by editors of Jefferson's papers. See *Founders Online*, National Archives, https://founders.archives.gov/.

45. "To Thomas Jefferson from Charles Willson Peale, 29 June 1801," *Founders Online*, National Archives, https://founders.archives.gov/documents/Jefferson/01-34-02-0378; "To Thomas Jefferson from Charles Willson Peale, 24 July 1801," *Founders Online*, National Archives, https://founders.archives.gov/documents/Jefferson/01-34-02-0478; Semonin, *American Monster*; Thomson, *Jefferson's Shadow*; Dugatkin, *Mr. Jefferson and the Giant Moose*.
46. "From Thomas Jefferson to Charles Willson Peale, 29 July 1801," *Founders Online*, National Archives, https://founders.archives.gov/documents/Jefferson/01-34-02-0521.
47. "To Thomas Jefferson from Charles Willson Peale, 12 January 1802," *Founders Online*, National Archives, https://founders.archives.gov/documents/Jefferson/01-36-02-0215-0001.
48. "From Thomas Jefferson to Charles Willson Peale, 16 January 1802," *Founders Online*, National Archives, https://founders.archives.gov/documents/Jefferson/01-36-02-0237.
49. Ibid; Castel., "Founding Fathers and the Vision of a National University"; Charles C. Sellers, *Mr. Peale's Museum*, 148–49.
50. Peale, *Collected Papers of Charles Willson Peale and His Family*, provides a snapshot to aid an understanding of the donations and donors to Peale's museum. See also, because Peale served as the APS's curator, Index to Curator's Record of Donors, AD 1769–1900, and Curator's Record of Donations to the Cabinet, 1769–1818, both in American Philosophical Society Archives. The literature on exploration of the West and the accumulation of scientific knowledge is vast, but I rely especially upon Coalwell McDonald and McDonald, "West from West Point"; Greene, *American Science in the Age of Jefferson*; Dupree, *Science in the Federal Government*; Cutright, *Lewis and Clark*, 350–92; and Mizelle, "Displaying the Expanding Nation to Itself," esp. 220.
51. "From Thomas Jefferson to Charles Willson Peale, 6 October 1805," *Founders Online*, National Archives, https://founders.archives.gov/documents/Jefferson/99-01-02-2444; Mizelle, "Displaying the Expanding Nation to Itself," 220.
52. "Advertisement—Donations and Additions to Peale's Museum," *Poulson's American Daily Advertiser* (Philadelphia), 6 October 1808.
53. "From Thomas Jefferson to Charles Willson Peale, 5 November 1807," in Peale, *Selected CWP*, 2:1041–43. The editors of Peale, *Selected CWP*, identify Rio Bravo as the name given to the Rio Grande by Mexico; see 1043n2.
54. Charles C. Sellers, *Mr. Peale's Museum*, 206–7; Mizelle, "Displaying the Expanding Nation to Itself," 224–25.

55. Kerber, *Federalists in Dissent*, 67–69.
56. Domestic Occurrences, *Port-Folio* (Philadelphia) 1, no. 29 (18 July 1801): 230.
57. "American Miracle," *Poulson's American Daily Advertiser* (Philadelphia), 18 February 1802, 3.
58. There is a significant literature on the idea of American degeneracy and Jefferson's determination to refute Buffon's theories. Some useful works are Semonin, *American Monster*, 1–14, 180–82, 280; Dugatkin, *Mr. Jefferson and the Giant Moose*; Gerbi, *Dispute of the New World*; and Regis, *Describing Early America*, 80–105. On the connection between race and these scientific theories, see Dain, *Hideous Monster of the Mind*. See also the important way in which science and history became interconnected in Peale's museum in Hattem, *Past and Prologue*, 226–30.
59. Samuel Ewing, "Original Poetry: American Miracle," *Port-Folio* (Philadelphia) 2, no. 9 (6 Mar. 1802): 71.
60. Irving N. Rothman, "Structure and Theme in Samuel Ewing's Satire," 307.
61. Semonin, *American Monster*; Irving N. Rothman, "Structure and Theme in Samuel Ewing's Satire"; Dowling, *Literary Federalism in the Age of Jefferson*.
62. Columbian Museum and Daniel Bowen, *Bowen's Columbian Museum at the Head of the Mall, Boston*.
63. Ibid. For the significance of the Jacobin violence in the French Revolution, see Cleves, *Reign of Terror in America*.
64. Peale, *Guide to the Philadelphia Museum*.
65. Ibid., 9.
66. Scudder, *Companion to the American Museum*, vi.
67. Ibid., vii.
68. Orosz, *Curators and Culture*, 71.
69. Diary entry, 4 June 1817, in Peale, *Selected CWP*, 3:511–12. For a recent biography of Hosack, see Johnson, *American Eden*.
70. Orosz, *Curators and Culture*, 71–80, 131–39.
71. "Advertisement—Peale's Museum," *Poulson's American Daily Advertiser* (Philadelphia), 18 July 1810, 3.
72. Brigham, *Public Culture in the Early Republic*, 88–89.
73. Ibid., 106; for a breakdown of his analysis of ticket holders, see chap. 5.
74. Charles C. Sellers, *Mr. Peale's Museum*, 74–77; Peale, *Selected CWP*, 2, pt. 1: 24–26; "Charles Willson Peale to Thomas Jefferson, 2 May 1815," *Founders Online*, National Archives, https://founders.archives.gov/documents/Jefferson/03-08-02-0367.
75. "Charles Willson Peale to Thomas Jefferson, 2 May 1815."

76. For Peale's use of the world-in-miniature concept, see Charles Willson Peale to American Philosophical Society, 7 March 1797, in Peale, *Selected CWP*, 2:176–77.
77. I am grateful to Rosemarie Zagarri, who first told me about the society, and to Tony Guidone for many useful conversations about the SEIMS and for allowing me to view his completed dissertation. Guidone, "Empire's City." See also the following scholarship on the SEIMS: Lindgren, "'That Every Mariner May Possess the History of the World'"; Schwartz, *Collecting the Globe*; and Whitehill, *East India Marine Society and the Peabody Museum of Salem*.
78. East India Marine Society, *East-India Marine Society of Salem*.
79. Ibid.
80. John Fitzpatrick Jefferie to The President and Members of the East India Marine Society, December 1802, East India Marine Society Records, Box 3, Folder 1.
81. "Peele's Museum; Specimen; Salem; East-India; Marine; Society," *Salem (MA) Register*, 12 November 1804, 3.
82. X, "To the East India Marine Society," *Salem (MA) Gazette*, 5 November 1805, 2.
83. East India Marine Society, *By-Laws and Regulations of the East India Marine Society*. The society's first published museum catalog, produced in 1821 by the superintendent of the museum, Dr. Nathaniel Wallich, was included in the publication East India Marine Society, *East-India Marine Society of Salem*. The catalog described the society's collection as containing seven volumes recording sixty-seven voyages to destinations in Asia and across the Atlantic and Pacific Oceans from 1798 to 1821. The catalog also made clear that some types of objects were so numerous that not all could be listed.
84. "Salem East-India Marine Society," *Salem (MA) Gazette*, 9 January 1801.
85. "East India Marine Accessions," East India Marine Society Records, Box 24, Folder 1.
86. Guidone, "Empire's City," 309–13; Schwartz, *Collecting the Globe*, 27, 79–80.
87. "The Following Are the Toasts Drank at the Anniversary Meeting of the Salem East India Marine Society, on Wednesday Last," *Essex Register* (Salem, MA), 9 November 1807, 3.
88. East India Marine Society, *By-Laws and Regulations of the East India Marine Society*, 5, 7–8.
89. East India Marine Society, *East-India Marine Society of Salem*, 3–4.
90. "Advertisement," *Star of Liberty*, 3 November 1812, 1.

91. "Academy of Natural Sciences," *Philadelphia Gazette*, 20 April 1815, 2; "Academy of Natural Sciences," *Poulson's American Daily Advertiser* (Philadelphia), 19 August 1815, 3; "Lectures on Chemistry," *Philadelphia Gazette*, 3 January 1816, 2.
92. Baatz, "Philadelphia Patronage," 122.
93. For a biography of Maclure, see Warren, *Maclure of New Harmony*.
94. Academy of Natural Sciences, *Circular to Captains and Voyagers*, 1.
95. Ibid., 7–8.
96. "List of Donations to the Museum of the Academy of Natural Sciences," *Journal of the Academy of Natural Sciences of Philadelphia* 1, no. 6 (Oct. 1817): 213–19.
97. Thomas Say, "The Present Collection of the Academy of Natural Sciences of Philadelphia," 17 January 1817, Academy of Natural Sciences of Philadelphia, Minutes and Related Documents, 1812–1925.
98. Baatz, "Philadelphia Patronage"; Bennett, "1817 Florida Expedition of the Academy of Natural Sciences"; Peck, "To the Ends of the Earth for Science."
99. Mansfield, *Memoirs of the Life and Services of Daniel Drake*, 134.
100. "Intelligence: Art. XXIII. An Address to the People of the Western Country," *American Journal of Science (1818–1819)* 1, no. 2 (1819): 203; Shapiro, "Western Academy of Natural Sciences of Cincinnati"; Hendrickson, "Western Museum Society of Cincinnati."
101. "Intelligence: Art. XXIII. An Address to the People of the Western Country," 203.
102. Ibid., 203–4.
103. "Science of the West," *Columbian* (NY), 27 July 1820, 2.
104. "Review: An Anniversary Discourse, on the State and Prospects of the Western Museum Society; Delivered by Appointment, in the Chapel of the Cincinnati College, June 10 1820, on the Opening of the Museum," *Western Review and Miscellaneous Magazine, a Monthly Publication, Devoted to Literature and Science* 2, no. 6 (July 1820): 363–69.
105. "Review 1—No Title," *Philadelphia Register and National Recorder* 1, no. 17 (24 Apr. 1819): 286; Benson, *From Pittsburgh to the Rocky Mountains*, xxi.
106. "Expedition up the Missouri," *Niles' Weekly Register* (Baltimore), 31 July 1819, 377–78.

4. NATIONAL AGRICULTURAL INSTITUTIONS

1. Tocqueville, *Democracy in America*, 896.
2. Ibid., 897.

3. Ibid., 902.
4. Branson, *Scientific Americans*, 4 and 7; Daniels, *American Science in the Age of Jackson*; Porter, *Eagle's Nest*; Greene, *American Science in the Age of Jefferson*; Oleson and Brown, *Pursuit of Knowledge in the Early American Republic*.
5. Dupree, *Science in the Federal Government*; Brown, *Strength of a People*.
6. Allgor, *Parlor Politics*; Constance McLaughlin Green, *Washington*; Costanzo, *George Washington's Washington*.
7. George Washington, Eighth Annual Message to Congress, 7 December 1796; Ragsdale, *Washington at the Plow*, 179–81, 207–11.
8. The literature on this topic is expansive, but my understanding is informed especially by Schiebinger, *Plants and Empire*; O'Neill, *Peter Collinson and the Eighteenth-Century Natural History Exchange*; and essays such as Schiebinger, "Prospecting for Drugs"; and Lewis, "Gathering for the Republic." On Washington, see Ragsdale, *Washington at the Plow*, 179–81, 207–11. See also Pawley, *Nature of the Future*, 1–19, which shows the important connections between agricultural improvement, scientific progress, and capitalism.
9. Branson, *Scientific Americans*, 162; Pinkett, "Early Agricultural Societies in the District of Columbia."
10. Maryland Agricultural Society, *Articles of Association of the Maryland Agricultural Society*, 5.
11. Ibid., 6.
12. Turner, "Virginia State Agricultural Societies, 1811–1860."
13. Ron, *Grassroots Leviathan*.
14. Pinkett, "Early Agricultural Societies in the District of Columbia," 35.
15. "Matrimony Notice," *Daily National Intelligencer* (Washington, DC), 18 May 1810, 3.
16. "Exhibition; Columbian; Agricultural; Society; Union Tavern; George Town," *Pittsfield (MA) Sun*, 30 November 1811, 3; "Exhibition; Columbian Agricultural Society; Union Tavern; Georgetown; Mr. Steinberger; Virginia; Steer," *Hagers-Town Gazette* (Halifax, MD), 26 November 1811.
17. Armstead, *Freedom's Gardener*.
18. "Advertisement," *Independent American* (Georgetown, DC), 15 May 1810, 3.
19. "Columbian Agricultural Society," *Spirit of 'Seventy-Six* (Washington, DC), 22 May 1810, 3.
20. "Washington City. Thursday, November 22," *Daily National Intelligencer* (Washington, DC), 22 November 1810, 2; "From the Agricultural Museum. Columbian Agricultural Society," ibid., 4 December 1810, 3.
21. "Botany," *Connecticut Mirror* (Hartford), 2 January 1830.
22. Poinsett, Pinckney, and State Agricultural Society of South Carolina, *Report of the Committee, Appointed by the South Carolina Agricultural Society*, 7.

23. Ibid., 8.
24. Ibid., 11.
25. "Art. 72.—Proceedings of the Inspecting Committee of the New-York Horticultural Society," *New York Farmer* 2, no. 5 (May 1829): 120; Schakenbach Regele, *Flowers, Guns, and Money*, 4–7, 104–6, 157–60; Rippy, *Joel R. Poinsett*, 204–5.
26. "Art. XX.—Notice of Scientific Societies in the United States. Communicated for This Journal," *American Journal of Science and Arts* 10, no. 2 (June 1826): 369–76; Baatz, "'Squinting at Silliman'"; Marti, "Early Agricultural Societies in New York"; Pinkett, "Early Agricultural Societies in the District of Columbia"; True, "Early Days of the Albemarle Agricultural Society"; Ron, *Grassroots Leviathan;* Neely, *Agricultural Fair;* Rossiter, *Emergence of Agricultural Science;* Rossiter, "Organization of Agricultural Improvement in the United States, 1785–1865"; Ellsworth, "Philadelphia Society for the Promotion of Agriculture and Agricultural Reform, 1785–1793"; Turner, "Virginia State Agricultural Societies, 1811–1860"; Lynn A. Nelson, "When Land Was Cheap, and Labor Dear."
27. O'Neill, *Peter Collinson and the Eighteenth-Century Natural History Exchange;* Collinson, "Forget Not Mee & My Garden—."
28. O'Malley, "'Your Garden Must Be a Museum to You,'" 208.
29. Ibid., 213.
30. O'Malley, "'Your Garden Must Be a Museum to You'"; Pinkett, "Early Agricultural Societies in the District of Columbia"; Guthrie, *New System of Modern Geography*, 448.
31. Rathbun, *Columbian Institute for the Promotion of Arts and Sciences*, 5.
32. Barlow, *Vision of Columbus;* Ganter, "Active Virtue of *The Columbian Orator*"; Kenney, "America Discovers Columbus."
33. "An Account of the Origin and Progress of the Royal Institution of Great Britain," *Monthly Magazine or, British Register* 9, no. 58 (May 1800): 378.
34. "institute, n.1," *OED Online*, https://doi.org/10.1093/OED/8151899925; Constance McLaughlin Green, *Washington*, 1:69.
35. C [possibly Edward Cutbush, MD, the organization's president], "For the National Intelligencer," *Daily National Intelligencer* (Washington, DC), 19 August 1816, 3.
36. "The Columbian Institute," *Otsego Herald* (Cooperstown, NY), 31 October 1816, 2.
37. "Washington; Columbian; Institute; Arts; Sciences; National University," *American Advocate* (Hallowell, ME), 7 September 1816.
38. C, "For the National Intelligencer."

39. Costanzo, *George Washington's Washington*, 138–43. Many see the institution as a failure because of the short time it was in existence, but this is a limited view. The Columbian Institute established a solid groundwork for future institutional endeavors, and meaningful contributions were made to the development of scientific knowledge by members, including Thomas Law, Andrew Ellicott, and others.
40. Cutbush, *Observations on the Means of Preserving the Health of Soldiers and Sailors*, 256–57; Dupree, *Science in the Federal Government*, 33–35; Constance McLaughlin Green, *Washington*, 1:69.
41. Cutbush, *Address, Delivered Before the Columbian Institute*, 13.
42. Ibid., 12.
43. Rathbun, *Columbian Institute for the Promotion of Arts and Sciences*; Solit, *History of the United States Botanic Garden, 1816–1991*, 1–16; Elliot, *Washington Guide*, 295–310.
44. Fullilove, *Profit of the Earth*, 23–88; Sarudy, "Nurserymen and Seed Dealers in the Eighteenth-Century Chesapeake." See also MacLean, "Nursery and Seed Trade Catalogs," on the special collections at the National Library of Agriculture.
45. Langdon, *Catalogue of English Kitchen-Garden and Fancy Flower Seeds*.
46. M'Mahon, *Catalogue of Garden, Grass, Herb, Flower, Tree, and Shrub-Seeds, Flower-Roots, Andc. Andc.*; Grundy, *Catalogue of Kitchen-Garden, Field, and Flower-Seeds, Plants, Andc.*
47. M'Mahon, *Catalogue of Garden, Herb, Flower, Tree, Shrub, and Grass Seeds, Gardening, Agricultural and Botanical Books, Garden Tools, Andc.*, 4–5.
48. Ian Dyck, "Cobbett, William (1763–1835), Political Writer and Farmer," *Oxford Dictionary of National Biography*, https://doi-org.mutex.gmu.edu/10.1093/ref:odnb/5734.
49. Cobbett, *List of Field Seeds and Garden Seeds, Contained in One of the Boxes*; "English Seeds," *Evening Post* (New York), 30 March 1819, 2.
50. Cobbett, *List of Field Seeds and Garden Seeds, Contained in One of the Boxes*.
51. Ibid., 4.
52. For a useful assortment of tasks and work conducted by consuls, see the thirty-four episodes created in 2020–22 of the podcast series "Consolation Prize: A podcast about consuls from the Roy Rosenzweig Center for History and New Media," https://consolationprize.rrchnm.org/. This work, led by Abby Mullen and Megan Brett, provides exceptional background information.
53. Schakenbach Regele, *Flowers, Guns, and Money*, 33–77; Rippy, *Joel R. Poinsett*, 10–34.
54. Andrew Rolle, "Poinsett, Joel Roberts (1779–1851), Diplomat and Statesman," *American National Biography Online*, https://doi-org.mutex.gmu

.edu/10.1093/anb/9780198606697.article.0300390. Rolle calls the position equivalent to that of a consul, while James Hammond in the South Carolina Encyclopedia calls him a "U.S. trade envoy to South America." See James T. Hammond, "Poinsett, Joel Roberts," South Carolina Encyclopedia, https://www.scencyclopedia.org/sce/entries/poinsett-joel-roberts/. The editors of The Papers of James Madison show that his title changed to consul general on 30 April 1811 in response to a desire of the revolutionary junta in Argentina. See note 2 in "To James Madison from the Junta of the Provinces of the Río de la Plata, 13 February 1811 (Abstract)," *Founders Online,* National Archives, https://founders.archives.gov/documents/Madison/03-03-02-0213.

55. "To James Madison from Albert Gallatin, 15 August 1810," *Founders Online,* National Archives, https://founders.archives.gov/documents/Madison/03-02-02-0600.
56. Fitz, *Our Sister Republics,* 21–22; Schakenbach Regele, *Flowers, Guns, and Money,* 33–54; Rippy, *Joel R. Poinsett.*
57. Joel R. Poinsett, "Report of Mr. Poinsett on the Condition of South America," American State Papers: Foreign Relations, 4:323, https://congressional-proquest-com.mutex.gmu.edu/congressional/docview/t47.d48.asp04_for.rel.305_6?accountid=14541.
58. Ibid., 4:323–48.
59. Fitz, *Our Sister Republics,* 1.
60. Rasmussen, "Diplomats and Plant Collectors."
61. Baldwin, *Short Practical Narrative of the Diseases Which Prevailed Among the American Seamen.* Baldwin represents a group of men who were ambitious and sought intellectual improvement. I rely on Joyce Oldham Appleby, *Inheriting the Revolution,* 90–128; and Opal, *Beyond the Farm,* for my understanding of these people.
62. Baldwin, *A Short Practical Narrative of the Diseases Which Prevailed Among the American Seamen.*
63. Baldwin and Muhlenberg, *Reliquiae Baldwinianae,* 245.
64. Ibid., 246. In fact, his letters are filled with significant details about plants and the regions in which they thrived.
65. "Bonpland's Useful Exertions in the Region Watered by the River La Plata," *American Farmer,* 25 August 1820, 176.
66. "Art. XVII.—Account of an Expedition from Pittsburgh to the Rocky Mountains," *North American Review,* April 1823, 243.
67. Lewis, "Gathering for the Republic"; Benson, *From Pittsburgh to the Rocky Mountains,* 69–70; Nichols, *Stephen Long and American Frontier Exploration;* Richard G. Wood, *Stephen Harriman Long.*
68. Daniel Walker Howe, *Political Culture of the American Whigs,* 13, 16, 43–68.

69. Daniel Walker Howe, *What Hath God Wrought*, 328–410; Charles G. Sellers, *Market Revolution*.
70. Hofstadter, *Anti-Intellectualism in American Life*, 154–71, remains a critically important text for this issue, as does Daniel Walker Howe, *What Hath God Wrought*, 447–82. See also Feller, *Jacksonian Promise*, 83–94; and Remini, *Andrew Jackson and the Course of American Freedom, 1822–1832*, 100–142.
71. John Quincy Adams, First Annual Message to Congress, 6 December 1825, "Presidential Speeches," UVA Miller Center, https://millercenter.org/the-presidency/presidential-speeches/december-6-1825-first-annual-message; Portolano, *Passionate Empiricist*, 53–76; Portolano, "John Quincy Adams's Rhetorical Crusade for Astronomy."
72. Daniel Walker Howe, *What Hath God Wrought*, 252–53; Castel, "Founding Fathers and the Vision of a National University."
73. Watkins, *Anniversary Discourse Delivered Before the Columbian Institute*, 3.
74. Ibid., 23.
75. Ibid., 15; for the broader arguments, see 15–21.
76. Remini, *Andrew Jackson and the Course of American Freedom, 1822–1832*, 186–87; Ebert, "Rise and Development of the American Medical Periodical, 1797–1850."
77. Ray, *Lyceum and Public Culture in the Nineteenth-Century United States*, 1–12.
78. Ray and Stob, Introduction; Eastman, "Conclusion: Placing Platform Culture in Nineteenth-Century American Life."
79. "County Meeting," *Spectator* (New York), 12 February 1819, 3.
80. "Advertisement," *Columbian* (New York), 22 April 1819, 3.
81. "Deligates; Colleges; Middle; Summoned; Important Work," *Utica (NY) Patriot, & Patrol*, 11 May 1819, 2.
82. Daniel Walker Howe, *What Hath God Wrought*, 619–20.
83. Wilson and Patia, "Authentic Imitation or Perverse Original?"; Eastman, *Nation of Speechifiers*, 212. The latter convincingly makes the case that local lyceums served as a means to promote the "star 'lecturers' by the 1850s."
84. Symmes, *Light Gives Light, to Light Discover*.
85. John Cleves Symmes, "Circular," *Boston Weekly Magazine & Ladies' Miscellany* 2, no. 33 (29 June 1818): 131.
86. Existing scholarship on Symmes is mostly from literary scholars and popular history. Lang and Lease, "Authorship of Symzonia"; Blum, "John Cleves Symmes and the Planetary Reach of Polar Exploration"; Madden, "John Cleves Symmes Revisited"; Gustaitis, "Hole Truth of John Cleves Symmes"; Standish, *Hollow Earth*. Michael A. Verney's important book *A Great*

and Rising Nation does deal with Symmes in a broader context; see pp. 23–24, 29–30.
87. Verney, *Great and Rising Nation*, 19–26.
88. James McBride, "James McBride's Scrapbook of Articles on the Hollow Earth Theory Lectures of John Symmes," 47–50, Academy of Natural Sciences of Philadelphia, Minutes and Related Documents, 1812–1925.
89. McBride and Symmes, *Symmes's Theory of Concentric Spheres*, iii,
90. "To Thomas Jefferson from Thomas Spottswood Hinde, 28 December 1824," *Founders Online*, National Archives, https://founders.archives.gov/documents/Jefferson/98-01-02-4817.
91. Henry Howe, "Romantic History of Jeremiah N. Reynolds."
92. Ibid.; Reynolds, *Beneath the American Renaissance*, 195; Verney, *Great and Rising Nation*, 25.
93. Andrew Jackson to John Branch, 3 March 1826, in The Papers of Andrew Jackson Digital Edition, https://rotunda.upress.virginia.edu/founders/JKSN-01-06-02-0103.
94. John Quincy Adams, First Annual Message to Congress, 6 December 1825; Parsons, *Birth of Modern Politics*, 114–15.
95. Pasley, *"Tyranny of Printers,"* esp. 356, 392; Parsons, *Birth of Modern Politics*, 134–37.
96. Richard Rush and United States Department of the Treasury, *Circular to Consuls*, 1, 5.
97. Ibid., 7–12.
98. Neely, *Agricultural Fair*, 83–87.
99. Dearborn, *Address Delivered Before the Massachusetts Horticultural Society*, 8.
100. Ibid., 10.
101. Rossiter, "Organization of Agricultural Improvement in the United States, 1785–1865."
102. Marti, "Early Agricultural Societies in New York." Under DeWitt Clinton's program of internal development, the Albany Lyceum received a state subsidy to underwrite its program, but this subsidy was cut off when the Clintonians were defeated in the mid-1820s. Further state aid was denied the agricultural societies until the 1840s, which seriously undermined their effectiveness. The promoters of these institutions beginning with Robert Livingston in 1794 saw these practices as part of the goal to establish all-inclusive improvements via civic society.
103. New York Board of Agriculture, preface to *Memoirs of the Board of Agriculture of the State of New-York* 3 (1826): 3.

104. Rossiter, "Organization of Agricultural Improvement in the United States, 1785–1865."
105. Henry, *Papers of Joseph Henry*, 4:167. On the basis of references made in the letter regarding the experiments that discredited Mr. Cross's claims about electricity being able to fertilize insect eggs, the editors of the *Papers of Joseph Henry* estimate that Henry wrote the letter after 1837. Interestingly, they also believe that Henry sent the letter to the editor of New York's *Genessee Farmer* or the editor of the *Cultivator* since they had printed the stories he was writing to discredit. Also these stories made the rounds in several newspapers. See 4:167n3.
106. Ibid. 4:167.
107. Ibid., 4:xviii.
108. Ibid., 4:97–99.
109. Ibid., 4:100.
110. Kohlstedt, *Formation of the American Scientific Community*, 25–58.
111. "A Dictionary of Terms Used in Agriculture and Its Kindred Sciences," *Cultivator* 7, no. 12 (Dec. 1840): 187.
112. Ibid.
113. Dearborn, *Address Delivered Before the Berkshire Agricultural Society at Pittsfield*, 22–24.
114. Poinsett, *Discourse, on the Objects and Importance of the National Institution for the Promotion of Science*, 6.
115. Henry Alexander Scammell Dearborn to J. R. Poinsett, 22 April 1841, National Institute, Records, Series 1, Box 1.
116. See Distributive Preemption Act, 1841, 5 Stat. 453.
117. US Congress, House, Select Committee on Smithsonian Bequest, "Memorial of Charles Lewis Fleischmann in Relation to the Smithsonian Legacy," H.R. Doc. 70, 25th Cong., 3rd sess. (1938), 2.
118. Dalrymple, "Smithsonian Bequest, Congress, and Nineteenth-Century Efforts to Increase and Diffuse Agricultural Knowledge in the United States"; Rossiter, "Organization of Agricultural Improvement in the United States, 1785–1865."

5. A NATIONAL RESEARCH INSTITUTION

1. James Smithson, "Last Will and Testament, October 23, 1826," in Rhees, *Smithsonian Institution*, 1:6.
2. Thomas, *Founders and the Idea of a National University*; Madsen, *National University*; Castel, "Founding Fathers and the Vision of a National University."

3. There is a rich and nuanced scholarship on the founding of the Smithsonian, of which the following have been very helpful: Ewing, *Lost World of James Smithson*; Oehser, *Smithsonian Institution*; Burleigh, *Stranger and the Statesman*; Goode, *Smithsonian Institution, 1846–1896*. Works about key people include Moyer, *Joseph Henry*; Jansen, *Alexander Dallas Bache*; Borome, *Charles Coffin Jewett*; and Matthews, *Rufus Choate*.
4. Ewing, *Lost World of James Smithson*, 280, 303–4, 313, 347.
5. *Christian Watchman* (Boston), 1 January 1836; *Pawtucket (RI) Chronicle and Manufacturers' and Artizans' Advocate*, 1 January 1836; *Easton (MD) Star*, 5 January 1836; *Columbian Centinel* (Boston), 6 January 836; *Hampshire Gazette* (Northampton, MA), 6 January 1836; "Bequest of James Smithson," *Alexandria (VA) Gazette*, 29 December 1835; "Bequest of James Smithson," *Evening Post* (New York), 29 December 1835; "Bequest of James Smithson," *Commercial Advertiser* (New York), 31 December 1835; "Bequest of James Smithson," *New-York American for the Country*, 1 January 1836; "Bequest of James Smithson," *Emporium and True American* (Trenton, NJ), 2 January 1836; *Portsmouth (NH) Journal of Literature & Politics*, 2 January 1836; "Congress," *Watchman* (Wilmington, DE), 5 January 1836; "Congressional Synopsis: The University," *Easton (MD) Star*, 2 January 1836; "District Affairs," *Alexandria (VA) Gazette*, 7 January 1836; "Indian; David Davis; New Haven; Sailors; Allen," *Massachusetts Spy* (Worcester), 6 January 1836; "Items," *Portland (ME) Daily Advertiser*, 6 January 1836; "James Smithson; United States; Congress," *North Carolina Sentinel* (Newbern), 13 January 1836; "Legislative Acts / Legal Proceedings," *Newport (RI) Mercury*, 26 December 1835; "Legislative Acts / Legal Proceedings," *Jeffersonian* (New Orleans), 28 December 1835; "Legislative Acts / Legal Proceedings," *Rhode-Island Republican* (Newport), 30 December 1835; "Legislative Acts / Legal Proceedings," *New-Bedford (MA) Mercury*, 1 January 1836; "Legislative Acts / Legal Proceedings," *Columbian Register* (New Haven), 2 January 1836; "Legislative Acts / Legal Proceedings," *Saturday Morning Transcript* (Concord, NH), 2 January 1836; "Legislative Acts / Legal Proceedings," *New Hampshire Patriot and State Gazette* (Concord), 4 January 1836; "Legislative Acts / Legal Proceedings," *The Age* (Augusta, ME), 6 January 1836; "Legislative Acts / Legal Proceedings; The Smithson Legacy," *Daily National Intelligencer* (Washington, DC), 30 December 1835; "Legislative Acts / Legal Proceedings: Bequest of James Smithson," *Baltimore Gazette and Daily Advertiser*, 28 December 1835; "Legislative Acts / Legal Proceedings: House of Representatives," *Alexandria (VA) Gazette*, 30 December 1835; "Legislative Acts / Legal Proceedings: National University," *Commercial Advertiser* (New Orleans), 7 January 1836; "Legislative Acts /

Legal Proceedings: New College," *Saratoga Sentinel* (Saratoga Springs, NY), 29 December 1835; "Legislative Acts / Legal Proceedings: Smithsonian Institution," *Southern Patriot* (Charleston, SC), 28 December 1835; "Monument to Washington," *Daily Commercial Bulletin* (Chicago), 25 March 1836; "National College," *Essex North Register* (Salem, MA), 8 January 1836; "New College," *Evening Star* (Washington, DC), 23 December 1835; "New College," *Daily Pennsylvanian* (Philadelphia), 24 December 1835; "President; Congress; Mr. James Smithson; London; United States; Washington; Smithsonian; Institution," *Pittsfield (MA) Sun*, 31 December 1835; "President; Congress; Mr. James; London; Smithsonian Institution," *Salem (MA) Gazette*, 29 December 1835; "Selected Summary," *Boston Traveler*, 1 January 1836; "Smithsonian Institution," *Newark (NJ) Daily Advertiser*, 30 December 1835; "The Bequest," *Lynchburg Virginian*, 4 January 1836; "The Following Is the Committee of the House of Representatives on the Bequest of James Smithson," *Daily National Intelligencer* (Washington, DC), 1 January 1836; "The National University," *New Bedford (MA) Gazette*, 28 December 1835; "The Smithson Bequest," *Albany (NY) Argus*, 5 January 1836; "The Smithson Bequest," *Ulster Republican* (Kingston, NY), 6 January 1836; "The University," *United States' Telegraph* (Washington, DC), 22 December 1835; "Twenty-Fourth Congress First Session," *Daily Commercial Advertiser* (Philadelphia), 29 December 1835; "Twenty-Fourth Congress First Session-Senate," *Daily Pennsylvanian* (Philadelphia), 7 January 1836; "Twenty-Fourth Congress First Session: Bequest of James Smithson," ibid., 30 December 1835; "Twenty-Fourth Congress First Session: New College," *Jerseyman* (Morris-Town, NJ), 30 December 1835; "Washington Correspondence," *Alexandria (VA) Gazette*, 24 December 1835; "What's in a Name," *Norfolk (VA) Advertiser*, 9 January 1836.

6. John Quincy Adams, House of Representatives, 19 January 1836, in Rhees, *Smithsonian Institution*, 1:130–34.

7. Goode, *Smithsonian Institution, 1846–1896*, 26; Dupree, *Science in the Federal Government*; Manning, *U.S. Coast Survey vs. Naval Hydrographic Office*.

8. William C. Preston, 30 April 1836, in Rhees, *Smithsonian Institution*, 1:136–37.

9. Rhees, *Smithsonian Institution*, 1:129.

10. The story of Richard Rush securing in just under two years of strategic maneuvering in the Court of Chancery the Smithson bequest in gold is told in several works, including Burleigh, *Stranger and the Statesman*, 181–205; Ewing, *Lost World of James Smithson*, 319–25; and Goode, *Smithsonian Institution, 1846–1896*, 28–31. It is important to note that the diplomat was the son of Benjamin Rush, the early advocate a the national university who first argued in 1787 that "The Revolution Is Not Over!" and stressed the paramount

need to create a national identity by "convert[ing] men into republican machines." See Benjamin Rush, "Address to the People of the United States," *American Museum; or, Repository of Ancient and Modern Fugitive Pieces &c. Prose and Poetical* 1, no. 1 (Jan. 1787): 8; and Rush, *Plan for the Establishment of Public Schools*, 27.

11. US Congress, House, Select Committee on Smithsonian Bequest, "Message from the President of the United States, upon the subject of the bequest of James Smithson to the United States," H.R. Doc. 11, 25th Cong., 3rd sess. (1838), 2.
12. Christman, *1846*; Walker, *Living Exhibition*; Ewing, *Lost World of James Smithson*; Hinsley, *Smithsonian and the American Indian*; Daniel Walker Howe, *What Hath God Wrought*, 468.
13. These eleven are designated in the official collections of documents related to the founding of the Smithsonian in Rhees, *Smithsonian Institution*, but there were many memorials and other proposals issues by individuals and organizations that were submitted to Congress or published in periodicals during this period.
14. "Letter from Thomas Cooper M.D. to John Forsyth," 20 July 1838, in Rhees, *Smithsonian Institution*, 1:337; US Congress, House, Select Committee on Smithsonian Bequest, "Message from the President of the United States, upon the subject of the bequest of James Smithson to the United States," 10–11.
15. "Letter from Francis Wayland to John Forsyth," 2 October 1838, in US Congress, House, Select Committee on Smithsonian Bequest, "Message from the President of the United States, upon the subject of the bequest of James Smithson to the United States," 5–10.
16. Congressman George M. Keim of Pennsylvania proposed in 1839 that Americans establish a "professorship of the German language as a part of the literary instruction in the intended Smithsonian Institute" to promote German-language expertise in the United States. Learning German would promote access to the scholarship and methods emerging at German universities. See Rhees, *Smithsonian Institution*, 1:169.
17. Walter R. Johnson, "Establishment of an Institution for Experiments in Physical Sciences: Memorial of Walter R. Johnson of Philadelphia," 21 May 1838, H.R. Doc. 896, 25th Cong., 2nd sess. (1838). See also Rhees, *Smithsonian Institution*, 1:146–55.
18. "IX. Walter R. Johnson: List of Publications by Walter R. Johnson. I. Educational. II. Scientific and Miscellaneous," *American Journal of Education* 15 (Dec. 1858): 780–98.
19. Walter R. Johnson, "Establishment of an Institution for Experiments in Physical Sciences," 11.

20. Ibid., 2–3; the nine objectives, listed on pp. 3–11, make up the bulk of the memorial.
21. See chapter 4; Dalrymple, "Smithsonian Bequest, Congress, and Nineteenth-Century Efforts to Increase and Diffuse Agricultural Knowledge in the United States"; and Rossiter, "Organization of Agricultural Improvement in the United States, 1785–1865."
22. Cahan, *From Natural Philosophy to the Sciences*, 313; Altar, *Reluctant Patron*, 1–12; Phillips, *Acolytes of Nature*, 11.
23. "Period; Rooms; Lodge; Americans; Civilized; Houses; Crowded; City," *Spooner's Vermont Journal* (Windsor), 6 November 1820, 1.
24. "German University," *Album, & Ladies' Weekly Gazette* 1, no. 35 (31 Jan. 1827): 5.
25. Here I rely on the important ideas of Chad Wellmon, in *Organizing Enlightenment*, who demonstrates the evolution of the modern research university as a tool for dealing with the information overload; see esp. pp. 3–19. See also Phillips, *Acolytes of Nature*, 5–25, esp. the case of Jacob Sturm on pp. 11–14.
26. National Institute for the Promotion of Science, *Bulletin of the Proceedings*, 3.
27. Peter S. DuPonceau to Francis Markoe Jr., November 1840, in National Institute for the Promotion of Science, *Bulletin of the Proceedings*, 10–11.
28. See esp. Achim, *From Idols to Antiquity*, 21–54. Poinsett secured numerous collections for the American Philosophical Society and other learned societies by engaging with Lucas Alamán, Mexico's minister of interior and exterior relations and founder of the National Museum of Mexico, on commercial treaties and conducting trades for specimens. For biographical accounts on Poinsett, see Schakenbach Regele, *Flowers, Guns, and Money*; and Rippy, *Joel R. Poinsett*.
29. See esp. "Notes on Mexico," *Port-Folio* (Philadelphia), December 1824, 1, where the editor claimed that Poinsett's work excited "our curiosity concerning [Mexico's] character and prospects," especially "its proximity to the United States, . . . a population of nearly seven millions; a territory capable of maintaining many times that number; . . . a fine climate and fruitful soil; rich and various productions; sea-ports of easy access; the possession of inexhaustible mines of precious metals are circumstances which powerfully attest our attention." See also Poinsett's book *Notes on Mexico: Made in the Autumn of 1822*.
30. "Museum: Of the Literary and Philosophical Society," *United States Catholic Miscellany*, 25 November 1826.
31. "Multiple News Items," *Daily National Journal* (Washington, DC), 8 June 1827.

32. Clement C. Moore, "Extract from the Minutes," 10 July 1828, United States Legation in Mexico Papers, 1824–1843; "Mexican Antiquities," *Transactions of the American Philosophical Society* 3 (1830): 510–11. See also the digitized collection of approximately 614 drawings of these Mexican antiquities on eighty-one sheets made available by the British Museum.
33. Prescott, *History of the Conquest of Mexico*, 143; Winterer, *American Enlightenments*, 107–9.
34. George Brown Goode, "Memorial of George Brown Goode," in Smithsonian Institution, Board of Regents, *Annual Report of the Board of Regents of the Smithsonian Institution* (1897), 2:106; "National Institute for the Promotion of Science: Circular," *Globe* (Washington, DC), 20 October 1842, 3.
35. "National Institute for the Promotion of Science: Circular," *Globe* (Washington, DC), 20 October 1842, 3.
36. Verney, *Great and Rising Nation*, 98.
37. National Institute for the Promotion of Science, *Second Bulletin of the Proceedings*, 69–70.
38. "Stated Meeting, August 9, 1841," in ibid., 100; "Legislative Acts / Legal Proceedings," *American Commercial Daily Advertiser* (Baltimore), 19 February 1841, 2; US Congress, Senate, "Text—S.259—26th Congress (1839–1841): A Bill to invest the proceeds of the Smithsonian fund, and to establish the Smithsonian Institution," 17 February 1841, in Rhees, *Smithsonian Institution*, 1:219.
39. Schakenbach Regele, *Flowers, Guns, and Money*, 150–60.
40. "Literary: From the Edinburg Journal of Science—Congress of Philosophers," *Boston Recorder*, 24 November 1830, 179.
41. "To the Editor of the Evening Post," *Evening Post* (New York), 30 September 1830, 1.
42. "Washington Liberty and Union Now and Forever One and Inseparable," *Daily National Intelligencer* (Washington, DC), 2 April 1844, 3.
43. "National Institute Third Day's Session," *Daily National Intelligencer* (Washington, DC), 4 April 1844, 3.
44. "Agriculture," *Baltimore Sun*, 8 September 1841; National Institute for the Promotion of Science, *Second Bulletin of the Proceedings of the National Institute for the Promotion of Science*, 131.
45. Kohlstedt, "Step toward Scientific Self-Identity in the United States."
46. Charles C. Sellers, *Mr. Peale's Museum*, 293. See also Antony Adler, "From the Pacific to the Patent Office," 55.
47. Stanton, *Great United States Exploring Expedition of 1838–1842*, 316–37.
48. U.S. Congress, Senate, *A Bill for the Preservation of the Collection of Natural Curiosities Furnished by the Exploring Squadron, and from Other Sources*, S. Doc. 116, 27th Cong., 3rd sess. (1843).

49. Michael Verney has done an amazing job exploring the publications related to the Exploration Expedition. See his *Great and Rising Nation*. Other interesting works on the changing nature of the naturalist collector and the scientific expert can be found in Bert Chapman, "Initial Visions of Paradise"; and Porter, *Eagle's Nest*, 125–34.
50. Barnum, *Life of P.T. Barnum*, 230–42; Greenberg, "The Nose, the Lie, and the Duel in the Antebellum South"; Cook, *Arts of Deception*, 73–118.
51. "American Museum," *New York Herald*, November 1842, 3.
52. Greenberg, *Honor and Slavery*, 3–23.
53. Harris, *Humbug*, 74–83.
54. "The Medical Faculty," *Alexandria (VA) Gazette*, 21 November 1849, 2.
55. John Torrey to Joseph Henry, 2 August 1838, in Henry, *Papers of Joseph Henry*, 4:85. See also the example in chapter 4. The edited volumes of Henry's papers have copious examples of charlatans and the concerns mentioned by those with whom Henry corresponded.
56. Joseph Henry to Samuel B. Morse, 24 February 1842, in Henry, *Papers of Joseph Henry*, 5:150.
57. Dupree, *Science in the Federal Government*, 76–79.
58. Ewing, *Lost World of James Smithson*, 330.
59. "An Act to establish the 'Smithsonian Institution,' for the Increase and Diffusion of Knowledge among Men," 10 August 1846, *United States Statutes at Large*, 9:102.
60. Ibid., 103. The initial board of regents included George M. Dallas, of Pennsylvania, vice president of the United States; Roger B. Taney, of Maryland, chief justice of the United States; William W. Seaton, mayor of the city of Washington; Senator George Evans of Maine; Senator Isaac S. Pennybacker of Virginia; Senator Sidney Breese of Illinois; Congressman Robert Dale Owen of Indiana; Congressman William J. Hough of New York; Congressman Henry W. Hilliard of Alabama; the Honorable Rufus Choate of Massachusetts; Dr. Gideon Hawley, of New York; Richard Rush, of Pennsylvania, citizens at large; and Dr. Alexander Dallas Bache and Colonel Joseph G. Totten, representing the National Institute of Washington.
61. Ibid.; Goode, *Smithsonian Institution, 1846–1896*, 25–60.
62. "An Act to establish the 'Smithsonian Institution,'" 105.
63. Moyer, *Joseph Henry*, 253–60; Jansen, *Alexander Dallas Bache*.
64. Moyer, *Joseph Henry*, 255.
65. Ibid., 256.
66. Alexander Dallas Bache to Joseph Henry, 4 December 1846, in Henry, *Papers of Joseph Henry*, 6:566; see also 6:544–55, 564–67.
67. Ibid., 564–67.

68. Joseph Henry to Harriet Henry, 22 December 1846, in ibid., 604.
69. Joseph Henry to Eliphalet Nott, 26 December 1846, in ibid., 608.
70. Ewing, *Lost World of James Smithson*, 315–42; Matthews, *Rufus Choate*, 106–46. For in-depth details on the various compromises and types of proposals throughout the decade, see Dupree, *Science in the Federal Government*, 66–90.
71. Smithsonian Institution, Board of Regents, *Annual Report of the Board of Regents of the Smithsonian Institution* (1848), 3–4.
72. Ibid., 6.
73. There needs to be a systematic study of this publication and its impact on scholarship in the transatlantic community. Hints of the importance of this work can be seen in works exploring racial pseudoscientific work, such as Fabian, *Skull Collectors*; Dain, *Hideous Monster of the Mind*; and Ragan Stanton, *Leopard's Spots*.
74. Smithsonian Institution, Board of Regents, *Annual Report of the Board of Regents of the Smithsonian Institution* (1848), 5.
75. John Quincy Adams, 18 October 1847, in John Quincy Adams diary 46, 14 August 1846–4 January 1848, p. 196, in *The Diaries of John Quincy Adams: A Digital Collection*, Massachusetts Historical Society, 2005, http://www.masshist.orh/jqadiaries. Henry did send his program to Adams for his feedback, which was what prompted the diary entry. There is no evidence of a response to Henry's request.
76. *Annual Report of the Board of Regents of the Smithsonian Institution.* (1848), report on 172–91, appendixes on 191–208.
77. Ibid., 174–75.
78. Ibid., 179–81. Here Henry speaks about the challenges scientists faced in trying to sell enough copies of their books to cover the costs of publication and said that often they did not.
79. Fleming, *Meteorology in America*, 23–73.
80. Smithsonian Institution, *Circular on Meteorology*, 1 November 1848, Smithsonian Institution Archives, SIA-SIA2012-2724.
81. Fleming, *Meteorology in America*, 76–77.
82. Ibid., 82.
83. Many newspapers report the language of the "Programme of Organization," but the following article is especially detailed: "Researches as to the Phenomena of American Storms," *Semi-Weekly Eagle* (Brattleboro, VT), 5 March 1849, 2. See also Grossman, "Gendering Nineteenth-Century Data," 89.
84. "Prof. Henry Secretary of the Smithsonian Institute," *Newark (NJ) Daily Advertiser*, 9 October 1849, 2. The article reports that New York committed to three thousand dollars.

85. Grossman, "Gendering Nineteenth-Century Data," 89.
86. Fleming, *Meteorology in America*, 81; Joseph Henry Collection, Pocket and Desk Diaries and Notebooks, Smithsonian Institution Archives, Record Unit 7001, Series 7, Box 13, Folder 9.
87. Grossman, "Gendering Nineteenth-Century Data," 85–86, 88–96.
88. Ibid., 99.
89. Ibid., 90, 108n88.
90. Smithsonian Institution, "Circular on Programme and Libraries," 17 November 1848, in Henry, *Papers of Joseph Henry*, 7:422–23.
91. Jewett, *Notices of Public Libraries*; Jewett, *On the Construction of Catalogues of Libraries*.
92. Charles C. Jewett, "'Plan for Stereotyping Catalogues by Separate Titles; and Forming a General Stereotyped Catalogue of Public Libraries in the United States,'" in *Proceedings of the American Association for the Advancement of Science* 4 (1854): 165–75. See also Jewett, *Plan for Stereotyping Catalogues by Separate Titles*.
93. "Librarians' Convention," *Norton's Literary Gazette* 2, no. 7 (15 July 1852): 128.
94. "The Result of the Librarians' Convention," *Norton's Literary Gazette* 3, no. 10 (15 Oct. 1853): 176.
95. "Proceedings of the Librarians' Convention, Held in New York, September 15, " ibid., 170–76.
96. Henry fired Jewett for insubordination as they clashed over the mission of the institution. This topic is well covered in works such as Ostrowski, *Books, Maps, and Politics*, 145–78. For more on libraries in the period, see Carpenter, "Libraries.". For more on Jewett, see Boromé, *Charles Coffin Jewett*; and Jewett, *Age of Jewett*.
97. "The Smithsonian Institute.—A Mystery," *Augusta (GA) Chronicle*, 5 January 1854. Here, the prairie is the empty space along the mall and the author is describing the unique characteristic of the Smithsonian building commonly called the castle.
98. Ibid.
99. Ibid.
100. "Smithsonian Institution," *Alexandria (VA) Gazette*, 30 December 1853, 3.
101. Joseph Henry, "The Lecture Room, Smithsonian Institution, Washington," *Canadian Journal of Industry, Science & Art* 3, no. 14 (Mar. 1858): 110–15.
102. "Literary Celebrities of Boston, U. S.," *Illustrated London News*, 20 March 1858; "The British Association," ibid., 14 September 1861; S. M. Gilliss, "An Account of Astronomical Observations Proposed to Be Made in South

America. By S. M. Gilliss, in an Extract of a Letter to Lieut.-Col. Sabine, R. A., For. Sec. R. S. Communicated by Lieut.-Col. Sabine," *Abstracts of the Papers Communicated to the Royal Society of London* 5 (Jan. 1997): 768–70.
103. Smithsonian Institution, Board of Regents, *Annual Report of the Board of Regents of the Smithsonian Institution* (1857), 59.
104. Smithsonian Institution, Board of Regents, *Tenth Annual Report of the Board of Regents of the Smithsonian Institution* (1855), 16.

CONCLUSION

1. Smithsonian Institution, "Human Remains Task Force Report to the Secretary, 10 January 2024," https://web.archive.org/web/20240222233557mp_/https://www.si.edu/sites/default/files/about/human-remains-task-force-report.pdf.
2. Exec. Order No. 14253, "Restoring Truth and Sanity to American History," 27 March 2025, https://www.whitehouse.gov/presidential-actions/2025/03/restoring-truth-and-sanity-to-american-history/.
3. Henson, "Spencer Baird's Dream."
4. Sorber, *Land-Grant Colleges and Popular Revolt*, 45–83.
5. Gilman, *Our National Schools of Science*, 4–7.

BIBLIOGRAPHY

PRIMARY SOURCES

Manuscript Collections

Academy of Natural Sciences of Philadelphia. Minutes and Related Documents, 1812–1925. Drexel University Library and Archives, Philadelphia.
American Philosophical Society Minutes, 1787–1798. American Philosophical Society Archives, Philadelphia.
Columbia Institute, Records. Record Unit 7051. Smithsonian Institution Archives.
Curator's Record of Donations to the Cabinet, 1769–1818. American Philosophical Society Archives, Philadelphia.
Derby Family Papers. Phillips Library, Rowley, MA.
East Indian Marine Society Records. Phillips Library, Peabody Essex Museum, Salem, MA.
Force, Peter. Papers and Collection. Manuscript Division, Library of Congress.
  Series VIII B. Ebenezer Hazard Collection.
  Series VIII D. Other Collections, 1632–1873
Jefferson, Thomas. The Thomas Jefferson Papers. Series 1, General Correspondence. Manuscript Division, Library of Congress.
Meehan, John Silva. Papers. Manuscript Division, Library of Congress.
National Institute, Records. Record Unit 7058. Smithsonian Institution Archives.
Thornton, William. Papers. Manuscript Division, Library of Congress.
United States Department of War. Papers of the War Department, 1784–1800. Roy Rosenzweig Center for History and New Media, George Mason University.
United States Legation in Mexico Papers, 1824–1843. Latin American Library at Tulane.
United States Military Philosophical Society Records, 1789–1813. New York Historical Society.
Vaughan, Benjamin. Papers. American Philosophical Society Archives, Philadelphia.
Vaughan, John. Papers. American Philosophical Society Archives, Philadelphia.
Watterston, George. Paper. Manuscript Division, Library of Congress.
Williams, Jonathan. Manuscripts. Lilly Library, Indiana University, Bloomington.

BIBLIOGRAPHY

Databases

American Antiquarian Periodicals Series 1–6
American History, 1493–1946. Gilder Lehrman Collection
    Henry Knox Papers
    Livingston Family Papers
American National Biography Online
American Periodicals Series I–II
American Philosophical Society Members Database
America's Historical Imprints
    Evans
    Library Company of Philadelphia Supplements 1 and 2
    Shaw-Shoemaker
Biographical Directory of the United States Congress
Founders Online, National Archives
    The Papers of John Adams
    The Papers of Alexander Hamilton
    The Papers of Thomas Jefferson
    The Papers of James Madison
    The Papers of George Washington
Frontier Life: Borderlands, Settlement and Colonial Encounters
    Papers of Joel Roberts Poinsett
HathiTrust
Mapping Early American Elections
Oxford Dictionary of National Biography
Oxford English Dictionary
ProQuest Congressional
    American State Papers
    Foreign Relations
    Miscellaneous
    Military Affairs
    Congressional Serial Set
    HeinOnline U.S. Congressional Documents
    Annals of Congress
    Congressional Globe
    Register of Debates
Sabin Americana
University of Virginia Press, Rotunda
    The Adams Papers Digital Edition

Correspondence of James K. Polk, the Digital Edition
Documentary History of the First Federal Congress of the United States of America
Documentary History of the Ratification of the Constitution
The Papers of Andrew Jackson Digital Edition
The Papers of Thomas Jefferson Digital Edition
The Papers of James Madison Digital Edition
The Papers of James Monroe Digital Edition
The Papers of the Revolutionary Era Pinckney Statesman Digital Edition
The Papers of George Washington Digital Edition
The People of the Founding Era

Published Collections of Papers

Hamilton, Alexander. *The Papers of Alexander Hamilton.* Edited by Harold C. Syrett. 27 vols. Columbia University Press, 1961–87.

Henry, Joseph. *The Papers of Joseph Henry.* Edited by Nathan Reingold and Marc Rothenberg. 12 vols. Smithsonian Institution Press, 1972–2008.

Latrobe, Benjamin Henry. *The Correspondence and Miscellaneous Papers of Benjamin Henry Latrobe.* Edited by John C. Van Horne. 3 vols. Published for the Maryland Historical Society by Yale University Press, 1984–88.

Latrobe, Benjamin Henry. *The Journals of Benjamin Henry Latrobe, 1799–1820: From Philadelphia to New Orleans.* Edited by Edward C. Carter II, Lee W. Formwalt, and John C. Van Horne. The Papers of Benjamin Henry Latrobe Series 1, Journals, vol. 3. Published for the Maryland Historical Society by Yale University Press, 1980.

Peale, Charles Willson. *The Collected Papers of Charles Willson Peale and His Family, 1735–1885.* Edited by Lillian B. Miller, Sidney Hart, and David C. Ward. Millwood, NY: KTO Microform, 1980.

Peale, Charles Willson. *The Selected Papers of Charles Willson Peale and His Family.* Edited by Lillian B. Miller with Sidney Hart, assistant editor, and Toby A. Appel, research historian. 5 vols. Published for the National Portrait Gallery, Smithsonian Institution, by Yale University Press, 1983.

Rush, Benjamin. *Letters of Benjamin Rush.* Edited by Lyman Henry Butterfield. 2 vols. Princeton University Press, 1951.

Thayer, Sylvanus. *The West Point Thayer Papers, 1808–1872.* Edited by Cindy Adams. West Point, NY: West Point Association of Graduates, 1965.

Thornton, William. *Papers of William Thornton.* Edited by Charles M. Harris and Daniel Preston. University Press of Virginia, 1995.

BIBLIOGRAPHY

Newspapers and Periodicals

The Age (Augusta, ME)
Albany (NY) Argus
Alexandria (VA) Gazette
American Advocate (Hallowell, ME)
American Commercial Daily Advertiser (Baltimore)
American Mercury (Hartford, CT)
Augusta (GA) Chronicle
Aurora General Advertiser (Philadelphia)
Baltimore American
Baltimore Gazette and Daily Advertiser
Baltimore Sun
Boston Recorder
Boston Traveler
Christian Watchman (Boston)
Columbian (New York)
Columbian Centinel (Boston)
Columbian Register (New Haven)
Commercial Advertiser (New Orleans)
Commercial Advertiser (New York)
Connecticut Gazette (New London)
Connecticut Mirror (Hartford)
Daily Commercial Advertiser (Philadelphia)
Daily Commercial Bulletin (Chicago)
Daily National Intelligencer (Washington, DC)
Daily National Journal (Washington, DC)
Daily Pennsylvanian (Philadelphia)
Easton (MD) Star
Emporium and True American (Trenton, NJ)
Essex North Register (Salem, MA)
Essex Register (Salem, MA)
Evening Post (New York)
Evening Star (Washington, DC)
Federal Gazette (Philadelphia)
Freeman's Journal; or, the North-American Intelligencer (Philadelphia)
General Advertiser (Philadelphia)
Globe (Richmond, KY)
Globe (Washington, DC)
Hagers-Town Gazette (Halifax, MD)

Hampshire Gazette (Northampton, MA)
Illustrated London News
Independent American (Georgetown, DC)
Independent Gazetteer (Philadelphia)
Jeffersonian (New Orleans)
Jerseyman (Morris-Town, NJ)
Lynchburg Virginian
Mail; or, Claypoole's Daily Advertiser (Philadelphia)
Maryland Gazette (Annapolis)
Massachusetts Centinel (Boston)
Massachusetts Gazette (Boston)
Massachusetts Spy (Worcester)
Mercantile Advertiser (New York)
Middlesex Gazette (Middletown, CT)
Newark (NJ) Daily Advertiser
New Bedford (MA) Gazette
New-Bedford (MA) Mercury
New Hampshire Patriot and State Gazette (Concord)
Newport (RI) Mercury
New-York American for the Country
New York Herald
Niles' Weekly Register (Baltimore)
Norfolk (VA) Advertiser
North Carolina Sentinel (Newbern)
Norwich (CT) Republican
Otsego Herald (Cooperstown, NY)
Pawtucket (RI) Chronicle and Manufacturers' and Artizans' Advocate
Pennsylvania Mercury, and Universal Advertiser (Philadelphia)
Pennsylvania Packet (Philadelphia)
Philadelphia Gazette
Philadelphia Register and National Recorder
Pittsfield (MA) Sun
Portland (ME) Daily Advertiser
Portsmouth (NH) Journal of Literature & Politics
Poulson's American Daily Advertiser (Philadelphia)
Raleigh (NC) Register
Rhode-Island Republican (Newport)
Salem (MA) Gazette
Salem (MA) Register

Saratoga Sentinel (Saratoga Springs, NY)
Saturday Morning Transcript (Concord, NH)
Semi-Weekly Eagle (Brattleboro, VT)
Southern Patriot (Charleston, SC)
Spectator (New York)
Spirit of 'Seventy-Six (Washington, DC)
Spooner's Vermont Journal (Windsor)
Star of Liberty (Philadelphia)
State Gazette of South-Carolina (Charleston)
Ulster Republican (Kingston, NY)
United States' Telegraph (Washington, DC)
Utica (NY) Patriot, & Patrol
Watchman (Wilmington, DE)

Magazines and Journals

Abstracts of the Papers Communicated to the Royal Society of London
Album and Ladies' Weekly Gazette
American Farmer, Containing Original Essays and Selections on Rural Economy and Internal Improvements, with Illustrative Engravings and Prices Current of County Produce
American Journal of Science
American Journal of Science and Arts
American Museum; or, Repository of Ancient and Modern Fugitive Pieces &c. Prose and Poetical
American Register; or, General Repository of History, Politics and Science
Boston Weekly Magazine & Ladies' Miscellany
Canadian Journal of Industry, Science & Art
Edinburgh Journal of Science
Journal of the Academy of Natural Sciences of Philadelphia
Medical Repository of Original Essays and Intelligence
Memoirs of the American Academy of Arts and Sciences
Memoirs of the Board of Agriculture of the State of New-York
Monthly Magazine or, British Register
New York Farmer
North American Review
Norton's Literary Gazette
Port-Folio (Philadelphia)
Proceedings of the American Association for the Advancement of Science
Proceedings of the American Philosophical Society

Transactions of the American Philosophical Society
United States Catholic Miscellany
Weekly Magazine of Original Essays, Fugitive Pieces, and Interesting Intelligence (1798–1799)
Western Review and Miscellaneous Magazine, a Monthly Publication, Devoted to Literature and Science

Published Papers, Pamphlets, and Books

Academy of Natural Sciences of Philadelphia. *Circular to Captains and Voyagers.* Philadelphia, 1817.

Baldwin, William. *A Short Practical Narrative of the Diseases Which Prevailed Among the American Seamen, at Wampoa in China, in the Year 1805.* Philadelphia: Thomas Stiles, printer, 1807.

Baldwin, William, and Henry Muhlenberg. *Reliquiae Baldwinianae: Selections from the Correspondence of the Late William Baldwin with Occasional Notes, and a Short Biographical Memoir.* Edited by William Darlington. Philadelphia: Kimber and Sharpless, 1843.

Barlow, Joel. *Letters from Paris.* London: Printed for J. Ridgway by A. Wilson, 1800.

Barlow, Joel. *The Political Writings of Joel Barlow.—Containing—Advice to the Privileged Orders. Letter to the National Convention. Letter to the People of Piedmont. The Conspiracy of Kings.* New ed., corrected. New York: Printed by Mott & Lyon. 1796.

Barlow, Joel. *Prospectus of a National Institution, to Be Established in the United States.* Washington, DC: Printed by Samuel H. Smith, 1806.

Barlow, Joel. *The Vision of Columbus: A Poem in Nine .* 2nd ed. Hartford, CT: Printed by Hudson & Goodwin for the author, 1787.

Barnum, P. T. *The Life of P.T. Barnum: Written by Himself.* New York: Redfield, 1855.

Blodget, Samuel. *Economica: A Statistical Manual for the United States of America.* City of Washington: Printed for the author, 1806.

Bonaparte, Napoleon. *Copies of Original Letters from the Army of General Bonaparte in Egypt, Intercepted by the Fleet Under the Command of Admiral Lord Nelson. Translated from the French. Part First.* Philadelphia: Andrew Way and Joseph Groff, 1799.

Chapman, George. *A Treatise on Education, with a Sketch of the Author's Method.* London: Printed for T. Cadell, 1784.

Clarkson, Matthew, Ebenezer Hazard, and Pierre Eugène Du Simitière. *For Sale at Public Vendue, on Thursday the 10th Day of March, at the Late Dwelling House of Pierre Eugene Du Simitiere.* Philadelphia: Printed by Charles Cist, at the corner of Fourth and Arch-Streets, 1785.

Cobbett, William. *List of Field Seeds and Garden Seeds, Contained in One of the Boxes, Sold for Five Dollars. Also, Hints Respecting the Sowing of Each Sort of Seed, and the Cultivation of the Plants. By William Cobbett. Sold at W. Cobbett's Seed and Book Store, No. 63 Fulton-Street, New-York; and by Mr. John Morgan, Philadelphia.* New York: Clayton & Kingsland, printer, 1819.

Collinson, Peter. *"Forget Not Mee & My Garden—": Selected Letters, 1725–1768, of Peter Collinson, F.R.S.* Edited and with an introduction by Alan W. Armstrong. American Philosophical Society, 2002.

Columbian Museum, and Daniel Bowen. *Bowen's Columbian Museum at the Head of the Mall, Boston, Is Opened Every Day: And Elegantly Illuminated Every Tuesday, Thursday, & Friday Evening. Paintings. . . . Figures of Wax-Work (Large as Life.) . . . With a Large Collection of Natural & Artificial Curiosities. . . .* Boston: Daniel Bowen, 1798.

Commission des sciences et arts d'Egypte and Emperor of the French Napoleon I, eds. *Description of Egypt. First Edition. Antiquities, Descriptions, Volume One.* Paris: Imprimerie impériale, 1809.

Commission des sciences et arts d'Egypte and Emperor of the French Napoleon I, eds. *Description of Egypt. First Edition. Antiquities, Descriptions, Volume Two.* Paris: Imprimerie royale, 1818.

Coram, Robert. *Political Inquiries: To Which Is Added, a Plan for the General Establishment of Schools Throughout the United States.* Wilmington, DE: Printed by Andrews & Brynberg in Market-Street, 1791.

Cutbush, Edward. *An Address, Delivered Before the Columbian Institute, for the Promotion of Arts and Sciences, at the City of Washington, on the 11th January, 1817.* Washington, DC: Printed by Gales and Seaton, 1817.

Cutbush, Edward. *Observations on the Means of Preserving the Health of Soldiers and Sailors and on the Duties of the Medical Department of the Army and Navy, with Remarks on Hospitals and Their Internal Arrangement.* Philadelphia: Printed for Thomas Dobson, at the Stone House, No. 41, South Second Street, Fry and Kammerer, printers, 1808.

Dallas, George Mifflin. *Address Delivered on Occasion of Laying the Corner Stone of the Smithsonian Institution, May 1, 1847.* Washington, DC: Printed at the Office of Blair and Rives, 1847.

Dearborn, H. A. S. *An Address Delivered Before the Berkshire Agricultural Society at Pittsfield, October 8, 1840.* Pittsfield, MA: Printed by P. Allen and Son, 1840.

Dearborn, H. A. S. *An Address Delivered Before the Massachusetts Horticultural Society, on the Celebration of Their First Anniversary.* Boston: From the Press of Isaac R. Butts, 1829.

East India Marine Society. *By-Laws and Regulations of the East India Marine Society, Massachusetts: An Association of Masters and Commanders of Vessels, and of Such*

Persons as May Be Hereafter Described, Who Have Been, or Are, Engaged in the East India Trade from the Town of Salem. Salem, MA: Thomas Croade Cushing, printer, 1800.

East India Marine Society. *The East-India Marine Society of Salem*. Salem, MA: Printed by W. Palfray, Jr., 1821.

Elliot, William. *The Washington Guide: Containing Capt. John Smith's Account of the Chesapeake Bay*. Washington City, 1837.

Farrand, Max, ed. *The Records of the Federal Convention of 1787*. 3 vols. Yale University Press, 1911.

Fisher, Joshua Francis. *Recollections of Joshua Francis Fisher: Written in 1864*. Arranged by Sophia Cadwalader. Boston, 1929. http://archive.org/details/recollectionsofj00fish.

Georgia Legislature. *Colonial Records of the State of Georgia, Compiled and Published under the Authority of the Legislature*, vol. 1. Atlanta: Franklin Printing and Publishing, 1904.

Gilman, Daniel. *Our National Schools of Science*. Boston: Ticknor and Fields, 1867.

Gross, Robert A., and Mary Kelley, eds. *An Extensive Republic: Print, Culture, and Society in the New Nation, 1790–1840*. 5 vols. Chapel Hill: Published in association with the American Antiquarian Society by the University of North Carolina Press, 2007–10.

Grundy, S[amuel]. *A Catalogue of Kitchen-Garden, Field, and Flower-Seeds, Plants, Andc. for Sale by S. Grundy, at No. 20 Nassau-Street, New-York, Exactly Opposite the New Dutch Church, and One Door from the Corner of Liberty-Street*. New York, 1815.

Hopkinson, Francis. *The Miscellaneous Essays and Occasional Writings of Francis Hopkinson, Esq*. 3 vols. Philadelphia: Printed by T. Dobson, at the Stone-House, no. 41, Second Street, 1792.

Howe, Henry. *Historical Collections of Ohio*. 2 vols. Columbus: H. Howe & Son, 1889.

Institut d'Égypte. *Memoirs Relative to Egypt, Written in That Country during the Campaigns of General Bonaparte, In the Years 1798 and 1799, by the Learned and Scientific Men Who Accompanied the French Expedition. Published in Paris by Authority*. London: Printed by T. Gillet, Salisbury-Square, for R. Phillips, 71, St. Paul's Church Yard; sold by T. Hurst, 32, Paternoster-Row; Messrs. Carpenter and Co. Old Bond-Street; E. Balfour, Edinburgh; and by J. Archer, Dublin, 1800.

Jewett, Charles C. *The Age of Jewett: Charles Coffin Jewett and American Librarianship, 1841–1868*. Edited by Michael H. Harris. Heritage of Librarianship Series, No. 1. Littleton, CO: Libraries Unlimited, 1975.

Jewett, Charles C. *Notices of Public Libraries in the U.S. of America*. Washington, DC, 1851.

Jewett, Charles C. *On the Construction of Catalogues of Libraries, and of a General Catalogue*. Smithsonian Institution, 1852.

Jewett, Charles C. *A Plan for Stereotyping Catalogues by Separate Titles, and for Forming a General Stereotyped Catalogue of Public Libraries of the United States*. Washington, DC, 1851.

Langdon, John. *A Catalogue of English Kitchen-Garden and Fancy Flower Seeds, Imported in the Snow, Hazard, from London, and for Sale at the Store of John Langdon, No. 6 Fletcher-Street, near the Fly-Market. Wholesale and Retail*. New York, 1798.

Long, Stephen H. *Account of an Expedition from Pittsburgh to the Rocky Mountains, Performed in the Years 1819 and '20, by Order of the Hon. J. C. Calhoun, Sec'y of War: Under the Command of Major Stephen H. Long. From the Notes of Major Long, Mr. T. Say, and Other Gentlemen of the Party*. London: Longman, Hurst, Pees, Orre & Brown, 1823.

Mansfield, Edward Deering. *Memoirs of the Life and Services of Daniel Drake*. Cincinnati: Applegate, 1860.

Maryland Agricultural Society. *Articles of Association of the Maryland Agricultural Society*. Easton, MD, 1818.

McBride, James, and John Cleves Symmes. *Symmes's Theory of Concentric Spheres: Demonstrating That the Earth Is Hollow, Habitable Within, and Widely Open About the Poles*. Cincinnati: Morgan, Lodge and Fisher, 1826.

M'Mahon, Bernard. *A Catalogue of Garden, Grass, Herb, Flower, Tree, & Shrub-Seeds, Flower-Roots, &c. &c.* Philadelphia, n.d.

M'Mahon, Bernard. *A Catalogue of Garden, Grass, Herb, Flower, Tree, and Shrub-Seeds, Flower-Roots, Andc. Andc. Sold by Bernard M'Mahon, Seedsman, No. 129, Chesnut-Street, Philadelphia*. Philadelphia, 1806.

M'Mahon, Bernard. *A Catalogue of Garden, Herb, Flower, Tree, Shrub, and Grass Seeds, Gardening, Agricultural and Botanical Books, Garden Tools, Andc., Sold by Bernard M'Mahon Who Has Likewise for Sale, Plants of above Fifty Varieties of the Most Superior English, Irish and Scotch Gooseberries*. Philadelphia: Printed by William Duane, 1813.

Moore, S. S. *The Traveller's Directory, or A Pocket Companion: Shewing the Course of the Main Road from Philadelphia to New York, and from Philadelphia to Washington*. Philadelphia: M. Carey, publisher, 1802.

National Institute for the Promotion of Science. *Bulletin of the Proceedings of the National Institute for the Promotion of Science*. Washington, DC, 1841.

National Institute for the Promotion of Science. *Second Bulletin of the Proceedings of the National Institute for the Promotion of Science: March, 1841 to February, 1842*. Washington, DC, 1842.

Norry, Charles. *An Account of the French Expedition to Egypt: Comprehending a View of the Country of Lower Egypt, Its Cities, Monuments, and Inhabitants, at the Time of the Arrival of the French.* London: Printed by S. Gosnell, Little Queen Street, Holborn, for James Ridgway, York Street, St. James's Square, 1800.

Peale, Charles Willson. *Guide to the Philadelphia Museum.* Philadelphia, 1805.

Peale, Charles Willson, and A. M. F. J. Beauvois. *A Scientific and Descriptive Catalogue of Peale's Museum, by C.W. Peale.* Philadelphia: Printed by Samuel H. Smith, no. 118 Chesnut-Street, 1796.

Pike, Zebulon Montgomery. *An Account of Expeditions to the Sources of the Mississippi, and Through the Western Parts of Louisiana, to the Sources of the Arkansaw, Kans, La Platte, and Pierre Jaun, Rivers; Performed by Order of the Government of the United States During the Years 1805, 1806, and 1807. And a Tour through the Interior Parts of New Spain, When Conducted Through These Provinces, by Order of the Captain-General, in the Year 1807. By Major Z. M. Pike. Illustrated by Maps and Charts.* Philadelphia: Lucas, Fielding, publisher, 1810.

Poinsett, Joel Roberts. *Discourse, on the Objects and Importance of the National Institution for the Promotion of Science, Established at Washington, 1840: Delivered at the First Anniversary.* Washington, DC: P. Force, printer, 1841.

Poinsett, Joel Roberts. *Notes on Mexico: Made in the Autumn of 1822.* London: John Miller, 1825.

Poinsett, Joel Roberts, Thomas Pinckney, and State Agricultural Society of South Carolina. *Report of the Committee, Appointed by the South Carolina Agricultural Society, to Consider What Beneficial Effects Would Result to the Agricultural Interests of the State, by Importing Foreign Seeds, Plants and Implements of Husbandry: To Which Is Added, Gen[Eral] Thomas Pinckney's Letter on the Water Culture of Rice.* Charleston: A. E. Miller, 1823.

Prescott, William Hickling. *History of the Conquest of Mexico, with a Preliminary View of the Ancient Mexican Civilization, and the Life of the Conqueror, Hernando Cortés.* Harper and Brothers, 1843.

Price, Richard. *The Evidence for a Future Period of Improvement in the State of Mankind, with the Means and Duty of Promoting It; Represented in a Discourse, Delivered on Wednesday the 25th of April, 1787, at the Meeting-House in the Old Jewry, London, to the Supporters of a New Academical Institution Among Protestant Dissenters.* London: Cadell, 1787.

Price, Richard. *Observations on the Importance of the American Revolution, and the Means of Making It a Benefit to the World. By Richard Price, D.D. L.L.D. and Fellow of the Royal Society of London, and of the Academy of Arts and Sciences in New-England.* London, 1784. Reprint, Boston: Powars and Willis, 1784.

The Records of the Federal Convention of 1787. 3 vols. Edited by Max Farrand. Yale University Press, 1911.

Rhees, William Jones. *The Smithsonian Institution: Documents Relative to Its Origin and History, 1835–1889.* 2 vols. Smithsonian Miscellaneous Collections. Smithsonian Institution, 1901.

Richardson, James D., comp. *A Compilation of the Messages and Papers of the Presidents.* Vol. 1. New York: Bureau of National Literature and Art, 1910.

Ripault, Louis-Madeleine. *Report of the Commission of Arts to the First Consul Bonaparte on the Antiquities of Upper Egypt, and the Present State of All the Temples, Palaces, Obelisks, Statues, Tombs, Pyramids, &c. of Philo, Syene, Thebes, Tentyris, Latopolis, Memphis, Heliopolis, &c. &c. From the Cataracts of the Nile to Cairo: With an Accurate Description of the Pictures with Which They Are Decorated, and the Conjectures That May Be Drawn from Them, Respecting the Divinities to Whom They Were Consecrated. Translated from the French of Citizen Ripaud, Librarian to the Institute of Egypt.* London: Printed for J. Debrett, opposite Burlington House, Piccadilly, 1800.

Rush, Benjamin. *A Plan for the Establishment of Public Schools and the Diffusion of Knowledge in Pennsylvania; to Which Are Added Thoughts upon the Mode of Education, Proper in a Republic: Addressed to the Legislature and Citizens of the State.* Philadelphia: Printed for Thomas Dobson, in Second-Street, two doors above Chesnut-Street, 1786.

Rush, Benjamin. *Thoughts upon Female Education, Accommodated to the Present State of Society, Manners, and Government, in the United States of America. Addressed to the Visitors of the Young Ladies' Academy in Philadelphia, 28 July, 1787, at the Close of the Quarterly Examination.* Philadelphia: William Pritchard, printer, 1787.

Rush, Benjamin, Thomas Jefferson, John Adams, and Alexander Biddle. *Old Family Letters: Copied from the Originals for Alexander Biddle.* 2 vols. Philadelphia: Press of J. B. Lippincott Company, 1892.

Rush, Richard, and United States Department of the Treasury. *Circular to Consuls.* Washington, DC: P. Force, 1827.

Scudder, John. *A Companion to the American Museum. . . .* New York: Printed by G. F. Hopkins, 1823.

Smithsonian Institution, Board of Regents. *Annual Report of the Board of Regents of the Smithsonian Institution.* Washington, DC, 1848.

Smithsonian Institution, Board of Regents. *Tenth Annual Report of the Board of Regents of the Smithsonian Institution.* Washington, DC, 1855.

Smithsonian Institution, Board of Regents. *Annual Report of the Board of Regents of the Smithsonian Institution.* Washington, DC, 1857.

Smithsonian Institution, Board of Regents. *Annual Report of the Board of Regents of the Smithsonian Institution.* 2 vols. Washington, DC, 1897.

Smithsonian Institution, Board of Regents. *Annual Report of the Board of Regents of the Smithsonian Institution . . . to July, 1897.* Washington, DC, 1898.

Sonnini, C. S. *Travels in Upper and Lower Egypt.* Translated by Henry Hunter. London: Printed for J. Stockdale, 1799.

State of Massachusetts. *An Act to Incorporate and Establish a Society for the Cultivation and Promotion of Arts and Sciences.* Boston: Printed by Benjamin Edes and Sons, 1780.

State of Virginia. *The Statutes at Large; Being a Collection of All the Laws of Virginia, from the First Session of the Legislature in the Year 1619.* Vol. 11. Published for the Jamestown Foundation of the Commonwealth of Virginia by the University Press of Virginia, 1969.

Symmes, John Cleves. *Light Gives Light, to Light Discover—"Ad Infinitum." St. Louis, (Missouri Territory,) North America, April 10, A.D. 1818. To All the World! I Declare the Earth Is Hollow, and Habitable Within . . . I Pledge My Life in Support of This Truth, and Am Ready to Explore the Hollow, If the World Will Support and Aid Me in the Undertaking. . . .* St. Louis, 1818.

Tocqueville, Alexis de. *Democracy in America.* Edited by Eduardo Nolla and James T. Schleifer. Translated by James T. Schleifer. Indianapolis: Liberty Fund, 2012.

United States. *Abridgment of the Debates of Congress, from 1789 to 1856. From Gales and Seatons' Annals of Congress; from Their Register of Debates; and from the Official Reported Debates, by John C. Rives.* Edited by Thomas Hart Benton. Vol. 2. D. Appleton, 1857.

United States, ed. *An Account of Louisiana: Laid Before Congress by Direction of the President of the United States, November 14, 1803; Comprising an Account of Its Boundaries, History, Cities, Towns, and Settlements.* Providence: Printed by Heaton & Williams, 1803.

Watkins, Tobias. *Anniversary Discourse Delivered Before the Columbian Institute on the 7th January, 1826.* Washington, DC: Printed by Davis and Force, 1826.

Wilson, Alexander, and George Ord. *American Ornithology, or, The Natural History of the Birds of the United States.* 9 vols. Philadelphia: Bradford and Inskeep, 1808–14.

SECONDARY SOURCES

Achim, Miruna. *From Idols to Antiquity: Forging the National Museum of Mexico.* The Mexican Experience. University of Nebraska Press, 2017.

Addis, Cameron. *Jefferson's Vision for Education, 1760–1845.* New York: Peter Lang, 2003.

Adler, Antony. "From the Pacific to the Patent Office: The US Exploring Expedition and the Origins of America's First National Museum." *Journal of the History of Collections* 23, no. 1 (May 1, 2011): 49–74.

Adler, William D. *Engineering Expansion: The U.S. Army and Economic Development, 1787–1860.* University of Pennsylvania Press, 2021.

Alder, Ken. *Engineering the Revolution: Arms and Enlightenment in France, 1763–1815.* Princeton University Press, 1997.

Alexander, Edward P. *Museum Masters: Their Museums and Their Influence.* Nashville: American Association for State and Local History, 1983.

Allgor, Catherine. *Parlor Politics: In Which the Ladies of Washington Help Build a City and a Government.* University Press of Virginia, 2000.

Altar, Peter. *The Reluctant Patron: Science and the State in Britain, 1850–1920.* Lemington Spa, UK: Berg, 1987.

American Academy of Arts and Sciences. *The American Academy of Arts and Sciences, 1780–1940.* Boston, 1940.

Appel, Toby A. "Science, Popular Culture and Profit: Peale's Philadelphia Museum." *Journal of the Society for the Bibliography of Natural History* 9, no. 4 (Jan. 1980): 619–34.

Appleby, Joyce Oldham. *Inheriting the Revolution: The First Generation of Americans.* Belknap Press of Harvard University Press, 2000.

Armstead, Myra Beth Young. *Freedom's Gardener: James F. Brown, Horticulture, and the Hudson Valley in Antebellum America.* New York University Press, 2012.

Arnebeck, Bob. *Through a Fiery Trial: Building Washington, 1790–1800.* Lanham, MD: Madison Books, 1991.

Augst, Thomas, and Kenneth E. Carpenter. *Institutions of Reading: The Social Life of Libraries in the United States.* University of Massachusetts Press, 2007.

Baatz, Simon. "Philadelphia Patronage: The Institutional Structure of Natural History in the New Republic, 1800–1833." *Journal of the Early Republic* 8, no. 2 (Summer 1988): 111–38.

Baatz, Simon. "'Squinting at Silliman': Scientific Periodicals in the Early American Republic, 1810–1833." *Isis* 82, no. 2 (1 June 1991): 223–44.

Bamford, T. W. "Public Schools and Social Class, 1801–1850." *British Journal of Sociology* 12, no. 3 (1 Sept. 1961): 224–35.

Beadie, Nancy. *Education and the Creation of Capital in the Early American Republic.* New York: Cambridge University Press, 2010.

Bennett, Thomas Peter. *Florida Explored: The Philadelphia Connection in Bartram's Tracks.* Mercer University Press, 2019.

Bennett, Thomas Peter. "The 1817 Florida Expedition of the Academy of Natural Sciences." *Proceedings of the Academy of Natural Sciences of Philadelphia* 152, no. 1 (Oct. 2002): 1–21.

Benson, Maxine. *From Pittsburgh to the Rocky Mountains: Major Stephen Long's Expedition, 1819–1820*. Lakewood, CO: Fulcrum, 1988.
Bilder, Mary Sarah. *Female Genius: Eliza Harriot and George Washington at the Dawn of the Constitution*. University of Virginia Press, 2022.
Binger, Carl. *Revolutionary Doctor: Benjamin Rush, 1746–1813*. Norton, 1966.
Bleichmar, Daniela, and Peter C. Mancall. *Collecting Across Cultures: Material Exchanges in the Early Modern Atlantic World*. University of Pennsylvania Press, 2011.
Blum, Hester. "John Cleves Symmes and the Planetary Reach of Polar Exploration." *American Literature* 84, no. 2 (1 June 2012): 243–71.
Boonshoft, Mark. *Aristocratic Education and the Making of the American Republic*. University of North Carolina Press, 2020.
Boromé, Joseph Alfred. *Charles Coffin Jewett*. Chicago: American Library Association, 1951.
Bowling, Kenneth R. *Creating the Federal City, 1774–1800: Potomac Fever*. Washington, DC: American Institute of Architects Press, 1988.
Bowling, Kenneth R. *The Creation of Washington, D.C.: The Idea and Location of the American Capital*. George Mason University Press, 1991.
Branson, Susan. "'Barnum Is Undone in His Own Province': Science, Race, and Entertainment in the Lectures of George Robins Gliddon." In *The Cosmopolitan Lyceum: Lecture Culture and the Globe in Nineteenth-Century America*, edited by Tom F. Wright, 151–67. University of Massachusetts Press, 2013.
Branson, Susan. *Scientific Americans: Invention, Technology, and National Identity*. Cornell University Press, 2021.
Brigham, David R. "'Ask the Beasts, and They Shall Teach Thee': The Human Lessons of Charles Willson Peale's Natural History Displays." *Huntington Library Quarterly* 59, no. 2/3 (1996): 183–206.
Brigham, David R. *Public Culture in the Early Republic: Peale's Museum and Its Audience*. Smithsonian Institution Press, 1995.
Brown, Richard D. "Bulwark of Revolutionary Liberty: Thomas Jefferson's and John Adams's Program for an Informed Citizenry." In *Thomas Jefferson and the Education of a Citizen*, edited by James Gilreath, 91–102. Library of Congress, 1999.
Brown, Richard D. *Knowledge Is Power: The Diffusion of Information in Early America, 1700–1865*. New York: Oxford University Press, 1989.
Brown, Richard D. *The Strength of a People: The Idea of an Informed Citizenry in America, 1650–1870*. University of North Carolina Press, 1996.
Budka, Metchie J. E. "Minerva Versus Archimedes." *Smithsonian Journal of History* 1, no. 1 (Jan. 1966): 61–64.
Buel, Richard. *Joel Barlow: American Citizen in a Revolutionary World*. Johns Hopkins University Press, 2011.

Burke, Peter. *A Social History of Knowledge. II, From the Encyclopédie to Wikipedia*. Polity Press, 2012.

Burleigh, Nina. *The Stranger and the Statesman: James Smithson, John Quincy Adams, and the Making of America's Greatest Museum; The Smithsonian*. William Morrow, 2003.

Cahan, David. *From Natural Philosophy to the Sciences: Writing the History of Nineteenth-Century Science*. University of Chicago Press, 2003.

Carney, Judith. "Out of Africa: Colonial Rice History in the Black Atlantic." In *Colonial Botany: Science, Commerce, and Politics in the Early Modern World*, edited by Londa L. Schiebinger and Claudia Swan, 204–20. University of Pennsylvania Press, 2005.

Carpenter, Kenneth. "Libraries." In *A History of the Book in America*, vol. 3, *The Industrial Book, 1840–1880*, edited by Scott E. Casper, Jeffrey D. Groves, Stephen W. Nisenbaum, and Michael Winship, 303–18. Chapel Hill: Published in association with the American Antiquarian Society by the University of North Carolina Press, 2007.

Carter, Edward Carlos. *"One Grand Pursuit": A Brief History of the American Philosophical Society's First 250 Years, 1743–1993*. American Philosophical Society, 1993.

Castel, Albert. "The Founding Fathers and the Vision of a National University." *History of Education Quarterly* 4, no. 4 (Winter 1964): 280–302.

Chapman, Bert. "Initial Visions of Paradise: Antebellum U.S. Government Documents on the South Pacific." *Journal of Government Information* 30, no. 5/6 (Nov. 2004): 727–50.

Christman, Margaret C. S. *1846: Portrait of the Nation*. Smithsonian Institution Press, 1996.

Cleves, Rachel Hope. *The Reign of Terror in America: Visions of Violence from Anti-Jacobinism to Antislavery*. New York: Cambridge University Press, 2009.

Coalwell McDonald, Christine, and Robert M. S. McDonald. "West from West Point: Thomas Jefferson's Military Academy and the 'Empire of Liberty.'" In *Light and Liberty: Thomas Jefferson and the Power of Knowledge*, edited by Robert M. S. McDonald, 116–36. University of Virginia Press, 2012.

Cohen, Henning. "Melville's Surgeon Cuticle and Surgeon Cutbush." *Studies in the Novel* 5, no. 2 (1 July 1973): 251–53.

Cohen, I. Bernard. *Science and the Founding Fathers: Science in the Political Thought of Jefferson, Franklin, Adams and Madison*. Norton, 1997.

Cole, John Y. "The Library of Congress Becomes a World Library, 1815–2005." *Libraries & Culture* 40, no. 3 (Summer 2005): 385–98.

Cook, James W. *The Arts of Deception: Playing with Fraud in the Age of Barnum*. Harvard University Press, 2001.

Costanzo, Adam. *George Washington's Washington: Visions for the National Capital in the Early American Republic.* University of Georgia Press, 2018.

Cotlar, Seth. "'Every Man Should Have Property': Robert Coram and the American Revolution's Legacy of Economic Populism." In *Revolutionary Founders: Rebels, Radicals, and Reformers in the Making of the Nation,* edited by Alfred F. Young, Gary B. Nash, and Ray Raphael, 337–53. Knopf, 2011.

Cotlar, Seth. *Tom Paine's America: The Rise and Fall of Transatlantic Radicalism in the Early Republic.* University of Virginia Press, 2011.

Crackel, Theodore J. "The Military Academy in the Context of Jeffersonian Reform." In *Thomas Jefferson's Military Academy: Founding West Point,* edited by Robert M. S. McDonald, 99–107. University of Virginia Press, 2004.

Crackel, Theodore J. *Mr. Jefferson's Army: Political and Social Reform of the Military Establishment, 1801–1809.* New York University Press, 1987.

Crackel, Theodore J. *West Point: A Bicentennial History.* Modern War Studies. University Press of Kansas, 2002.

Cremin, Lawrence A. *American Education: The Colonial Experience, 1607–1783.* Harper and Row, 1970.

Cremin, Lawrence A. *American Education: The National Experience, 1783–1876.* Harper and Row, 1980.

Cutright, Paul Russell. *Lewis and Clark: Pioneering Naturalists.* University of Illinois Press, 1969.

Dain, Bruce R. *A Hideous Monster of the Mind: American Race Theory in the Early Republic.* Harvard University Press, 2002.

Dalrymple, Dana G. "The Smithsonian Bequest, Congress, and Nineteenth-Century Efforts to Increase and Diffuse Agricultural Knowledge in the United States." *Agricultural History Review* 57, no. 2 (2009): 207–35.

Daniels, George H. *American Science in the Age of Jackson.* University of Alabama Press, 1994.

Davidson, Cathy N. *Reading in America: Literature and Social History.* Johns Hopkins University Press, 1989.

DeLucia, Christine M. "Antiquarian Collecting and the Transits of Indigenous Material Culture: Rethinking 'Indian Relics' and Tribal Histories." *Common-Place* 17, no. 2 (2017), https://commonplace.online/article/antiquarian-collecting-and-the-transits-of-indigenous-material-culture/.

DeLucia, Christine M. "Fugitive Collections in New England Indian Country: Indigenous Material Culture and Early American History Making at Ezra Stiles's Yale Museum." *William and Mary Quarterly* 75, no. 1 (6 Feb. 2018): 109–50.

DeLucia, Christine M. *Memory Lands: King Philip's War and the Place of Violence in the Northeast.* Yale University Press, 2018.

Donner, Irah. "The Copyright Clause of the U.S. Constitution: Why Did the Framers Include It with Unanimous Approval?" *American Journal of Legal History* 36, no. 3 (1992): 361-78.

Dowling, William C. *Literary Federalism in the Age of Jefferson: Joseph Dennie and "The Port Folio," 1801-1812.* University of South Carolina Press, 1999.

Dugatkin, Lee Alan. *Mr. Jefferson and the Giant Moose: Natural History in Early America.* University of Chicago Press, 2009.

Dupree, A. Hunter. "The National Pattern of American Learned Societies, 1769-1863." In *The Pursuit of Knowledge in the Early American Republic: American Scientific and Learned Societies from Colonial Times to the Civil War*, edited by Alexandra Oleson and Sanborn Conner Brown, 21-32. Johns Hopkins University Press, 1976.

Dupree, A. Hunter. *Science in the Federal Government: A History of Policies and Activities.* Johns Hopkins University Press, 1986.

Dzurec, David. "Of Salt Mountains, Prairie Dogs, and Horned Frogs: The Louisiana Purchase and the Evolution of Federalist Satire, 1803-1812." *Journal of the Early Republic* 35, no. 1 (19 Feb. 2015): 79-108.

Eastman, Carolyn. "Conclusion: Placing Platform Culture in Nineteenth-Century American Life." In *Thinking Together: Lecturing, Learning, and Difference in the Long Nineteenth Century*, edited by Angela G. Ray and Paul Stob, 187-202. Pennsylvania State University Press, 2018.

Eastman, Carolyn. *A Nation of Speechifiers: Making an American Public After the Revolution.* University of Chicago Press, 2010.

Eastman, Carolyn. "'The Powers of Debate Should Be Sedulously Cultivated': The Importance of Eloquence in Early American Education and the University of Virginia." In *The Founding of Thomas Jefferson's University*, edited by John A. Ragosta, Peter S. Onuf, and Andrew J. O'Shaughnessy, 287-305. University of Virginia Press, 2019.

Ebert, Myrl. "The Rise and Development of the American Medical Periodical, 1797-1850." *Journal of the Medical Library Association: JMLA* 100, no. S4 (2012): 243-73.

Edling, Max M. *A Revolution in Favor of Government: Origins of the U.S. Constitution and the Making of the American State.* New York: Oxford University Press, 2003.

Ellis, Richard P. "The Founding History, and Significance of Peale's Museum in Philadelphia, 1785-1841." *Curator* 9, no. 3 (July 1966): 235-58.

Ellsworth, Lucius F. "The Philadelphia Society for the Promotion of Agriculture and Agricultural Reform, 1785-1793." *Agricultural History* 42, no. 3 (Summer 1968): 189-99.

Estes, Todd. *The Jay Treaty Debate, Public Opinion, and the Evolution of Early American Political Culture.* University of Massachusetts Press, 2006.

Ewing, Heather P. *The Lost World of James Smithson: Science, Revolution, and the Birth of the Smithsonian*. Bloomsbury, 2007.

Fabian, Ann. *The Skull Collectors: Race, Science, and America's Unburied Dead*. University of Chicago Press, 2010.

Fairchild, Herman L. *A History of the New York Academy of Sciences, Formerly the Lyceum of Natural History*. New York: The author, 1887.

Feller, Daniel. *The Jacksonian Promise: America, 1815–1840*. Johns Hopkins University Press, 1995.

Fernandez-Sacco, Ellen. "Framing 'The Indian': The Visual Culture of Conquest in the Museums of Pierre Eugene Du Simitiere and Charles Willson Peale, 1779–96." *Social Identities* 8, no. 4 (1 Dec. 2002): 571–618.

Fernandez-Sacco, Ellen. "Spectacular Masculinities: The Museums of Peale, Baker and Bowen in the Early Republic." PhD diss., University of California, Los Angeles, 1998.

Fichter, James R. *So Great a Proffit: How the East Indies Trade Transformed Anglo-American Capitalism*. Harvard University Press, 2010.

Fitting, Peter, ed. *Subterranean Worlds: A Critical Anthology*. Wesleyan University Press, 2004.

Fitz, Caitlin. *Our Sister Republics: The United States in an Age of American Revolutions*. Liveright, 2016.

Fleming, James Rodger. *Meteorology in America, 1800–1870*. Johns Hopkins University Press, 1990.

Forman, Sidney. "The United States Military Philosophical Society, 1802–1813: Scientia in Bello Pax." *William and Mary Quarterly*, 3rd ser., 2, no. 3 (1945): 273–85.

Forman, Sidney. "Why the United States Military Academy Was Established in 1802." *Military Affairs* 29, no. 1 (1 Apr. 1965): 16–28.

Fredriksen, John C. "Williams, Jonathan." American National Biography, http://www.anb.org/articles/03/03-00620.html.

Fullilove, Courtney. *The Profit of the Earth: The Global Seeds of American Agriculture*. University of Chicago Press, 2017.

Ganter, Granville. "The Active Virtue of *The Columbian Orator*." *New England Quarterly* 70, no. 3 (Sept. 1997): 463–76.

George Washington University, Office of the University Historian. *The Fate of Washington's Bequest to a National University*. Washington, DC, 1968.

Gerbi, Antonello. *The Dispute of the New World: The History of a Polemic, 1750–1900*. Translated by Jeremy Moyle. Revised and enlarged ed. University of Pittsburgh Press, 1973.

Gibson, Robert S. "Medical Education in the Nineteenth Century: Jefferson and Flexner Revisited." In *The Founding of Thomas Jefferson's University*, edited by

John A. Ragosta, Peter S. Onuf, and Andrew J. O'Shaughnessy, 151–89. University of Virginia Press, 2019.

Gillispie, Charles Coulston. "Scientific Aspects of the French Egyptian Expedition, 1798–1801." *Proceedings of the American Philosophical Society* 133, no. 4 (1989): 447–74.

Gilreath, James, ed. *Thomas Jefferson and the Education of a Citizen*. Library of Congress, 1999.

Glover, Lorri. *Founders as Fathers: The Private Lives and Politics of the American Revolutionaries*. Yale University Press, 2014.

Gochberg, Reed. *Useful Objects: Museums, Science, and Literature in Nineteenth-Century America*. New York: Oxford University Press, 2021.

Goetzmann, William H. *Exploration and Empire: The Explorer and the Scientist in the Winning of the American West*. Knopf, 1966.

Goldstein, Paul. *Copyright's Highway: From Gutenberg to the Celestial Jukebox*. Revised ed. Stanford University Press, 2003.

Goode, G. Brown. *The Smithsonian Institution, 1846–1896: The History of Its First Half Century*. Washington, DC, 1897.

Grasso, Christopher. *A Speaking Aristocracy: Transforming Public Discourse in Eighteenth-Century Connecticut*. Published for the Omohundro Institute of Early American History and Culture, Williamsburg, Virginia, by the University of North Carolina Press, 1999.

Green, Constance McLaughlin. *Washington: Village and Capital, 1800–1878*. 2 vols. Princeton University Press, 1962.

Green, James N. "The Rise of Book Publishing." In *An Extensive Republic: Print, Culture, and Society in the New Nation, 1790–1840*, edited by Robert A. Gross and Mary Kelley, 2:75–127. Chapel Hill: Published in association with the American Antiquarian Society by the University of North Carolina Press, 2010.

Green, Jennifer R. *Military Education and the Emerging Middle Class in the Old South*. New York: Cambridge University Press, 2008.

Green, Jennifer R. ""Practical Progress Is the Watchword": Military Education and the Expansion of Opportunity in the Old South." *Journal of the Historical Society* 5, no. 3 (Fall 2005): 363–90.

Greenberg, Kenneth S. *Honor and Slavery: Lies, Duels, Noses, Masks, Dressing as a Woman, Gifts, Strangers, Humanitarianism, Death, Slave Rebellions, the Proslavery Argument, Baseball, Hunting, and Gambling in the Old South*. Princeton University Press, 1996.

Greenberg, Kenneth S. "The Nose, the Lie, and the Duel in the Antebellum South." *American Historical Review* 95, no. 1 (1990): 57–74.

Greene, John C. *American Science in the Age of Jefferson*. Iowa State University Press, 1984.

Greene, John C. "Science, Learning and Utility: Patterns of Organization in the Early American Republic." In *The Pursuit of Knowledge in the Early American Republic: American Scientific and Learned Societies from Colonial Times to the Civil War*, edited by Alexandra Oleson and Sanborn Conner Brown, 1–20. Johns Hopkins University Press, 1976.

Grossman, Sara J. "Gendering Nineteenth-Century Data: The Women of the Smithsonian Meteorological Project." *Journal of Women's History* 33, no. 1 (Spring 2021): 85–109.

Groves, Jeffrey D. "Periodicals and Serial Publication: Introduction." In *A History of the Book in America*, vol. 3, *The Industrial Book, 1840–1880*, edited by Scott E. Casper, Jeffrey D. Groves, Stephen W. Nisenbaum, and Michael Winship, 303–18. Chapel Hill: Published in association with the American Antiquarian Society by the University of North Carolina Press, 2007.

Guidone, Anthony Edward. "The Empire's City: A Global History of Salem, Massachusetts, 1783–1820." PhD diss., George Mason University, 2023.

Gustaitis, Joseph. "The Hole Truth of John Cleves Symmes." *American History Illustrated* 19, no. 7 (1984): 32–33.

Guthrie, William. *A New System of Modern Geography*: Philadelphia: Printed by Mathew Carey, 1794.

Hahn, Roger. *The Anatomy of a Scientific Institution: The Paris Academy of Sciences, 1666–1803*. University of California Press, 1971.

Harris, Neil. *Humbug: The Art of P. T. Barnum*. Little, Brown, 1973.

Harrison, Adrienne M. *A Powerful Mind: The Self-Education of George Washington*. Potomac Books, 2015.

Hart, Sidney. "'To Encrease the Comforts of Life': Charles Willson Peale and the Mechanical Arts." *Pennsylvania Magazine of History and Biography* 110, no. 3 (July 1986): 323–58.

Hart, Sidney, and David C. Ward. "The Waning of an Enlightenment Ideal: Charles Willson Peale's Philadelphia Museum, 1790–1820." *Journal of the Early Republic* 8, no. 4 (1988): 389–418.

Hattem, Michael D. *Past and Prologue: Politics and Memory in the American Revolution*. Yale University Press, 2020.

Hayes, Kevin J. *George Washington: A Life in Books*. New York: Oxford University Press, 2017.

Hayes, Kevin J. *The Road to Monticello: The Life and Mind of Thomas Jefferson*. New York: Oxford University Press, 2007.

Headrick, Daniel R. *When Information Came of Age: Technologies of Knowledge in the Age of Reason and Revolution, 1700–1850*. New York: Oxford University Press, 2000.

Hearl, Trevor. "Military Education and the School Curriculum, 1800–1870." *History of Education*, 5, no. 3 (1976): 251–64.

Heine Barnett, Janet. "Mathematics Goes Ballistic: Benjamin Robins, Leonhard Euler, and the Mathematical Education of Military Engineers." *BSHM Bulletin: Journal of the British Society for the History of Mathematics* 24, no. 2 (1 July 2009): 92–104.

Hendrickson, Walter B. "The Western Museum Society of Cincinnati." *Scientific Monthly* 63, no. 1 (1946): 66–72.

Henkin, David M. *City Reading: Written Words and Public Spaces in Antebellum New York*. Columbia University Press, 1998.

Henle, Alea R. *Rescued from Oblivion: Historical Cultures in the Early United States*. University of Massachusetts Press, 2020.

Henson, Pamela. "Spencer Baird's Dream: A U.S. National Museum." In *Cultures and Institutions of Natural History: Essays in the History and Philosophy of Science*, edited by Michael T. Ghiselin and Alan E. Leviton. California Academy of Sciences, 2000.

Higginbotham, Don. "Military Education Before West Point." In *Thomas Jefferson's Military Academy: Founding West Point*, edited by Robert M. S. McDonald. 23–53. University of Virginia Press, 2004.

Hindle, Brooke. *The Pursuit of Science in Revolutionary America, 1735–1789*. Published for the Institute of Early American History and Culture, Williamsburg, Va., by the University of North Carolina Press, 1956.

Hindle, Brooke, Lillian B. Miller, and E. P. Richardson, eds. *Charles Willson Peale and His World*. Abrams, 1983.

Hinsley, Curtis M. *The Smithsonian and the American Indian: Making a Moral Anthropology in Victorian America*. Smithsonian Institution Press, 1994.

Hofstadter, Richard. *Anti-Intellectualism in American Life*. Knopf, 1963.

Hofstadter, Richard. *The Idea of a Party System: The Rise of Legitimate Opposition in the United States, 1780–1840*. University of California Press, 1969.

Howe, Daniel Walker. *The Political Culture of the American Whigs*. University of Chicago Press, 1979.

Howe, Daniel Walker. *What Hath God Wrought: The Transformation of America, 1815–1848*. New York: Oxford University Press, 2007.

Hoyt, John Wesley. *A National University: Review of the Paper Read Before the Higher Department of the National Educational Association at Elmira, N.Y., August 5, 1873*. Madison, WI: National Education Association, 1874.

Hoyt, John Wesley. *Memorial in Regard to a National University*. Government Printing Office, 1892.

Huth, Hans. "Pierre Eugène Du Simitière and the Beginnings of the American Historical Museum." *Pennsylvania Magazine of History and Biography* 69, no. 4 (1945): 315–25.

Huxley, Robert. "Natural History Collectors and Their Collections: 'Simpling Macaronis' and Instruments of Empire." In *Enlightenment: Discovering the*

World in the Eighteenth Century, edited by Kim Sloan and Andrew Burnett, 80–91. Smithsonian Books, 2003.

Iannini, Christopher P. *Fatal Revolutions: Natural History, West Indian Slavery, and the Routes of American Literature.* Published for the Omohundro Institute of Early American History and Culture, Williamsburg, Virginia, by the University of North Carolina Press, 2012.

Isaac, Amanda. *Take Note! George Washington the Reader.* Mount Vernon Ladies Association, 2013.

Jansen, Axel. *Alexander Dallas Bache: Building the American Nation Through Science and Education in the Nineteenth Century.* New York: Campus Verlag, 2011.

John, Richard R. *Spreading the News: The American Postal System from Franklin to Morse.* Harvard University Press, 1995.

Johnson, Victoria. *American Eden: David Hosack, Botany, and Medicine in the Garden of the Early Republic.* Liveright, 2018.

Justice, Benjamin. "'The Great Contest': The American Philosophical Society Education Prize of 1795 and the Problem of American Education." *American Journal of Education* 114, no. 2 (2008): 191–213.

Justice, Benjamin, ed. *The Founding Fathers, Education, and "The Great Contest": The American Philosophical Society Prize of 1797.* Palgrave Macmillan, 2013.

Kaestle, Carl F. *Pillars of the Republic: Common Schools and American Society, 1780–1860.* Hill and Wang, 1983.

Kaplan, Catherine O'Donnell. *Men of Letters in the Early Republic: Cultivating Forums of Citizenship.* Published for the Omohundro Institute of Early American History and Culture, Williamsburg, Virginia, by the University of North Carolina Press, 2008.

Kayser, Elmer Louis. *Bricks Without Straw: The Evolution of George Washington University.* Appleton-Century-Crofts, 1970.

Kayser, Elmer Louis. *Washington's Bequest to a National University.* George Washington University, Office of the University Historian, 1965.

Kelley, Mary. *Learning to Stand and Speak: Women, Education, and Public Life in America's Republic.* Chapel Hill: Published for the Omohundro Institute of Early American History and Culture, Williamsburg, Virginia, by the University of North Carolina Press, 2006.

Kenney, Alice P. "America Discovers Columbus: Biography as Epic, Drama, History." *Biography: An Interdisciplinary Quarterly* 4, no. 1 (Winter 1981): 45–65.

Kerber, Linda K. *Federalists in Dissent; Imagery and Ideology in Jeffersonian America.* Cornell University Press, 1970.

Kerber, Linda K. *Women of the Republic: Intellect and Ideology in Revolutionary America.* Published for the Institute of Early American History and Culture by the University of North Carolina Press, 1980.

Kimball, Bruce A. *Orators and Philosophers: A History of the Idea of Liberal Education*. Teachers College, Columbia University, 1986.
Kohlstedt, Sally Gregory. "Curiosities and Cabinets: Natural History Museums and Education on the Antebellum Campus." *Isis: Journal of the History of Science in Society* 79, no. 3 (1 Sept. 1988): 405–26.
Kohlstedt, Sally Gregory. *The Formation of the American Scientific Community: The American Association for the Advancement of Science, 1848–60*. University of Illinois Press, 1976.
Kohlstedt, Sally Gregory. "The National Academy of Sciences: The First Hundred Years, 1863–1963." *ISIS: Journal of the History of Science in Society* 71, no. 1 (Mar. 1980): 155–57.
Kohlstedt, Sally Gregory. "Parlors, Primers, and Public Schooling: Education for Science in Nineteenth-Century America." *Isis* 81, no. 3 (1 Sept. 1990): 424–45.
Kohlstedt, Sally. "A Step toward Scientific Self-Identity in the United States: The Failure of the National Institute, 1844." *ISIS: Journal of the History of Science in Society* 62, no. 3 (1971): 339–62.
Kohn, Richard H. *Eagle and Sword: The Federalists and the Creation of the Military Establishment in America, 1783–1802*. Free Press, 1975.
Kuritz, Hyman. "Benjamin Rush: His Theory of Republican Education." *History of Education Quarterly* 7, no. 4 (Winter 1967): 432–51.
Lang, Hans-Joachim, and Benjamin Lease. "The Authorship of Symzonia: The Case for Nathaniel Ames." *New England Quarterly* 48, no. 2 (1975): 241–52.
Leibiger, Stuart Eric. *Founding Friendship: George Washington, James Madison, and the Creation of the American Republic*. University Press of Virginia, 1999.
Leopold, Richard William. *Robert Dale Owen: A Biography*. Harvard University Press, 1940.
Lewis, Andrew J. *A Democracy of Facts: Natural History in the Early Republic*. University of Pennsylvania Press, 2011.
Lewis, Andrew J. "Gathering for the Republic : Botany in Early Republic America." In *Colonial Botany: Science, Commerce, and Politics in the Early Modern World*, edited by Londa L. Schiebinger and Claudia Swan, 66–80. University of Pennsylvania Press, 2005.
Library of Congress. *Librarians of Congress, 1802–1974*. Government Printing Office, 1977.
Lindgren, James M. "'That Every Mariner May Possess the History of the World': A Cabinet for the East India Marine...." *New England Quarterly* 68, no. 2 (June 1995): 179–205.
Longmore, Paul K. *The Invention of George Washington*. University Press of Virginia, 1999.

Lucas, Frederic A. *The Story of Museum Groups.* Variation: Guide Leaflet Series of the American Museum of Natural History, no. 53. American Museum of Natural History, 1921.

MacLean, Jayne. "Nursery and Seed Trade Catalogs." *Journal of NAL Associates* 5, no. 3/4 (1980): 88–92.

Madden, E. F. "John Cleves Symmes Revisited." *American History Illustrated* 20, no. 2 (1985): 40–43.

Madsen, David. *The National University: Enduring Dream of the USA.* Wayne State University Press, 1966.

Manning, Thomas G. *U.S. Coast Survey vs. Naval Hydrographic Office: A 19th-Century Rivalry in Science and Politics.* University of Alabama Press, 1988.

Marti, Donald B. "Early Agricultural Societies in New York: The Foundations of Improvement." *New York History* 48, no. 4 (October 1967): 313–31.

Martin, Robert W. T. *Government by Dissent: Protest, Resistance, and Radical Democratic Thought in the Early American Republic.* New York University Press, 2013.

Matheson, William. "George Watterston: Advocate of the National Library." In *Librarians of Congress 1802–1974*, by Library of Congress, 57–75. Government Printing Office, 1977.

Matthews, Jean V. *Rufus Choate: The Law and Civic Virtue.* Temple University Press, 1980.

Mauviel, Maurice. "Volney, Constantin-François de Chasseboeuf." In *Encyclopedia of the Enlightenment,* edited by Alan Charles Kors. Oxford: Oxford University Press, 2005. https://www-oxfordreference-com.mutex.gmu.edu/view/10.1093/acref/9780195104301.001.0001/acref-9780195104301-e-738.

May, Henry F. *The Enlightenment in America.* New York: Oxford University Press, 1976.

Mayer, David N. "'Necessary and Proper' West Point and Jefferson's Constitutionalism." In *Thomas Jefferson's Military Academy: Founding West Point,* edited by Robert M. S. McDonald, 54–76. University of Virginia Press, 2004.

McDonald, Robert M. S., ed. *Light and Liberty: Thomas Jefferson and the Power of Knowledge.* University of Virginia Press, 2012.

McDonald, Robert M. S., ed. *Sons of the Father: George Washington and His Protégés.* University of Virginia Press, 2013.

McDonald, Robert M. S., ed. *Thomas Jefferson's Military Academy: Founding West Point.* University of Virginia Press, 2004.

McDonough, John. "John Silva Meehan: A Gentleman of Amiable Manners." In *Librarians of Congress 1802–1974,* by Library of Congress, 77–102. Government Printing Office, 1977.

McMullen, Haynes. *American Libraries Before 1876.* Greenwood Press, 2000.

Messerli, Jonathan. "The Columbian Complex: The Impulse to National Consolidation." *History of Education Quarterly* 7, no. 4 (1967): 417–31.

Mizelle, Brett. "Displaying the Expanding Nation to Itself: The Cultural Work of Public Exhibitions of Western Fauna in Lewis and Clark's Philadelphia." In *The Shortest and Most Convenient Route: Lewis and Clark in Context*, edited by Robert S. Cox, 215–35. Transactions of the American Philosophical Society 94, pt. 5. American Philosophical Society, 2004.

Moyer, Albert E. *Joseph Henry: The Rise of an American Scientist*. Smithsonian Institution Press, 1997.

Mucher, Christen. *Before American History: Nationalist Mythmaking and Indigenous Dispossession*. University of Virginia Press, 2022.

Nash, Gary B. "The American Clergy and the French Revolution." *William and Mary Quarterly* 22 (July 1965): 392–412.

Nash, Gary B. *First City: Philadelphia and the Forging of Historical Memory*. Early American Studies. University of Pennsylvania Press, 2002.

National Capital Planning Commission. "Foggy Bottom / Northwest Rectangle Heritage Trail Assessment Report." Washington, DC, 2014.

Naughton, Patrick. "Professional Military Education: Proven in Combat During the Mexican War." *Military Review* 97, no. 4 (7 Aug. 2017): 84–91.

Neely, Wayne Caldwell. *The Agricultural Fair*. Columbia University Press, 1935.

Neem, Johann N. *Creating a Nation of Joiners: Democracy and Civil Society in Early National Massachusetts*. Harvard University Press, 2008.

Neem, Johann N. *Democracy's Schools: The Rise of Public Education in America*. John Hopkins University Press, 2017.

Neem, Johann N. "From 'Ancients and Axioms' to 'Every Branch of Science': Thomas Jefferson's Philosophy of Liberal Education." In *The Founding of Thomas Jefferson's University*, edited by John A. Ragosta, Peter S. Onuf, and Andrew J. O'Shaughnessy, 306–24. University of Virginia Press, 2019.

Neem, Johann N. "'To Diffuse Knowledge More Generally through the Mass of the People': Thomas Jefferson on Individual Freedom and the Distribution of Knowledge." In *Light and Liberty: Thomas Jefferson and the Power of Knowledge*, edited by Robert M. S. McDonald, 47–74. University of Virginia Press, 2012.

Nelson, Adam R. "The Perceived Dangers of Study Abroad, 1780–1800: Nationalism, Internationalism, and the Origins of the American University." In *The Founding Fathers, Education, and "The Great Contest": The American Philosophical Society Prize of 1797*, edited by Benjamin Justice, 175–97. Palgrave Macmillan, 2013.

Nelson, Lynn A. "When Land Was Cheap, and Labor Dear: James Madison's 'Address to the Albemarle Agricultural Society' and the Problem of Southern Agricultural Reform." *History Compass* 6, no. 3 (2008): 917–33.

Nichols, Roger L. *Stephen Long and American Frontier Exploration*. University of Delaware Press, 1980.
O'Malley, Therese. "'Your Garden Must Be a Museum to You': Early American Botanic Gardens." *Huntington Library Quarterly* 59, no. 2/3 (Mar. 1996): 207–31.
O'Neill, Jean. *Peter Collinson and the Eighteenth-Century Natural History Exchange*. American Philosophical Society, 2008.
O'Shaughnessy, Andrew Jackson. *The Illimitable Freedom of the Human Mind: Thomas Jefferson's Idea of a University*. University of Virginia Press, 2021.
Oberle, George D. "institutionalizing the Information Revolution: Debates over Knowledge Institutions in the Early American Republic." PhD diss., George Mason University, 2016.
Odle, Mairin. "Buried in Plain Sight: Indian 'Curiosities' in Du Simitière's American Museum." *Pennsylvania Magazine of History and Biography* 136, no. 4 (2012): 499–502.
Oehser, Paul H. *The Smithsonian Institution*. Routledge, 2019.
Oleson, Alexandra, and Sanborn Conner Brown, eds. *The Pursuit of Knowledge in the Early American Republic: American Scientific and Learned Societies from Colonial Times to the Civil War*. Johns Hopkins University Press, 1976.
Onuf, Peter S. *The Mind of Thomas Jefferson*. University of Virginia Press, 2007.
Opal, J. M. *Beyond the Farm: National Ambitions in Rural New England*. University of Pennsylvania Press, 2008.
Opal, J. M. "Exciting Emulation: Academies and the Transformation of the Rural North, 1780s–1820s." *Journal of American History* 91, no. 2 (Sept. 2004): 445–70.
Orosz, Joel J. *Curators and Culture: The Museum Movement in America, 1740–1870*. University of Alabama Press, 1990.
Orosz, Joel J. *The Eagle That Is Forgotten: Pierre Eugène Du Simitière, Founding Father of American Numismatics*. Wolfeboro, NH: Bowers and Merena Galleries, 1988.
Orsi, Jared. *Citizen Explorer: The Life of Zebulon Pike*. Oxford University Press, 2014.
Ostrowski, Carl. *Books, Maps, and Politics: A Cultural History of the Library of Congress, 1783–1861*. University of Massachusetts Press, 2004.
Pangle, Lorraine Smith, and Thomas L. Pangle. *The Learning of Liberty: The Educational Ideas of the American Founders*. American Political Thought. University Press of Kansas, 1993.
Parrington, Vernon Louis. *The Colonial Mind, 1620–1800*. Volume 1 of *Main Currents in American Thought*. University of Oklahoma Press, 1987.
Parrish, Susan Scott. *American Curiosity: Cultures of Natural History in the Colonial British Atlantic World*. University of North Carolina Press, 2006.

Parsons, Lynn Hudson. *The Birth of Modern Politics: Andrew Jackson, John Quincy Adams, and the Election of 1828*. New York: Oxford University Press, 2009.

Parsons, Lynn Hudson. "In Which the Political Becomes the Personal, and Vice Versa: The Last Ten Years of John Quincy Adams and Andrew Jackson." *Journal of the Early Republic* 23, no. 3 (2003): 421–43.

Pasley, Jeffrey L. "The Cheese and the Words: Popular Political Culture and Participatory Democracy in the Early American Republic." In *Beyond the Founders: New Approaches to the Political History of the Early American Republic*, edited by Jeffrey L. Pasley, Andrew W. Robertson, and David Waldstreicher, 31–56. University of North Carolina Press, 2004.

Pasley, Jeffrey L. *"The Tyranny of Printers": Newspaper Politics in the Early American Republic*. University Press of Virginia, 2001.

Patterson, L. Ray. *Copyright in Historical Perspective*. Vanderbilt University Press, 1968.

Pawley, Emily. *The Nature of the Future: Agriculture, Science, and Capitalism in the Antebellum North*. University of Chicago Press, 2020.

Peck, Robert McCracken. "To the Ends of the Earth for Science: Research Expeditions of the Academy of Natural Sciences; The First 150 Years, 1812–1962." *Proceedings of the Academy of Natural Sciences of Philadelphia* 150 (14 Apr. 2000): 15–46.

Phillips, Denise. *Acolytes of Nature: Defining Natural Science in Germany, 1770–1850*. University of Chicago Press, 2012.

Pinkett, Harold T. "Early Agricultural Societies in the District of Columbia." *Records of the Columbia Historical Society, Washington, D.C.* 51/52 (1 Jan. 1951): 32–45.

Pleadwell, Frank Lester. *Edward Cutbush, M. D.: The Nester of the Medical Corps of the Navy*. New York: P. B. Hoeber, 1923.

Porter, Charlotte M. "The American West Described in Natural History Journals, 1819–1836." *Midwest Review* 2 (Mar. 1980): 18–37.

Porter, Charlotte M. *The Eagle's Nest: Natural History and American Ideas, 1812–1842*. University of Alabama Press, 1986.

Portolano, Marlana. "John Quincy Adams's Rhetorical Crusade for Astronomy." *ISIS: Journal of the History of Science in Society* 91, no. 3 (2000): 480–503.

Portolano, Marlana. *The Passionate Empiricist: The Eloquence of John Quincy Adams in the Service of Science*. State University of New York Press, 2009.

Potts, William John, and Pierre Eugene Du Simitiere. "Du Simitiere: Artist, Antiquary, and Naturalist, Projector of the First American Museum, with Some Extracts from His Note-Book." *Pennsylvania Magazine of History and Biography* 13, no. 3 (1889): 341–75.

Puls, Mark. *Henry Knox: Visionary General of the American Revolution*. Palgrave Macmillan, 2008.

Quattlebaum, Charles Albert. *The National University Movement in the United States: A Report Prepared in the Legislative Reference Service of the Library of Congress.* Library of Congress, 1961.

Rader, Karen A, and Victoria E. M. Cain. *Life on Display: Revolutionizing U.S. Museums of Science and Natural History in the Twentieth Century.* University of Chicago Press, 2014.

Ragosta, John A., Peter S. Onuf, and Andrew J. O'Shaughnessy, eds. *The Founding of Thomas Jefferson's University.* University of Virginia Press, 2019.

Ragsdale, Bruce A. *Washington at the Plow: The Founding Farmer and the Question of Slavery.* Belknap Press of Harvard University Press, 2021.

Rasmussen, Wayne D. "Diplomats and Plant Collectors: The South American Commission, 1817–1818." *Agricultural History* 29, no. 1 (1955): 22–31.

Rathburn, Richard. *The Columbian Institute for the Promotion of Arts and Sciences: A Washington Society of 1816–1838, Which Established a Museum and Botanic Garden Under Government Patronage.* Government Printing Office, 1917.

Rathburn, Richard. *The United States National Museum.* . . . Washington, DC, 1905.

Ray, Angela G. *The Lyceum and Public Culture in the Nineteenth-Century United States.* Michigan State University Press, 2005.

Ray, Angela G., and Paul Stob, eds. *Thinking Together: Lecturing, Learning, and Difference in the Long Nineteenth Century.* Rhetoric and Democratic Deliberation. Pennsylvania State University Press, 2018.

Ray, Angela G., and Paul Stob. Introduction to *Thinking Together: Lecturing, Learning, and Difference in the Long Nineteenth Century,* edited by Angela G. Ray and Paul Stob, 1–20.

Regis, Pamela. *Describing Early America: Bartram, Jefferson, Crèvecoeur, and the Rhetoric of Natural History.* Northern Illinois University Press, 1992.

Reingold, Nathan. "Definitions and Speculations: The Professionalization of Science in America in the Nineteenth Century." In *The Pursuit of Knowledge in the Early American Republic: American Scientific and Learned Societies from Colonial Times to the Civil War,* edited by Alexandra Oleson and Sanborn Conner Brown, 33–69. Johns Hopkins University Press, 1976.

Remini, Robert V. *Andrew Jackson and the Course of American Freedom, 1822–1832.* Harper and Row, 1981.

Reynolds, David S. *Beneath the American Renaissance: The Subversive Imagination in the Age of Emerson and Melville.* Knopf, 1988.

Rippy, J. Fred. *Joel R. Poinsett, Versatile American.* Duke University Press, 1935.

Robson, David W. "Pennsylvania's 'Lost' National University: Johann Forster's Plan." *Pennsylvania Magazine of History and Biography* 102, no. 3 (1978): 364–74.

Ron, Ariel. *Grassroots Leviathan: Agricultural Reform and the Rural North in the Slaveholding Republic.* Johns Hopkins University Press, 2020.

Ron, Ariel. "Summoning the State: Northern Farmers and the Transformation of American Politics in the Mid-Nineteenth Century." *Journal of American History* 103, no. 2 (1 Sept. 2016): 347–74.

Ronda, James P. *Beyond Lewis & Clark: The Army Explores the West*. Tacoma: Washington State Historical Society, 2003.

Rose, Mark. *Authors and Owners: The Invention of Copyright*. Harvard University Press, 1993.

Rossiter, Margaret W. *The Emergence of Agricultural Science: Justus Liebig and the Americans, 1840–1880*. Yale University Press, 1975.

Rossiter, Margaret. "The Organization of Agricultural Improvement in the United States, 1785–1865." In *The Pursuit of Knowledge in the Early American Republic: American Scientific and Learned Societies from Colonial Times to the Civil War*, edited by Alexandra Oleson and Sanborn Conner Brown, 279–98. Johns Hopkins University Press, 1976.

Rothman, Adam. *Slave Country: American Expansion and the Origins of the Deep South*. Harvard University Press, 2005.

Rothman, Irving N. "Structure and Theme in Samuel Ewing's Satire, the *American Miracle*." *American Literature* 40, no. 3 (Nov. 1968): 294–308.

Rudolph, Frederick. *The American College and University: A History*. Knopf, 1968.

Sarudy, Barbara Wells. "Nurserymen and Seed Dealers in the Eighteenth-Century Chesapeake." *Journal of Garden History* 9, no. 3 (1 July 1989): 111–17.

Schakenbach Regele, Lindsay. *Flowers, Guns, and Money: Joel Roberts Poinsett and the Paradoxes of American Patriotism*. American Beginnings, 1500–1900. University of Chicago Press, 2023.

Schiebinger, Londa L. *Plants and Empire: Colonial Bioprospecting in the Atlantic World*. Harvard University Press, 2004.

Schiebinger, Londa. "Prospecting for Drugs: European Naturalists in the West Indies." In *Colonial Botany: Science, Commerce, and Politics in the Early Modern World*, edited by Londa L. Schiebinger and Claudia Swan, 119–33. University of Pennsylvania Press, 2007.

Schiebinger, Londa L., and Claudia Swan, eds. *Colonial Botany: Science, Commerce, and Politics in the Early Modern World*. University of Pennsylvania Press, 2005.

Schofield, Robert E. "The Science Education of an Enlightened Entrepreneur: Charles Willson Peale and His Philadelphia Museum, 1784–1827." *American Studies* 30, no. 2 (1989): 21–40.

Schwartz, George H. *Collecting the Globe: The Salem East India Marine Society Museum*. University of Massachusetts Press, 2020.

Scott, Pamela. *Capital Engineers: The U.S. Army Corps of Engineers in the Development of Washington, D.C., 1790–2004*. U.S. Army Corps of Engineers, Office of History, 2005.

Sellers, Charles Coleman. *Mr. Peale's Museum: Charles Willson Peale and the First Popular Museum of Natural Science and Art*. Norton, 1980.

Sellers, Charles Grier. *The Market Revolution: Jacksonian America, 1815–1846*. New York: Oxford University Press, 1991.

Semonin, Paul. *American Monster : How the Nation's First Prehistoric Creature Became a Symbol of National Identity*. New York University Press, 2000.

Shapiro, Henry D. "The Western Academy of Natural Sciences of Cincinnati and the Structure of Science in the Ohio Valley, 1810–1850." In *The Pursuit of Knowledge in the Early American Republic: American Scientific and Learned Societies from Colonial Times to the Civil War*, edited by Alexandra Oleson and Sanborn Conner Brown, 219–47. Johns Hopkins University Press, 1976.

Shawen, Neil McDowell. "Thomas Jefferson and a 'National' University: The Hidden Agenda for Virginia." *Virginia Magazine of History and Biography* 92, no. 3 (1984): 309–35.

Shera, Jesse Hauk. *Foundations of the Public Library; the Origins of the Public Library Movement in New England, 1629–1885*. Hamden, Conn.: Shoe String Press, 1965.

Shera, Jesse Hauk. "Jewett and Spofford—National Librarians: A Review Article." *Library Quarterly* 47, no. 1 (Jan. 1977): 58–61.

Sifton, Paul G. "A Disordered Life: The American Career of Pierre Eugène Du Simitière." *Manuscripts* 25 (Fall 1973): 235–53.

Sifton, Paul G. "Pierre Eugene Du Simitiere (1737–1784): Collector in Revolutionary America." PhD diss., University of Pennsylvania, 1960.

Sioli, Marco. "Breaking into the Trans-Mississippian Frontiers: Thomas Jefferson's Expeditions to the West." *European Contributions to American Studies* 58 (Aug. 2004): 69–87.

Sloan, Kim, and Andrew Burnett, eds. *Enlightenment: Discovering the World in the Eighteenth Century*. Smithsonian Books, 2003.

Smith, Mark A. *Engineering Security: The Corps of Engineers and Third System Defense Policy, 1815–1861*. University of Alabama Press, 2009.

Smith, Richard Norton. *Patriarch: George Washington and the New American Nation*. Houghton Mifflin, 1993.

Snead, James E. *Relic Hunters: Archaeology and the Public in Nineteenth-Century America*. Oxford: Oxford University Press, 2018.

Solit, Karen. *History of the United States Botanic Garden, 1816–1991*. Government Printing Office, 1993.

Sorber, Nathan M. *Land-Grant Colleges and Popular Revolt: The Origins of the Morrill Act and the Reform of Higher Education*. Cornell University Press, 2018.

Spero, Patrick. "The Other Presidency: Thomas Jefferson and the American Philosophical Society." *Proceedings of the American Philosophical Society* 162, no. 4 (Dec. 2018): 321–60.

Spero, Patrick. *The Scientist Turned Spy: André Michaux, Thomas Jefferson, and the Conspiracy of 1793*. Jeffersonian America. University of Virginia Press, 2024.

Standish, David. *Hollow Earth: The Long and Curious History of Imagining Strange Lands, Fantastical Creatures, Advanced Civilizations, and Marvelous Machines Below the Earth's Surface*. Da Capo Books, 2006.

Stanton, William Ragan. *American Scientific Exploration, 1803–1860: Manuscripts in Four Philadelphia Libraries*. American Philosophical Society, 1991.

Stanton, William Ragan. *The Great United States Exploring Expedition of 1838–1842*. University of California Press, 1975.

Stanton, William Ragan. *The Leopard's Spots: Scientific Attitudes Toward Race in America, 1815–59*. University of Chicago Press, 1960.

Steele, Brian. "'The Yeomanry of the United States Are Not the Canaille of Paris': Thomas Jefferson, American Exceptionalism and the 'Spirit' of Democracy." In *Light and Liberty: Thomas Jefferson and the Power of Knowledge*, edited by Robert M. S. McDonald, 19–46. University of Virginia Press, 2012.

Strang, Cameron B. *Frontiers of Science: Imperialism and Natural Knowledge in the Gulf South Borderlands, 1500–1850*. Published for the Omohundro Institute of Early American History and Culture, Williamsburg, Virginia, by the University of North Carolina Press, 2018.

Terrell, Colleen E. "'Republican Machines': Franklin, Rush, and the Manufacture of Civic Virtue in the Early Republic." *Early American Studies* 1, no. 2 (2003): 100–132.

Thelin, John R. *A History of American Higher Education*. 2nd ed. Johns Hopkins University Press, 2011.

Thomas, George. *The Founders and the Idea of a National University: Constituting the American Mind*. New York: Cambridge University Press, 2015.

Thomson, Keith Stewart. *Jefferson's Shadow: The Story of His Science*. Yale University Press, 2012.

Tolley, Kim. "Learning from Nature: Alexander von Humboldt's Influence on Young Women's Geography and Natural History Education in Nineteenth-Century America." *Paedagogica Historica* 56, no. 1–2 (3 Mar. 2020): 101–20.

True, Rodney H. "Early Days of the Albemarle Agricultural Society." *Agricultural History Society Papers* 1 (1921): 241–59.

Tucher, Andie. "Periodical Press: Newspapers, Magazines, and Reviews." In *An Extensive Republic: Print, Culture, and Society in the New Nation, 1790–1840*, edited by Robert A. Gross and Mary Kelley, 2:389–408. Chapel Hill: Published in association with the American Antiquarian Society by the University of North Carolina Press, 2010.

Turner, Charles W. "Virginia State Agricultural Societies, 1811–1860." *Agricultural History* 38, no. 3 (Summer 1964): 167–77.

Tyack, David B. *Law and the Shaping of Public Education, 1785–1954.* University of Wisconsin Press, 1987.

United States Army Corps of Engineers. *The U.S. Army Corps of Engineers: A History.* Revised ed. Alexandria, VA, 2007.

Verney, Michael A. *A Great and Rising Nation: Naval Exploration and Global Empire in the Early US Republic.* American Beginnings, 1500–1900. University of Chicago Press, 2022.

Wade, Arthur P. "A Military Offspring of the American Philosophical Society." *Military Affairs* 38, no. 3 (1 Oct. 1974): 103–7.

Wagoner, Jennings L. *Jefferson and Education.* Chapel Hill: Thomas Jefferson Foundation; Distributed by The University of North Carolina Press, 2004.

Wagoner, Jennings L., and Christine Coalwell McDonald. "Mr. Jefferson's Academy: An Educational Interpretation." In *Thomas Jefferson's Military Academy: Founding West Point,* edited by Robert M.S. McDonald, 118–53. University of Virginia Press, 2004.

Waldstreicher, David. *In the Midst of Perpetual Fetes: The Making of American Nationalism, 1776–1820.* Published for the Omohundro Institute of Early American History and Culture, Williamsburg, Virginia, by the University of North Carolina Press, 1997.

Walker, William S. *A Living Exhibition: The Smithsonian and the Transformation of the Universal Museum.* University of Massachusetts Press, 2013.

Ward, David C. *Charles Willson Peale: Art and Selfhood in the Early Republic.* University of California Press, 2004.

Warren, Leonard. *Maclure of New Harmony: Scientist, Progressive Educator, Radical Philanthropist.* Indiana University Press, 2009.

Webb, Lester Austin. "The Origin of Military Schools in the United States Founded in the Nineteenth Century." PhD diss., University of North Carolina at Chapel Hill, 1958.

Wellmon, Chad. *Organizing Enlightenment: Information Overload and the Invention of the Modern Research University.* Johns Hopkins University Press, 2015.

Wells, Colin. *The Devil and Doctor Dwight: Satire and Theology in the Early American Republic.* Published for the Omohundro Institute of Early American History and Culture, Williamsburg, Virginia, by the University of North Carolina Press, 2002.

Wells, Jonathan Daniel. *The Origins of the Southern Middle Class, 1800–1861.* University of North Carolina Press, 2004.

Wells, Jonathan Daniel, and Jennifer R. Green, eds. *The Southern Middle Class in the Long Nineteenth Century.* Louisiana State University Press, 2011.

Whitehill, Walter Muir. *The East India Marine Society and the Peabody Museum of Salem: A Sesquicentennial History.* Peabody Museum, 1949.

Wilder, Craig Steven. *Ebony and Ivy: Race, Slavery, and the Troubled History of America's Universities.* Bloomsbury, 2013.

Wilson, Kirt H., and Kaitlyn G. Patia. "Authentic Imitation or Perverse Original? Learning About Race from America's Popular Platforms." In *Thinking Together: Lecturing, Learning, and Difference in the Long Nineteenth Century,* edited by Angela G. Ray and Paul Stob, 72–94. Pennsylvania State University Press, 2018.

Winterer, Caroline. *American Enlightenments: Pursuing Happiness in the Age of Reason.* Yale University Press, 2016.

Wolff, Katherine. *Culture Club: The Curious History of the Boston Athenaeum.* University of Massachusetts Press, 2009.

Wonders, Karen. *Habitat Dioramas: Illusions of Wilderness in Museums of Natural History.* Uppsala: Acta Universitatis Upsaliensis, 1993.

Wood, Gordon S. *Empire of Liberty: A History of the Early Republic, 1789–1815.* New York: Oxford University Press, 2009.

Wood, Richard George. *Stephen Harriman Long, 1784–1864: Army Engineer, Explorer, Inventor.* Glendale, CA: A. H. Clark, 1966.

Woodress, James Leslie. *A Yankee's Odyssey: The Life of Joel Barlow.* Lippincott, 1958.

Wooster, Robert. *The American Military Frontiers: The United States Army in the West, 1783–1900.* University of New Mexico Press, 2009.

Wright, Tom F., ed. *The Cosmopolitan Lyceum: Lecture Culture and the Globe in Nineteenth-Century America.* University of Massachusetts Press, 2013.

Yokota, Kariann Akemi. *Unbecoming British: How Revolutionary America Became a Postcolonial Nation.* New York: Oxford University Press, 2011.

Zagarri, Rosemarie. *Revolutionary Backlash: Women and Politics in the Early American Republic.* University of Pennsylvania Press, 2007.

Zuersher, Dorothy J. Schoeberlein. "Benjamin Franklin, Jonathan Williams, and the United States Military Academy." PhD diss., University of North Carolina at Greensboro, 1974.

INDEX

Italicized page numbers refer to illustrations.

AAAS (American Academy of Arts and Sciences), 38, 44–48, 62, 146
AAAS (American Association for the Advancement of Science), 135, 146
Abert, John James, 127
Academy of Natural Sciences (ANS), 66, 85–87, 89–90, 118
Adams, John: as AAAS president, 38, 45, 62; Geneva faculty scheme and, 26; Jefferson as vice president to, 37; Randolph's correspondence with, 156n68; wax representation in Columbian Museum, 78
Adams, John Quincy: Henry's plan for Smithsonian, 132, 187n75; on national observatory, 105, 116, 129; scientific agenda of, 104–5, 107–9, 118; as Secretary of State, 101; USMPS membership of, 54
African Americans. *See* Black Americans
agricultural knowledge, 9, 92–96, 100, 103, 109, 113–15, 143
agricultural research, 92, 97, 114, 116, 120
agricultural societies: agricultural knowledge shared through, 9, 95; democratization of knowledge in, 96, 112; elite participation in, 95, 96, 100; experimentation by, 92, 93, 110, 113; fairs held by, 93–95, 110; horticultural, 91, 94, 109; journals published by, 110–13, *112*; national, 113–14, 120, 125, 126; proliferation of, 93, 96, 100, 109, 115; in public-private partnerships, 93; seed exchanges among, 92, 96; specialized, 91–92, 109; on specimen collection through fieldwork, 103; at state level, 110–13, *112*, 179n102; Washington on establishment of, 93. *See also specific organizations*
Agricultural Society of Prince George's County, 93
Alamán, Lucas, 184n28
Albany Lyceum, 110, 179n102
American Academy of Arts and Sciences (AAAS), 38, 44–48, 62, 146
American Antiquarian Society, 91
American Association for the Advancement of Science (AAAS), 135, 146
American degeneracy argument, 77, 171n58
American Journal of Science, 111
American Museum (New York), 78–80
American Philosophical Society (APS): collections secured by Poinsett for, 122–23, 184n28; dissemination of information by, 37; European learned societies as models for, 44; Hopkinson's address to, 64; Indigenous populations studied by, 51, 52; institutional apparatus of, 49; Jefferson as president of, 37–38; as knowledge institution, 49; mammoth excavation and, 76; Mexican artifacts given to, 123, *123*; Peale and, 49–50, 52, 67, 68, 72; publications by, 44–45, 47–50; scientific expeditions

American Philosophical Society (APS) (*continued*)
and, 45–51, 89; South American interests of, 101; USMPS ties with, 53, 62, 164n74; Washington as member of, 22–23

American Revolution: foreign assistance during, 40, 42; Peale's service during, 66–67; print culture and, 5–6, 149n12; Rush on incompleteness of, 16, 17; views on meaning of, 13, 30; Washington's service during, 26, 155n57

ANS (Academy of Natural Sciences), 66, 85–87, 89–90, 118

APS. *See* American Philosophical Society (APS)

Armstrong, John, 42

Army Corps of Engineers. *See* United States Army Corps of Engineers

Arnold, Benedict, 67

arts: domestic, 16; polite, 30; promotion of, 19, 21, 29, 73, 97, 105; Smithsonian Institution and, 130, 132; specialized knowledge in, 36; uniting science with, 55, 113

Association of American Geologists and Naturalists, 91, 126, 146

Bache, Alexander Dallas, 111, 129–31, 186n60

Bachman, John, 128

Baird, Spencer F., 133, 142

Baldwin, William, 102–3, 177n61, 177n64

Barlow, Joel, 35, 41, 54, 55, 122

Barnum, P. T., 80, 127–28

Barton, Benjamin Smith, 49–50

Bartram, John, 96

Beauvois, A. M. F. J., 71–72

Belknap, Jeremey, 18

Black Americans: American Museum admission for, 79; enslavement of, 94, 119, 141; in horticultural societies, 94; negative portrayals of, 79

Bland, Theodorick, 101
Blodget, Lorin, 135
Blodget, Samuel, 23–24, *24*, 33–34, 155n57
Bonaparte, Napoleon, 41–44, 48
Bonpland, Aimé, 102–3
Boston Athenaeum, 91
botanical gardens, 95–99, 103, 113
Bowen, Daniel, 78
Brackenridge, Henry, 101–2
Branch, John, 108
Breese, Sidney, 186n60
Brett, Megan, 176n52
Brown, James F., 94
Buffon, Comte de, 77, 171n58
Butterfield, Lyman Henry, 153n22

CAAS (Connecticut Academy of Arts and Sciences), 44, 47–48
Calhoun, John C., 88, 118–19
CAS (Columbian Agricultural Society), 91, 93–95, 97
Catalogue of the Mount Airy Agricultural Institute, 114, 115
Centennial Exposition (1876), 147
Chapin, Steven, 119
Chapman, George, 22, 154n41
charlatans, 9, 39, 47, 128–31, 138, 145, 186n55
Charleston Literary and Philosophical Society, 122
Chesapeake and Ohio Canal Company, 35, 151n2
Choate, Rufus, 130–31, 186n60
citizenry: educated, 2, 8, 12, 17, 20; engaged, 2–4, 6, 9, 88, 145; homogenous, 3, 17, 35, 144; information needs of, 5, 7; informed, 2–3, 6, 8, 12, 17, 64, 141, 147; privileges and duties of, 2, 6, 17, 144; republican, 6, 11, 13, 17, 19
citizen science, 9, 90, 91, 117, 134–35, 138, 144–46
citizen-soldiers, 43

civic societies, 3, 6, 85, 179n102
Clark, George Rogers, 45–46, 50, 66, 74, 124
Clinton, DeWitt, 54, 110, 179n102
Clinton, George, 54
Cobbett, William, 100
Collin, Nicholas, 15, 16, 21, 152n11
colonialism, 7, 13, 84, 88, 92, 96
Columbian Agricultural Society (CAS), 91, 93–95, 97
Columbian College (Washington, DC), 35, 98, 119
Columbian Institute for the Promotion of Arts and Sciences, 97–99, 102, 105, 109, 176n39
Columbian Museum (Boston), 78
Commission of Science and Arts (France), 41
concentric spheres theory, 106–7
Confederation period, 13, 14, 16
Connecticut Academy of Arts and Sciences (CAAS), 44, 47–48
Constitutional Convention (1787), 15, 17, 19–20, 22
consuls, 95, 100, 108, 176n52, 177n54
Cooper, Thomas, 119
Copyright Act of 1790, 154n35
Coram, Robert, 30–31
Corps of Engineers. *See* United States Army Corps of Engineers
corruption: education as source of, 17, 26; of European institutions, 144; in federal government, 108; intellectual, 76, 104; of knowledge, 49, 104; monarchical, 14, 17, 20
Craik, William, 32–33
creation of knowledge: in binding nation together, 3; centralization of, 28; debates regarding, 5, 65, 116, 141; democratization of, 96, 144–45; by learned societies, 44, 45; national university for, 36; participation in, 2, 5, 8, 39, 45, 63, 86, 92–93, 121, 144; print culture and, 4; scientific, 6, 13, 28, 39–40, 49, 92; specialized, 39, 51, 103, 142; useful, 2, 95
crested helmet (Hawaiian mahiole), 71
Cultivator (journal), 110–13, *112*
cultural nationalism, 39
curriculum: at European military academies, 40–41; Federalist views of, 13–14, 27–28, 64; Jeffersonian views of, 13–14, 27, 28, 64; for national university, 13–14, 18, 25, 27–29; republican values promoted through, 119; scientific knowledge and, 7, 9, 14, 25, 27–28; useful knowledge and, 14; at West Point, 7, 38, 44, 51, 53, 61–63; for women's education, 16
Cutbush, Edward, 98, 102

Dallas, George M., 1, 186n60
D'Anmour, Chevalier, 70
Dearborn, Henry Alexander Scammell, 109, 113
de Masson, Francis, 55, 58
Dennie, Joseph, 76
Department of Agriculture, 143
Derby, Elias, 69
digital technology, 147–48
dissemination of knowledge: agricultural, 100, 109; in binding nation together, 3; debates regarding, 5, 13, 27, 65, 116, 141; democratization of, 96, 144–45; digital technology and, 147–48; knowledge institutions for, 1, 5–6, 17, 35; by learned societies, 37, 39, 44, 45; libraries and, 136; museums and, 65, 78, 88–90; national university for, 36; participation in, 2, 5, 6, 8, 39, 45, 92, 121, 144; politicization of, 66; Price on opportunities created by, 15; scientific, 4, 28, 43, 63, 65, 87, 120; by Smithsonian Institution, 132–33, 135, 138–39; specialized, 39; universal, 49; useful, 20, 89, 118
Drake, Daniel, 88

Dunbar, William, 47, 66
Du Ponceau, Peter Stephen, 122
Du Pont de Nemours, Pierre Samuel, 41
Du Simitière, Pierre Eugène, 71
Dwight, Timothy, 61

Edling, Max, 51
education: access to, 25, 160n14; agricultural colleges, 147; classical, 22, 25, 39, 40, 65, 77–78, 119–20; colonial-era institutions, 13; equality through, 30–31; foreign, 11, 16–17, 20, 31; land-grant colleges, 143; models proposed for, 12, 152n18; at private academies, 12, 30; proposals for using Smithson bequest for, 119–20; public, 12–17, 25, 30, 119, 120, 133, 136; purpose of, 6, 15, 28, 30; as source of corruption, 17, 26; state's role in, 17, 21, 108, 153n20; technical colleges, 147; for women, 16. *See also* curriculum; military academies; national university; *specific institutions*
Egyptian Scientific Institute (Institut d'Égypte), 41, 43, 160n23
electricity, 110–12, 180n105
elites: in agricultural societies, 95, 96, 100; classical knowledge and, 14, 40, 77–78; communication infrastructure created by, 6; in creation and dissemination of knowledge, 2; in debates over information needs, 3, 4; on educated and informed citizenry, 8, 64; learned societies and, 38, 39, 44, 90, 95, 96; national university and, 24–25, 27, 29–30, 35, 144; Peale's Museum supported by, 67, 70, 86; private academies for, 12, 30; promotion of knowledge to, 7; research agenda created by, 10; on self-improvement, 19; Smithsonian Institution and, 9, 10, 117, 138
Ellicott, Andrew, 50, 61, 176n39
Elliot, William, 99
Ellsworth, Henry L., 126

Emerson, Ralph Waldo, 106
engineers: civil, 145, 146; expertise of, 44, 159n8; land-grant colleges for, 143; military, 40, 42, 44, 59, 144–45; training at West Point, 7, 144. *See also* United States Army Corps of Engineers
Eustis, William, 94
Evans, George, 186n60
Ewing, Samuel, 76, 77
expertise: agricultural, 95, 96, 110; credentialed, 2, 117, 131, 142, 146; demonstrations of, 83; engineering, 44, 159n8; financial, 24; German-language, 183n16; medical, 41, 122; military, 40, 42, 61, 87; natural history, 52, 109, 128; scientific, 9, 25, 47, 50, 65, 99, 120, 132, 186n49

Featherstonhaugh, George William, 110
Federalists: on curriculum, 13–14, 27–28, 64; debates over need for standing army, 51; on Geneva faculty scheme, 26; learned societies and, 39, 45–47, 49–50, 61–62; on military training models, 40; on Napoleon's scientific endeavors, 42–43; on national university, 8, 13–14, 21, 27–28, 144; on natural history, 49, 76–78; private academies promoted by, 30
Feejee Mermaid, 127–28
Fenno, John, 21
Fichter, James, 169n28
Fitz, Caitlin, 101
Fleischmann, Charles Lewis, 113–14, 120, 121
Forster, Johann, 152n18
Forsyth, John, 119
Franklin, Benjamin, 52, 67, 70, 78, 159n1
French Revolution, 78, 156n68, 171n63
Fulton, Robert, 54

Gallatin, Albert, 94, 101
gardens. *See* botanical gardens
Gates, Horatio, 42

Geneva faculty scheme, 25–27, 156n61
German research universities, 9
Gilman, Daniel Coit, 143
Goodrich, Chauncy, 32
Graham, John, 101
Graham, Martha P., 94
Gray, Robert, 71
Gundy, Samuel, 99

Hamilton, Alexander, 13, 22, 29, 31, 72, 157n79
Hamilton, William, 96
Hammond, James, 177n54
Harriot, Eliza, 16
Harrison, George, 70
Harvard University, 46, 68
Hassler, Ferdinand, 58
Hawaiian mahiole (crested helmet), 71
Hawley, Gideon, 186n60
Heckelwelder, John, 49
Henry, Joseph: on charlatans, 129, 186n55; dismissal of Jewett, 138, 188n96; on electricity, 110, 180n105; as leader of Smithsonian, 129–42, 146, 187n75; on popular scientific activities, 115; on publications by scientists, 133, 187n78; Silliman criticized by, 111
Hilliard, Henry W., 186n60
Hinde, Thomas Spottswood, 107
hollow-earth theory, 106–7
Hopkinson, Francis, 64
horticultural societies, 91, 94, 109
Hosack, David, 79, 171n69
Hough, William J., 186n60
Humboldt, Alexander von, 102–3
Hungerford, Henry James, 118
Hunter, George, 47, 66

Indigenous populations: APS studies of, 51, 52; artifacts obtained by Lewis and Clark, 74; colonialism and, 7, 84; historiographical framework for contact with Europeans, 123; knowledge and resources of, 7; medicinal plants used by, 99; negative portrayals of, 79
information revolution: inclusiveness of, 3; intellectual needs during, 64, 90, 143; knowledge institutions and, 1–2, 5, 7–8; management of, 117, 145, 148; print culture and, 4, 5
Institut d'Égypte (Egyptian Scientific Institute), 41, 43, 160n23
Irving, Washington, 76

Jackson, Andrew, 104, 108, 109, 118
Jacksonian Democrats, 104, 105, 107, 108, 115, 119
Jacobin societies, 61, 171n63
James River Company, 156n64
Jefferie, John Fitzpatrick, 82
Jefferson, Thomas: on access to education, 25, 160n14; *An Account of Louisiana*, 45; as APS president, 37–38; Bill 79 education plan, 12; botanical garden planned for by, 96; on "empire of liberty," 39, 160n13; expansionism of, 46–47; Federalist attacks on, 49, 76; Geneva faculty scheme of, 25–27, 156n61; on knowledge institutions, 35; on Napoleon's scientific endeavors, 41, 43; on national university, 13–14, 25–28, 36; natural history as interest of, 45, 49, 76; *Notes on the State of Virginia*, 76; Peale's correspondence with, 73–74, 80, 169n44; Peale's Museum supported by, 67, 68, 72, 73; retirement to Monticello, 61; scientific production under, 45–47; on students studying abroad, 17; USMPS membership of, 54, 56; Washington's correspondence with, 25–26; West Point and, 43, 51, 53, 59–60, 62, 166n101; Williams's correspondence with, 52, 53
Jeffersonian Republicans: on curriculum, 13–14, 27, 28, 64, 119; debates over need for standing army, 51; learned

Jeffersonian Republicans (*continued*)
societies and, 39, 45; on military training models, 40; on Napoleon's scientific endeavors, 43; on national university, 8, 13–14, 25–28, 33, 36
Jewett, Charles C., 131–33, 135–36, 138, 139, 188n96
Johns Hopkins University, 12, 143
Johnson, Thomas, 24
Johnson, Walter R., 120, 121

Keim, George M., 183n16
Kerber, Linda, 39
knowledge: access to, 4–5, 9, 13, 65, 73, 79–80, 82, 128, 145; authentic, 2, 65, 127–29; authority over, 45, 111, 115, 148; classical, 14, 40, 56, 77–78, 112–13; collection of, 1, 5–6, 35, 39, 66, 86, 89, 100; corruption of, 49, 104; democratization of, 72, 76–82, 91, 96, 112, 115, 128, 144–48; expansion of, 3, 16, 20, 66, 88–89, 92, 98, 105, 143, 146; of Indigenous populations, 7; as means of self-improvement, 19; politicization of, 45, 66, 73, 117; universal, 2, 3, 11, 38, 56, 144. *See also* creation of knowledge; dissemination of knowledge; education; expertise; promotion of knowledge; scientific knowledge; specialized knowledge; useful knowledge
knowledge institutions: botanical gardens and, 103; for collection of knowledge, 1, 5, 6; debates over purpose and nature of, 138–39; for dissemination of knowledge, 1, 5–6, 17, 35; economic progress through, 67; emergence and growth of, 5, 7–9, 87, 90, 145; free from biases, 141; Henry and Jewett as builders of, 136; information revolution and, 1–2, 5, 7–8; national, 8, 90, 105. *See also* agricultural societies; learned societies; libraries; lyceums; museums; *specific institutions*
Knox, Henry, 20

Lafayette, Marquis de, 68
Laming, Benjamin, 70
land-grant colleges, 143
Langdon, Jon, 99
Latrobe, Benjamin Henry, 55–56
Law, Thomas, 176n39
learned societies: active engagement of faculty in, 28; adult learning opportunities through, 44; agricultural, 9, 92–96; creation of knowledge by, 44, 45; dissemination of knowledge by, 37, 39, 44, 45; elite participation in, 38, 39, 44, 90, 95, 96; Federalists and, 39, 45–47, 49–50, 61–62; fusion of military's work and work of, 38, 44, 63; ideological differences among, 39; as information systems, 39, 159n8; Jeffersonians and, 39, 45; national, 116, 125, 129; natural history and, 47–48, 50, 66, 86–88; publications by, 44–45, 47–50; in public-private partnerships, 47, 88, 93; science-focused, 29, 38, 45–48, 121; useful knowledge promoted by, 91. *See also* specialized learned societies; *specific organizations*
Lerebours, Alexandre, 49
Lewis, Joseph, 60–61
Lewis, Lawrence, 151n2
Lewis, Meriwether, 45–46, 50, 61, 66, 74, 124
libraries: adult learning opportunities through, 3–4; Cutbush on importance of access to, 98; dissemination of knowledge and, 136; national, 50, 116, 129, 131, 133, 138, 147; Smithsonian Institution and, 130–33, 135–36, 138, 142; useful knowledge promoted by, 91; Washington's utilization of, 22, 154n46. *See also specific libraries*
Library Company of Philadelphia, 22
Linn, Lewis, 125
Linnaeus, Carl, 73
Literary and Scientific Convention, 125–26

Livingston, Edward, 33
Livingston, Robert, 42, 179n102
Long, Stephen H., 47, 66, 88–89, 103
Louis XVI (king of France), 68
lyceums: adult learning opportunities through, 3–4; lectures at, 105–7, 128, 178n83; natural history and, 61, 106; useful knowledge promoted by, 91. *See also specific organizations*

Maclure, William, 85–87, 118, 173n93
Madison, James: as advisor to Washington, 22; CAS exhibition attended by, 93; military science promoted by, 62; on national university, 19, 32; scientific production under, 45; USMPS membership of, 54
mammoth excavation, 73, 75, 76–77, 80
Marat, Jean-Paul, 78
Marbury, William, 94
Markoe, Francis, 130
Mason, John, 94
Mason, Sarah M. C., 94
Massachusetts Horticultural Society, 91, 109
Masters, Josiah, 60
McBride, James, 107
Medical Society of the District of Columbia, 91
Melville, Herman, 107
Michaux, Andre, 45–46
middling classes, 3, 7, 80, 89, 90, 127
military: citizen-soldiers, 43; engineering and, 40, 42, 44, 59, 144–45; expertise involving, 40, 42, 61, 87; fusion of learned society's work and work of, 38, 44, 63; Knox on national university and viability of, 20; in public-private partnerships, 88; readiness of, 59, 60; scientific expeditions and, 7, 47, 50, 63, 87–89; westward expansion and, 47, 51, 162n49. *See also* United States Army Corps of Engineers

military academies: European, 40–42, 44; proliferation of, 3, 7, 63; Washington on formation of, 42. *See also* United States Military Academy at West Point
military science, 14, 40–43, 53–54, 56, 58–63, 137
misinformation, 8, 111, 112
Mitchill, Samuel, 58
M'Mahon, Bernard, 99–100
Monroe, James, 54, 62, 101, 104
Montalembert, Marquis of, 57
Moore, Clement Clarke, 76
Morrill Act of 1862, 143
Morris, Gouverneur, 19–20
Morris, Robert, 70
Morse, Samuel B., 129
Mount Airy Agricultural Society, *114*, 115
Muhlenberg, Henry, 102
Mullen, Abby, 176n52
Murray, William, 32
museums, 64–90; adult learning opportunities through, 3–4; catalogs created for, 71–73, 78–79, 85, 172n83; Cutbush on importance of access to, 98; dissemination of knowledge and, 65, 78, 88–90; educational nature in early republic, 85, 167n6; items collected through scientific expeditions, 66, 74, 124; national, 72–74, 79, 81–82, 122, 142; natural history, 67–75, 78–81, 86–88, 90, 122; scientific knowledge and, 72, 78, 85; Smithsonian Institution and, 130, 132–33, 135, 138, 142, 146–47; of specialized learned societies, 82–90, 172n83. *See also specific museums*

Napoleon Bonaparte, 41–44, 48
national agricultural society, 113–14, 120, 125, 126
national botanical garden, 95–99
National Institute for the Promotion of Science, 122–27, 130–31, 145–46

National Institute of Sciences and Arts (France), 44, 48–49, 97, 105
nationalism, 26, 39, 65
national learned society, 116, 125, 129
national library, 50, 116, 129, 131, 133, 138, 147
national museum, 72–74, 79, 81–82, 122, 142
National Museum of Mexico, 123, 184n28
national observatory, 105, 116, 129
National Republicans, 104, 108
national unity, 15, 32, 39, 121, 122
national university, 11–36; advocacy for, 14–19, 48, 116, 182n10; curriculum for, 13–14, 18, 25, 27–29; debates over, 2–3, 5, 8, 12–14, 20, 32–34, 147, 158n98; failure to materialize, 3, 6, 8, 12, 34, 147; Federalists on, 8, 13–14, 21, 27–28, 144; Jeffersonians on, 8, 13–14, 25–28, 33, 36; land appropriated for, 32, 33, 34; purpose of, 6, 14–16, 18, 24, 27; Washington on, 2–3, 11–13, 19–27, 29–36, 97, 104, 117, 137, 144
Native Americans. *See* Indigenous populations
natural history: commodification of, 127–28; expertise in, 52, 109, 128; Federalist views of, 49, 76–78; fields related to, 64; in French military education, 40; intellectual debates within, 77; Jefferson's interest in, 45, 49, 76; learned societies and, 47–48, 50, 66, 86–88; lyceums and, 61, 106; museums of, 67–75, 78–81, 86–88, 90, 122; in national university curriculum, 18; participation in, 64–65, 77; Peale's lecture series on importance of, 72–73; physicians' lack of knowledge of, 98; Smithsonian Institution and, 130, 131, 133, 142, 146; South American specimens, 101, 102; in West Point curriculum, 51; Williams's knowledge of, 52, 53
Nelson, Horatio, 43

Nestor (pseudonym), 14–15
New York Agriculture Society, 111–13, *112*
New York Historical Society, 101
New York Lyceum of Natural History, 61, 106
New York Society Library, 22, 154n46
Northwest Ordinances, 12–13
Nott, Eliphalet, 131

observatories, 105, 116, 129, 142
Ord, George, 87, 168n12
Oswald, Eleazer, 15, 152n11
Owen, Robert Dale, 120, 129, 186n60

Partridge, Alden, 62
Partridge, William, 59
patriotism, 17, 54, 65–66, 70, 77, 94, 98, 104
Patterson, Robert, 67
Peale, Charles Willson: in American Revolution, 66–67; APS and, 49–50, 52, 67, 68, 72; *Exhumation of the Mastodon, 75*; Federalist attacks on, 76–77; Jefferson's correspondence with, 73–74, 80, 169n44; lecture series on importance of natural history, 72–73; mammoth excavation by, 73, *75*, 76–77, 80; on national museum, 72–74, 82; preservation methods, 68, 90, 168n14, 168n17; world-in-miniature concept of, 74, 81, 172n76. *See also* Peale's Museum (Philadelphia Museum)
Peale, Rembrandt, 76
Peale, Titian, 87, 89, 127, 168n14
Peale's Museum (Philadelphia Museum): admission tickets and fees, 80, *81*, 89; advertisements for, 68–71, 168n20; catalogs created for, 71–73, 78; demographics of visitors, 80, 171n73; display techniques at, 67–68, 72, 168n13; donations to, 53, 68–70, *71*, 73–74, 78, 124, 170n50; live specimens added to, 74–75; patronage and support for, 67–70,

73, 80, 86; public garden on grounds of, 96; as public good, 72, 81, 89
Pennybacker, Isaac S., 186n60
physiognotrace machine, 79
Pike, Zebulon M., 47, 59, 75
Pinckney, Charles C., 19, 54
Poinsett, Joel Roberts, 95–96, 101, 113, 122–25, 127, 130, 184nn28–29
Polk, James K., 1, 130
Polysophic Society, Barlow's proposal for, 35
Post, Alfred, 128–29
Potomac Company, 11–12, 26–27, 32, 35, 151n2, 156n64
Prescott, William, 123
Preston, William C., 118–19, 124–25
Price, Richard, 15–16
print culture, 3–6, 149n12
promotion of knowledge: in arts, 29; citizen science and, 134; congressional laws for, 21; education for, 30; museums for, 66; national institution for, 3, 11; scientific, 4, 7, 29, 39, 62, 106, 110, 112; by specialized learned societies, 84; universal, 2; useful, 4, 6, 8, 91, 143
public-private partnerships, 47, 88, 93, 105
public sphere, 3, 6, 21, 28, 39, 44, 145, 157n70

Quincy, Josiah, 49–50, 76

racism, scientific, 141
Ramsay, David, 69
Randolph, Edmund, 26, 72, 156n68
Rawle, William, 22
Reich, Johann Mathias, 55–56
Republicans. *See* Jeffersonian Republicans
research: AAAS sponsorship of, 46; agricultural, 92, 97, 114, 116, 120; collection and dissemination of, 6; cultivating knowledge through, 65; fusion of learning and, 9; Jefferson's agenda for, 47; national institution for, 122; Smithsonian's agenda for, 5, 10, 130–33, 138, 142, 146; in universities, 9, 146, 184n25; at West Point, 51, 54, 60; westward exploration and, 48. *See also* scientific expeditions
Revolutionary War. *See* American Revolution
Reynolds, Jeremiah N., 107
Richmond, Christopher, 69
Rittenhouse, David, 37, 67, 159n1
Rodney, Ceaser Augustus, 101
Rolle, Andrew, 177n54
Rothman, Adam, 162n49
Royal Academy of Britain, 105, 118
Royal Institution of Great Britain, 97
Royal Society of London, 44, 97, 138
Rush, Benjamin: on converting men into republican machines, 15, 183n10; on education system, 13, 15–19, 21, 153n20, 182n10; on incompleteness of American Revolution, 16, 17; on Jefferson as APS president, 37; tone and style of writing, 153n22
Rush, Richard, 119, 182n10, 186n60

Salem East India Marine Society (SEIMS), 66, 82–85, 89, 172n83
Say, Thomas, 87, 89
SCAS (South Carolina Agricultural Society), 91–92, 95, 124, 125
schools. *See* education; *specific institutions*
science: advancements in, 4, 5, 65, 81, 109, 118, 122; applied, 9, 28, 40, 54, 58, 62–63, 129; authority in, 27, 45, 68, 105, 128; citizen, 9, 90, 117, 134–35, 138, 144–46; expertise in, 9, 25, 47, 50, 65, 99, 120, 132, 186n49; infrastructure for, 7, 9, 64, 93, 98, 118, 122; learned societies focused on, 29, 38, 45–48, 121; military, 14, 40–43, 53–54, 56, 58–63, 137; non-elite participation in, 65, 166n4; professionalization of, 111, 130;

science (*continued*)
promotion of, 19–21, 29, 73, 97, 105, 154n35; uniting art with, 55, 113. *See also* natural history; research

Science (journal), 111

scientific expeditions: agricultural specimens from, 95–96, 102–3; APS and, 45–51, 89; dissemination of knowledge through, 65; Jacksonian views of, 108; of Lewis and Clark, 45–46, 50, 66, 74, 124; military and, 7, 47, 50, 63, 87–89; museum collections gathered through, 66, 74, 124; of specialized learned societies, 66, 85, 87; Symmes's proposal for, 106–8

scientific knowledge: advancement of, 42, 64, 76–77, 100, 110, 120; agricultural, 9, 92–96, 100, 103, 109, 113–15, 143; authentic, 65, 127–29; Columbian Institute's agenda of, 97, 176n39; creation of, 6, 13, 28, 39–40, 49, 92; curriculum and, 7, 9, 14, 25, 27–28; democratization of, 72, 76–82, 91, 96, 112, 128; dissemination of, 4, 28, 43, 63, 65, 87, 120; epistemological framework for, 38, 121; European, 14, 17, 25, 157n76; Jefferson on, 41, 43, 56, 60; museums and, 72, 78, 85; promotion of, 4, 7, 29, 39, 62, 106, 110, 112; research agendas and, 5, 54; specialized, 27, 36, 53, 54, 138; training in, 50, 117, 144; for US defense, 52

scientific racism, 141

Scudder, John, Jr., 80

Scudder, John, Sr., 78–80, 90

Seaton, William W., 1, 186n60

Sebert, Adam, 52

seed exchanges, 92, 96, 99–100, 103

SEIMS (Salem East India Marine Society), 66, 82–85, 89, 172n83

self-improvement, 3–4, 16, 19, 27, 82, 106

settler colonialism, 84, 88

Sherman, Roger, 20, 21, 120–21

Short, William, 48

Sibley, John, 47

Silliman, Benjamin, 96, 111

Simond, Louis, 55

slavery and enslaved people, 94, 119, 141

Smith, Robert, 94

Smith, William Loughton, 21

Smithson, James, 3, 116–20, 182n10

Smithsonian Institution: arts and, 130, 132; board of regents for, 130, 186n60; the "Castle," 120, 138, 188n97; ceremony to lay cornerstone for, 1; compromises related to, 129–30, 138, 187n70; credentialed expertise and, 2, 131; criticisms of, 136–37; debates regarding, 9, 116–21, 183n13; dissemination of knowledge by, 132–33, 135, 138–39; elitism of, 9, 10, 117, 138; Henry as leader of, 129–42, 146, 187n75; lecture room of, 137, *137*; libraries and, 130–33, 135–36, 138, 142; Meteorological Project, 133–35, 187nn83–84; museums and, 130, 132–33, 135, 138, 142, 146–47; National Institute and, 125, 130–31; natural history and, 130, 131, 133, 142, 146; publications of, 132, 133, 187n73; purpose of, 1, 3, 5, 117, 132, 138; research agenda of, 5, 10, 130–33, 138, 142, 146; scientific racism and, 141; Smithson's bequest for founding of, 3, 116–20, 182n10

Society of German Naturalists and Philosophers, 125

South American Commission, 101–3

South Carolina Agricultural Society (SCAS), 91–92, 95, 124, 125

specialized knowledge: acquisition of, 7, 28, 63, 64; APS encouragement of, 52; in arts, 36; creation of, 39, 51, 103, 142; dissemination of, 39; information needs and, 3; scientific, 27, 36, 53, 54, 138

specialized learned societies: agricultural, 91–92, 109; emergence of models for,

38; museums of, 82–90, 172n83; scientific expeditions of, 66, 85, 87; West Point graduates in, 62. *See also specific organizations*
Spofford, Ainsworth Rand, 147
Stiles, Ezra, 78
Stone, Michael, 21, 154n35
Strang, Cameron B., 161n40
Stuart, David, 155n57
supercargo, 70, 82, 169n28
Swift, Joseph Gardner, 61, 62
Symmes, John Cleves, Jr., 106–8, 178–79n86

Taney, Roger B., 186n60
Tappan, Benjamin, 127
technology: advancements in, 43, 64, 65, 112; digital, 147–48; infrastructure for, 7; for preserving animal skins, 168n14; USMPS discussions of, 59
Thayer, Sylvanus, 62
Thornton, William, 28–29, 31–33, 35, 48
Tocqueville, Alexis de, 91
Torrey, John, 129
Totten, Joseph G., 186n60
Trumbull, John, 24
Tyler, John, 125

United States Agricultural Society, 125
United States Army Corps of Engineers: establishment of, 51; fieldwork undertaken by, 59; infrastructure expertise of, 159n8; topographical engineers, 127; USMPS ties with, 53–54, 58, 164n74
United States Coast Survey, 58, 118
United States Exploration Expedition, 124, 126–27, 131, 142, 186n49
United States Military Academy at West Point: curriculum at, 7, 38, 44, 51, 53, 61–63; debates over relocation of, 60–61; dissemination of scientific knowledge at, 43; engineers trained at, 7, 144; impact on scientific advancements, 118; Jefferson and, 43, 51, 53, 59–60, 62, 166n101; Williams's plan for expansion of, 59–60, 166n101
United States Military Philosophical Society (USMPS): APS and, 53, 62, 164n74; certificate of membership for, 54–56, 57; Corps of Engineers and, 53–54, 58, 164n74; dissolution and transfer of funds, 61; establishment and growth of, 53–54, 56, 58, 59, 164n74; motto developed for, 54, 57; purpose of, 53, 54, 56, 59; seal of, 54–56, 55
unity. *See* national unity
University of Edinburg, 28, 101, 157n76
University of Geneva, 25–28, 156n61, 157n76
University of Göttingen, 121
University of Pennsylvania, 22, 72, 98, 102
University of Virginia, 35, 93
Upshur, Abel, 124
useful knowledge: acquisition of, 67; advancement of, 19; in antebellum period, 119; collection of, 89; creation of, 2, 95; curriculum focused on, 14; debates regarding, 92, 143; dissemination of, 20, 89, 118; ideological debates on, 25, 36; as marriage of science and art, 55; participation in, 40; promotion of, 4, 6, 8, 91, 143
USMPS. *See* United States Military Philosophical Society

Van Buren, Martin, 119, 121, 122
Van de Kemp, F. A., 45
Van Ness, John Peter, 34
Verney, Michael, 186n49
Volney, Constantine, 28, 41, 48

Wallich, Nathaniel, 172n83
Ward, William, 83
War of 1812, 61, 95, 106

Washington, DC: agricultural fairs in, 93; commissioners for, 23–24, 26–28, 31–33; map of (1802), 33, 34

Washington, George: on agriculture, 93, 113; in American Revolution, 26, 155n57; APS membership of, 22–23; Blodget's relationship with, 23–24, 155n57; botanical garden planned for by, 96; at Constitutional Convention, 19, 22; on Geneva faculty scheme, 26, 27; Hamilton's correspondence with, 29, 31, 157n79; honorary degree received by, 23; Jefferson's correspondence with, 25–26; lack of formal education received by, 21–22; libraries utilized by, 22, 154n46; on military academy formation, 42; on national university, 2–3, 11–13, 19–27, 29–36, 97, 104, 117, 137, 144; Peale's Museum supported by, 67, 68, 71; personal library of, 22, 153n26, 154n41; Potomac Company shares given to, 11–12, 26–27, 32, 151n2, 156n64; wax representation in Columbian Museum, 78

Washington, George Steptoe, 22

Washington, Laurence, 22
Washington Botanical Society, 91
Washington College (Maryland), 23
Watkins, Tobias, 105
Wayland, Francis, 120
Webster, Noah, 16, 17, 61
Wellmon, Chad, 184n25
West Point. *See* United States Military Academy at West Point
westward expansion, 46–51, 162n49, 167n7
Whig Party, 104, 131
White, Alexander, 32
Wilkes, Charles, 126, 127
Wilkinson, James, 52, 53
Williams, Jonathan, 52–62, 166n101
Williams, Moses, 79
Williams, Samuel, 46
Wilson, Alexander, 67–68, 168n12
Wilson, James, 19
Wistar, Caspar, 52
women: at agricultural fairs, 94; education for, 16; at Literary and Scientific Convention, 125; scientists' exploitation of, 134–35

FROM PAMPHLETS TO PODCASTS
An Institute for Thomas Paine Studies Series

This series takes its cue from Thomas Paine, who wrote that "America . . . replenished the world with more useful knowledge and sounder maxims of civil government" than any other society. It is intended to encompass a balanced mix of titles designed to advance a new and innovative approach to scholarship on the contests over knowledge making and the pursuit of informed, democratic citizenship in Thomas Paine's time, and about these processes' relevance to our own. It is open to intellectual histories, projects on Indigenous ways of knowing, scholarship that historicizes concepts of expertise, propaganda, and information, and studies that make transparent the methodologies (including digital) that undergird that work.

Archival Communities: Constructing the Past in the Early United States
Derek Kane O'Leary

www.ingramcontent.com/pod-product-compliance
Lightning Source LLC
Chambersburg PA
CBHW031328140426
43117CB00033B/238